Frommer's

PORTABLE

Washington, D.C.

5th Edition

by Elise Hartman Ford

D1045505

Here's what critics say about Frommer's:

"Amazingly easy to use. Very portable, very complete."

—*Booklist*

"Detailed, accurate, and easy-to-read information for all price ranges."

—*Glamour Magazine*

WILEY

Wiley Publishing, Inc.

Published by:

WILEY PUBLISHING, INC.

111 River St.
Hoboken, NJ 07030-5774

ISBN 0-7645-7291-1

Editor: Elizabeth Heath
Production Editor: Suzanna R. Thompson
Photo Editor: Richard Fox
Cartographer: Roberta Stockwell
Production by Wiley Indianapolis Composition Services

For information on our other products and services or to obtain technical
support, please contact our Customer Care Department within the U.S. at
800/762-2974, outside the U.S. at 317/572-3993 or fax 317/572-4002.

Wiley also publishes its books in a variety of electronic formats. Some con-
tent that appears in print may not be available in electronic formats.

Manufactured in the United States of America

5 4 3 2

Contents

List of Maps

To Jim, Caitlin, and Lucy

ABOUT THE AUTHOR

Elise Hartman Ford has been a freelance writer in the Washington, D.C., area since 1985. Her writing has appeared in the *Washington Post, Washingtonian* magazine, the London-based *Bradman's North America Guide, The Essential Guide to Business Travel, Ladies' Home Journal,* and other national, regional, and trade publications. In addition to this guide, she is the author of *Frommer's Washington, D.C., from $80 a Day, Frommer's Memorable Walks in Washington, D.C.,* and *Unique Meeting, Wedding, and Party Places in Greater Washington.*

AN INVITATION TO THE READER

In researching this book, we discovered many wonderful places—hotels, restaurants, shops, and more. We're sure you'll find others. Please tell us about them, so we can share the information with your fellow travelers in upcoming editions. If you were disappointed with a recommendation, we'd love to know that, too. Please write to:

Frommer's Portable Washington, D.C., 5th Edition
Wiley Publishing, Inc. • 111 River St. • Hoboken, NJ 07030-5774

AN ADDITIONAL NOTE

Please be advised that travel information is subject to change at any time—and this is especially true of prices. We therefore suggest that you write or call ahead for confirmation when making your travel plans. The authors, editors, and publisher cannot be held responsible for the experiences of readers while traveling. Your safety is important to us, however, so we encourage you to stay alert and be aware of your surroundings. Keep a close eye on cameras, purses, and wallets, all favorite targets of thieves and pickpockets.

FROMMER'S STAR RATINGS, ICONS & ABBREVIATIONS

Every hotel, restaurant, and attraction listing in this guide has been ranked for quality, value, service, amenities, and special features using a **star-rating system.** In country, state, and regional guides, we also rate towns and regions to help you narrow down your choices and budget your time accordingly. Hotels and restaurants are rated on a scale of zero (recommended) to three stars (exceptional). Attractions, shopping, nightlife, towns, and regions are rated according to the following scale: zero stars (recommended), one star (highly recommended), two stars (very highly recommended), and three stars (must-see).

In addition to the star-rating system, we also use **seven feature icons** that point you to the great deals, in-the-know advice, and unique experiences that separate travelers from tourists. Throughout the book, look for:

Finds	Special finds—those places only insiders know about
Fun Fact	Fun facts—details that make travelers more informed and their trips more fun
Kids	Best bets for kids—advice for the whole family
Moments	Special moments—those experiences that memories are made of
Overrated	Places or experiences not worth your time or money
Tips	Insider tips—some great ways to save time and money
Value	Great values—where to get the best deals

The following **abbreviations** are used for credit cards:

AE	American Express	DISC	Discover	V	Visa
DC	Diners Club	MC	MasterCard		

FROMMERS.COM

Now that you have the guidebook to a great trip, visit our website at **www.frommers.com** for travel information on more than 3,000 destinations. With features updated regularly, we give you instant access to the most current trip-planning information available. At Frommers.com, you'll also find the best prices on airfares, accommodations, and car rentals—and you can even book travel online through our travel booking partners. At Frommers.com, you'll also find the following:

- Online updates to our most popular guidebooks
- Vacation sweepstakes and contest giveaways
- Newsletter highlighting the hottest travel trends
- Online travel message boards with featured travel discussions

Planning Your Trip to Washington, D.C.

Planning can be the most intimidating part about taking a trip. The task of organizing yourself, and assorted loved ones, to depart one location without forgetting anything ("Did we stop the newspapers? Close the windows? Remember the camera?") and arrive at another location, luggage and loved ones intact—well, that's asking a lot.

If the job has fallen to you to plan a trip to Washington, and you're still in the sorting-it-all-out, not-sure-where-to-begin stage, these pages cover the essentials about what to bring, what's going on in D.C. throughout the year, how to get here, how to plan your trip online, and other salient points. This chapter also refers you to a number of helpful sources for additional and timely information.

But don't stop with this chapter: The rest of the book aims to assist you in selecting your lodging, dining, shopping, entertainment, and sightseeing preferences.

1 Visitor Information

Before you leave, contact the **Washington, D.C. Convention and Tourism Corporation,** 901 7th St. NW, Washington, DC 20001-3719 (© **800/422-8644** or 202/789-7000; www.washington. org), and ask for a free copy of the *Washington, D.C. Visitors Guide,* which details hotels, restaurants, sights, shops, and more. At the local number, you can speak directly to a staff "visitor specialist" and get answers to your specific questions about the city. You should also consult the WCTC website, which provides the latest news and information, including upcoming exhibits at the museums and anticipated closings of tourist attractions.

For more information about Washington's most popular tourist spots, check out the National Park Service website, **www.nps.gov/ nacc** (the Park Service maintains Washington's monuments, memorials, and other sites), and the Smithsonian Institution's **www.si.edu**.

Destination: Washington, D.C.— Red Alert Checklist

- Have you packed a photo ID? You'll need one to board a plane, of course, but even if you are not flying, you will probably be asked for a photo ID once you're here.
- Did you bring ID cards that may entitle you to discounts? Proof of AAA, AARP, or other membership, or of your status as a student can gain you special treatment or rates.
- Have you booked theater and restaurant reservations?
- Have you checked that your favorite attraction is open?
- Would you like to avoid the wait of a long line or the ultimate disappointment of missing a tour altogether? A number of sightseeing attractions permit you to reserve a tour slot in advance. The Supreme Court, the Library of Congress, and the Kennedy Center all direct you to your senator or representative's office to request advance reservations for "congressional" tours at each of their sites.

  The switchboard for the **Senate** is ☎ 202/224-3121; for the **House** switchboard, call ☎ 202/225-3121. You can also correspond by e-mail; check out the websites www.senate.gov and www.house.gov for e-mail addresses, individual member information, and much more. Or address written requests to representatives as follows: name of your representative, U.S. House of Representatives, Washington, DC 20515; or name of your senator, U.S. Senate, Washington, DC 20510. Don't forget to include the exact dates of your Washington trip.

Also helpful is the *Washington Post* site, **www.washingtonpost.com**, which gives you up-to-the-minute news, weather, visitor information, restaurant reviews, and nightlife insights.

2 When to Go

The city's peak seasons generally coincide with two activities: the sessions of Congress and springtime, starting with the appearance of the cherry blossoms along the Potomac. Specifically, when Congress is "in," from about the second week in September until Thanksgiving, and again from about mid-January through June, hotels are full with guests whose business takes them to Capitol Hill or to conferences. Mid-March through June traditionally is the most frenzied season, when families and school groups descend upon the city to see the cherry blossoms and enjoy Washington's sensational spring. This is also a popular season for protest marches. Hotel rooms are at a premium, and airfares tend to be higher.

If crowds turn you off, consider visiting Washington at the end of August or in early September, when Congress is still "out" and families return home to get their children back to school, or between Thanksgiving and mid-January, when Congress leaves again and many people are busy with the holidays. Hotel rates are cheapest at this time, too, and many hotels offer attractive packages.

If you're thinking of visiting in July and August, be forewarned: The weather is very hot and humid. Many of Washington's performance stages go dark in summer, although outdoor arenas and parks pick up some of the slack by featuring concerts, festivals, parades, and more (see chapter 7 for details about performing arts schedules). And, of course, Independence Day (July 4th) in the capital is a spectacular celebration.

WASHINGTON CALENDAR OF EVENTS

Washington's most popular annual events are the Cherry Blossom Festival in spring, the Fourth of July celebration in summer, the Taste of D.C. food fair in the fall, and the lighting of the National Christmas Tree in winter. But there's some sort of special event almost daily. For the latest schedules, check **www.washington.org**.

January

Presidential Inauguration. Every four years, on the steps of the U.S. Capitol. After the swearing-in, crowds line the sidewalks as the newly elected president of the United States proceeds by motorcade down Pennsylvania Avenue to the White House. Parades, concerts, parties, inaugural balls, and other festivities herald the occasion. For details, call © **202/789-7000.** January 20, 2005.

February

Black History Month. Features numerous events, museum exhibits, and cultural programs celebrating the contributions of African Americans to American life, including a celebration of abolitionist Frederick Douglass' birthday. For details, check the *Washington Post* or call © **202/357-2700.** For additional activities at the Martin Luther King, Jr. Memorial Library, call © **202/727-0321.**

Chinese New Year Celebration. A friendship archway, topped by 300 painted dragons and lighted at night, marks Chinatown's entrance at 7th and H streets NW. The celebration begins the day of the Chinese New Year and continues for 10 or more days, with traditional firecrackers, dragon dancers, and colorful street parades. For details, call © **202/789-7000.** Early February.

George Washington's Birthday. A series of celebratory events centered around the Washington Monument. Call © **202/619-7222** for details and to confirm the celebration is taking place; the Washington Monument remains open, although its grounds may be off limits because of ongoing construction of security barriers.

March/April

St. Patrick's Day Parade, on Constitution Avenue NW from 7th to 17th streets. A big parade with floats, bagpipes, marching bands, and the wearin' o' the green. For parade information, call © **202/789-7000.** The Sunday before March 17.

Cherry Blossom Events. Washington's best-known annual event: the blossoming of more than 3,700 famous Japanese cherry trees by the Tidal Basin in Potomac Park. Festivities include a major parade (marking the end of the festival) with floats, concerts, celebrity guests, and more. There are also special ranger-guided tours departing from the Jefferson Memorial. For information, call © **202/547-1500** or check the website, www.nps.gov/nacc/cherry. See p. 143 for more information about the cherry blossoms. Late March or early April (national and local news programs monitor the budding).

White House Easter Egg Roll. The biggie for little kids. The White House Easter Egg Roll continues a tradition begun in 1878. Entertainment on the White House South Lawn and the Ellipse may included clog dancers; clowns; Ukrainian egg-decorating exhibitions; puppet and magic shows; military drill teams; an egg-rolling contest; and a hunt for 1,000 or so wooden eggs, many of them signed by celebrities, astronauts, or the president. Call © **202/208-1631** for details. Easter Monday.

African-American Family Day at the National Zoo. This tradition extends back to 1889, when the zoo opened. The National Zoo celebrates African-American families the day after Easter with music, dance, Easter egg rolls, and other activities. Admission is free. Call © **202/357-2700** for details. Easter Monday.

Smithsonian Craft Show. Held in the National Building Museum, 401 F St. NW, this juried show features one-of-a-kind limited-edition crafts by more than 100 noted artists from all over the country. There's an entrance fee of about $12 per adult, free for children under 12 (strollers not allowed), each day. For details, call ℂ **202/357-4000** (TDD 202/357-1729). Four days in late April.

May

Georgetown Garden Tour. View the remarkable private gardens of one of the city's loveliest neighborhoods. Admission (about $25) includes light refreshments. Some years there are related events such as a flower show at a historic home. Call ℂ **202/789-7000** or browse the website, www.gtowngarden.org, for details. Early to mid-May.

Washington National Cathedral Annual Flower Mart. In a tradition more than 65 years old, the flower mart takes place on cathedral grounds, featuring displays of flowering plants and herbs, decorating demonstrations, ethnic food booths, children's rides and activities (including an antique carousel), costumed characters, puppet shows, and other entertainment. Free admission. Call ℂ **202/537-6200** for details. First Friday and Saturday in May, rain or shine.

Memorial Day. At 11am, a wreath-laying ceremony takes place at the Tomb of the Unknowns in Arlington National Cemetery, followed by military band music, a service, and an address by a high-ranking government official (sometimes the president); call ℂ **703/695-3175** for details. There are ceremonies at the World War II and Vietnam Veterans memorials, including a wreath-laying, speakers, and the playing of taps (ℂ **202/619-7222** for details), and activities at the U.S. Navy Memorial (ℂ **202/737-2300**). On the Sunday before Memorial Day, the National Symphony Orchestra performs a free concert at 8pm on the West Lawn of the Capitol to officially welcome summer to Washington; call ℂ **202/619-7222** for details. Last Monday in May.

June/July

Shakespeare Theatre Free For All. This free theater festival presents a Shakespeare play each year for a 2-week run at the Carter Barron Amphitheatre in upper northwest Washington. Tickets are required, but they're free. Call ℂ **202/334-4790.** Evenings in mid-June.

Smithsonian Festival of American Folklife. A major event with traditional American music, crafts, foods, games, concerts, and exhibits, staged the length of the National Mall. All events are free; most take place outdoors. Call ℂ **202/357-2700,** or check the listings in the *Washington Post* for details. For 5 to 10 days in late June and early July, always including July 4th.

Independence Day. There's no better place to be on the Fourth of July than in Washington, D.C. The festivities include a massive National Independence Day Parade down Constitution Avenue, celebrity entertainers, and concerts. A morning program in front of the National Archives includes military demonstrations, period music, and a reading of the Declaration of Independence. In the evening, the National Symphony Orchestra plays on the west steps of the Capitol with guest artists, and big-name entertainment also precedes the fabulous fireworks display behind the Washington Monument. You can also attend a free 11am organ recital at the Washington National Cathedral. Consult the *Washington Post* or call ✆ **202/789-7000** for details. July 4th, all day.

September

Labor Day Concert. West Lawn of the Capitol. The National Symphony Orchestra closes its summer season with a free performance at 8pm; call ✆ **202/619-7222** for details. Labor Day. (Rain date: Same day and time at Constitution Hall.)

Kennedy Center Open House Arts Festival. A festival of the performing arts, featuring local and national artists on the front plaza and river terrace (which overlooks the Potomac), and throughout stages of the Kennedy Center. Festivals have featured the likes of Los Lobos, Mary Chapin Carpenter, and Washington Opera soloists. Activities usually include a National Symphony Orchestra "petting zoo," where children get to bow, blow, drum, or strum a favorite instrument. Free admission, although you may have to wait in line for performances. Check the *Washington Post* or call ✆ **800/444-1324** or 202/467-4600 for details. A Sunday in early to mid-September, noon to 6pm.

Black Family Reunion. Performances, food, and fun are part of this celebration of the African-American family and culture, held on the Mall. Free admission. Call ✆ **202/737-0120.** Mid-September.

Hispanic Heritage Month. Various museums and other institutions host activities celebrating Hispanic culture and traditions. Call ✆ **202/789-7000.** Mid-September to mid-October.

Washington National Cathedral's Open House. Celebrates the anniversary of the laying of the foundation stone in 1907. Events include demonstrations of stone carving and other crafts utilized in building the cathedral; carillon and organ demonstrations; and performances by dancers, choirs, strolling musicians, jugglers, and puppeteers. This is the only time visitors are allowed to ascend to the top of the central tower to see the bells; it's a tremendous climb, but you'll be rewarded with a spectacular view. For details, call ✆ **202/537-6200.** A Saturday in late September or early October.

October

Taste of D.C. Festival. Pennsylvania Avenue, between 9th and 14th streets NW. Dozens of Washington's restaurants offer food tastings, along with live entertainment, dancing, storytellers, and games. Admission is free; food and drink tickets are sold in bundles, usually $6 for 5 tickets or $25 for 25 tickets. Call ✆ **202/789-7000** for details. Three days, including Columbus Day weekend.

White House Fall Garden Tours. For 2 days, visitors have an opportunity to see the famed Rose Garden and South Lawn. Admission is free. A military band provides music. For details, call ✆ **202/208-1631.** Mid-October.

Marine Corps Marathon. More than 16,000 runners compete in the fourth-largest marathon in the United States. It begins at the Marine Corps Memorial (the Iwo Jima statue) and passes major monuments. Call ✆ **800/RUN-USMC** or 703/784-2225 for details. Anyone can enter; register online at www.marine marathon.com. Fourth Sunday in October.

Halloween. There's no official celebration, but costumed revels seem to get bigger every year. Giant block parties take place in the Dupont Circle area and Georgetown. Check the *Washington Post* for special parties and activities. October 31.

November

Veterans Day. The nation's war dead are honored with a wreath-laying ceremony at 11am at the Tomb of the Unknowns in Arlington National Cemetery followed by a memorial service. The president of the United States or a very high-ranking government personage officiates. Call ✆ **202/685-2951** for information. At the Vietnam Veterans Memorial (✆ **202/619-7222**), observances include speakers, wreath placement, a color guard, and the playing of taps; a wreath laying is among the ceremonies performed at the World War II Memorial. November 11.

December

Christmas Pageant of Peace/National Tree Lighting. At the northern end of the Ellipse, the president lights the national

Christmas tree to the accompaniment of orchestral and choral music. The lighting inaugurates the 4-week Pageant of Peace, a tremendous holiday celebration with seasonal music, caroling, a nativity scene, 50 state trees, and a burning yule log. Call ⓒ **202/208-1631** for details. A select Wednesday or Thursday in early December at 5pm.

3 Specialized Travel Resources

TRAVELERS WITH DISABILITIES

Washington, D.C., is one of the most accessible cities in the world for travelers with disabilities. The best overall source of information about accessibility at specific Washington hotels, restaurants, shopping malls, and attractions is the nonprofit organization **Access Information.** You can read the information (including restaurant reviews) online at www.disabilityguide.org, or order a free copy of the *Washington, DC Access Guide* by calling ⓒ **301/528-8664,** or by writing to Access Information, 21618 Slidell Rd., Boyds, MD 20841.

The **Washington Metropolitan Transit Authority** publishes accessibility information on its website **www.wmata.com,** or you can call ⓒ **202/962-1245** with questions about services for travelers with disabilities, including how to obtain a Disabled ID card that entitles you to discounted fares. (Call at least 3 weeks ahead to allow enough time to obtain an ID card.) For up-to-date information about how Metro is operating on the day you're using it (for instance, to verify that the elevators are operating at the stations you'll be traveling to), call ⓒ **202/962-1212.**

Major Washington museums, including all **Smithsonian museum buildings** are accessible to wheelchair visitors. A comprehensive free publication called "Smithsonian Access" lists all services available to visitors with disabilities, including parking, building access, sign-language interpreters, and more. To obtain a copy, call ⓒ **202/357-2700** (TTY 202/357-1729) or visit www.si.edu/opa/accessibility. You can also use the TTY number to get information on all Smithsonian museums and events.

Likewise, all of the memorials, including the **Lincoln, Jefferson, Franklin Delano Roosevelt, Vietnam Veterans, Korean War Veterans,** and **World War II memorials** and the **Washington Monument,** are each equipped to accommodate visitors with disabilities and keep wheelchairs on the premises. There's limited parking for visitors with disabilities on the south side of the Lincoln Memorial.

Call ahead to other sightseeing attractions (© 202/426-6842 or 202/426-6841) for accessibility information and special services.

The White House is accessible to those in wheelchairs and requires no advance notice or special tour instructions for wheelchair-bound tourists. Call your senator or representative to arrange wheelchair-accessible tours of the **Capitol.** For further information about Capitol tours, call © 202/224-4048. Your congressperson can also arrange special tours for the blind or deaf at both the Capitol and at the White House. The TDD phone number for the Members of Congress Visitors Office is © 202/456-2121.

GAY & LESBIAN TRAVELERS

Washington, D.C., has a strong gay and lesbian community and welcomes gay and lesbian visitors. The Washington, D.C. Convention and Tourism Corporation website, www.washington.org, includes a link to information for gay and lesbian tourists: Click on "Pride in DC," which appears on the site's home page. You can also order the WCTC's publication, *The Gay, Lesbian, Bisexual and Transgender Travelers Guide to Washington, D.C.,* by calling © 202/789-7000.

While in Washington, you'll want to get your hands on the *Washington Blade,* a comprehensive weekly newspaper distributed free at many locations in the District. You can subscribe to the *Blade* for $90 a year, check out **www.washingtonblade.com**, or pick up a free copy at Olsson's Books/Records, 1307 19th St. NW; Borders, 18th and L streets; and Kramerbooks, 1517 Connecticut Ave. NW, at Dupont Circle. Call the *Blade* office at © 202/797-7000 for other locations.

Washington's gay bookstore, **Lambda Rising,** 1625 Connecticut Ave. NW (© 202/462-6969), also informally serves as an information center for the gay community, which centers in the Dupont Circle neighborhood.

SENIOR TRAVEL

Always mention the fact that you're a senior when you make your travel reservations, on the chance that you may be eligible for a discount. Several airlines offer discounts to "mature" travelers, including America West, Frontier, Southwest, US Airways, Air Canada, and Air France, all of which fly to Washington, D.C. America West's discount program is typical: Anyone who is 62 or older is eligible for a 10% discount off the published airfare; a traveling companion of any age may receive the 10% discount, too. Many hotels offer discounts for seniors.

In Washington, you'll find discounted admission prices for seniors at theaters and at those few museums that charge for entry, and discounted travel on Metro, although the designated "senior" age differs slightly from place to place. To obtain discounted farecards to ride Metro, you must visit a Metro sales office—there's one in the Metro Center subway station at 13th and G Streets NW—flash your photo ID with your birthdate on it, and pay half-price for your farecard; call © **202/962-1245** for more information.

Members of **AARP** (© **888/687-2277** or 202/434-2277; www. aarp.org) get discounts on hotels, airfares, and car rentals. AARP offers members a wide range of benefits, including *AARP, The Magazine* and a monthly newsletter. Anyone over 50 can join; annual membership is $13.

4 Internet Access Away from Home

Travelers have any number of ways to check e-mail and access the Internet on the road. Of course, using your own laptop—or even a PDA (personal digital assistant) or electronic organizer with a modem—gives you the most flexibility. But you may be able to leave your laptop at home, if you want, since other computer options may be available.

Washington, D.C., has at least two cybercafes: Cyberlaptops.com, on the second floor at 1636 R St. NW (© **202/462-7195**), providing Internet access and also laptop repairs; and Cyberstop Café, 1513 17th St. NW (© **202/234-2470**). For other listings, as well as the locations of **Internet kiosks** throughout the D.C. area, check the website, **www.cybercaptive.com**.

All three of Washington's airports offer some variation of Internet access. Each of National's 150 public phones has a data jack to which you can connect your laptop for the price of a phone call (50¢). Dulles has only six such kiosks, and the connection charge is $3.50, plus $4 per 10 minutes. BWI has three locations where high-speed wireless Internet access is available; you can borrow for a short period or purchase (for 25¢ per min. or $7.95 for unlimited daily access) a network card to plug into your laptop to connect you. Elsewhere, you'll find Internet kiosks in shopping malls, hotel lobbies, and tourist information offices, which give you basic Web access for a per-minute fee that's usually higher than cybercafe prices.

5 Getting There

BY PLANE

Domestic airlines flying into all three of Washington, D.C.'s airports, Washington Dulles International (Dulles), Ronald Reagan Washington National (National), and Baltimore-Washington International (BWI), include **American** (© 800/433-7300; www.aa.com), **Continental** (© 800/525-0280; www.continental.com), **Delta** (© 800/221-1212; www.delta.com), **Northwest** (© 800/225-2525; www.nwa.com), **United** (© 800/241-6522; www.united.com), and **US Airways** (© 800/428-4322; www.usairways.com).

Low-fare airlines seem to be most successful and dependable these days. Two of the newest to arrive in Washington are United Airline's **Ted Airlines** (© 800/225-5833; www.flyted.com), which debuted in April 2004, and **Independence Air** (www.flyi.com).

SHUTTLE SERVICE FROM NEW YORK, BOSTON & CHICAGO

Delta and US Airways continue to dominate the lucrative D.C.–East Coast shuttle service. The two airlines operate hourly or almost hourly shuttle service between Boston's Logan Airport and Washington, D.C., and New York's La Guardia Airport and Washington, D.C. The **Delta Shuttle** (© **800/933-5935**) travels daily between New York and Washington, while the **US Airways Shuttle** (© **800/428-4322**) flies daily between Boston and Washington, D.C., and New York and Washington, D.C. Both airlines fly into Ronald Reagan Washington National Airport. **Southwest** offers nearly hourly service daily between BWI and Chicago's Midway Airport, Providence, Hartford, Long Island, Manchester (New Hampshire), Orlando, and Nashville.

D.C. AREA AIRPORTS

Ronald Reagan Washington National Airport (airport code DCA; everyone calls it simply "National") lies across the Potomac River in Virginia, a few minutes by car and 15 to 20 minutes by Metro from downtown in non-rush-hour traffic. Its proximity to the District and its direct access to the Metro rail system are reasons to fly into National. The Metropolitan Washington Airports Authority oversees both National and Dulles airports, so the website is the same for the two facilities: www.metwashairports.com. Check there for airport information, or call © **703/417-1806.**

Washington Dulles International Airport (airport code IAD; aka "Dulles") lies 26 miles outside the capital, in Chantilly, Virginia, a 35- to 45-minute ride to downtown in non-rush-hour traffic. Of the three airports, Dulles handles the most daily flights and its airlines fly to the most destinations, about 69 U.S. and 37 foreign cities. Visit its website at www.metwashairports.com, or call ℂ **703/572-2700.**

Last but not least is **Baltimore–Washington International Airport** (airport code BWI; goes by "BWI"), which is located about 45 minutes from downtown, a few miles outside of Baltimore. One factor especially recommends BWI to travelers: Southwest Airlines, with its bargain fares, commands a major presence here, pulling in nearly half of BWI's business. BWI destinations via Southwest total at least 31. If you want to save some money, check if your city is one of them. Call ℂ **800/435-9294** for airport information, or point your browser to www.bwiairport.com.

GETTING INTO TOWN FROM THE AIRPORT

Taxi service: For a trip to downtown D.C., you can expect a taxi to cost anywhere from $8 to $15 for the 10- to 15-minute ride from National Airport; $44-plus for the 30- to 40-minute ride from Dulles Airport; and $55 for the 45-minute ride from BWI.

SuperShuttle buses (ℂ **800/258-3826;** www.supershuttle.com) offer shared-ride, door-to-door service between the airport and your destination, be it in the District or in a suburban location. You can't reserve space on the van for a ride from the airport, which means that you probably will have to wait 15 to 30 minutes before boarding so that your driver can fill his van with other passengers and make his trip worthwhile. This also means that you'll be taken to your destination in a roundabout way, as the driver drops off other passengers en route. If you arrive after midnight, call the toll-free number above from National Airport, ℂ **703/416-7884** from Dulles, and ℂ **888/826-2700** from BWI. The 24-hour service bases its fares on zip code, so, to reach downtown, expect to pay about $10, plus $8 for each additional person from National; $22, plus $10 per additional person from Dulles; and $26 to $32, plus $8 per additional person from BWI. If you're calling the Super-Shuttle for a ride from a D.C. area location to one of the airports, you must reserve a spot at least 24 hours in advance.

Individual transportation options at each airport are as follows:

FROM RONALD REAGAN WASHINGTON NATIONAL AIRPORT If you are not too encumbered with luggage, you should take **Metrorail** (ℂ **202/637-7000**) into the city. Metro's

Yellow and Blue lines stop at the airport and connect via an enclosed walkway to level two, the concourse level, of the main terminal, adjacent to terminals B and C.

FROM WASHINGTON DULLES INTERNATIONAL AIRPORT The **Washington Flyer Express Bus** runs between Dulles and the West Falls Church Metro station, where you can board a train to D.C. Buses to the West Falls Church Metro station run every 30 minutes, and cost $8 one-way. (**"Washington Flyer"** is also the name under which the taxi service operates at Dulles.)

More convenient is the **Metrobus** service that runs between Dulles and the L'Enfant Plaza Metro station, located near Capitol Hill and within walking distance of the National Mall and the Smithsonian museums. The bus departs daily on the hour, costs only $2.50, and takes about 45 to 50 minutes.

FROM BALTIMORE–WASHINGTON INTERNATIONAL AIRPORT BWI offers a daily **Express Metro Bus service** that runs to and from the Greenbelt Metro station. In the airport, look for "Public Transit" signs to find the service, which departs every 40 minutes, and costs $2.50 At the Greenbelt station, you purchase a farecard and board a Metro train, which takes you into the city.

BY CAR

Major highways approach Washington, D.C., from all parts of the country. Specifically, these are I-270, I-95, and I-295 from the north; I-95, I-395, Route 1, and Route 301 from the south; Route 50/301 and Route 450 from the east; and Route 7, Route 50, I-66, and Route 29/211 from the west.

No matter which road you take, there's a good chance you will have to navigate some portion of the **Capital Beltway** (I-495 and I-95) to gain entry to D.C. The Beltway girds the city, 66 miles around, with 56 interchanges or exits, and is nearly always congested, but especially during weekday morning and evening rush hours, roughly between 6 to 9:30am and 3 to 7pm. Commuter traffic on the Beltway now rivals that of L.A. freeways, and drivers can get a little crazy, weaving in and out of traffic.

If you're planning to drive to Washington, get yourself a good map before you do anything else. The **American Automobile Association** (**AAA;** *C* **800/763-9900** for emergency road service and for connection to the mid-Atlantic office; www.aaa.com) provides its members with maps and detailed Trip-Tiks that give precise directions to a destination, including up-to-date information about areas of construction. AAA also provides towing services should you have car trouble during your trip. If you are driving to a hotel in D.C. or its suburbs, contact the establishment to find out the best route to the hotel's address and other crucial details concerning parking availability and rates.

The District is 240 miles from New York City, 40 miles from Baltimore, 700 miles from Chicago, nearly 500 miles from Boston, and about 630 miles from Atlanta.

BY TRAIN

Amtrak (© **800/USA-RAIL;** www.amtrak.com) offers daily service to Washington, D.C., from New York, Boston, Chicago, and Los Angeles (you change trains in Chicago). Amtrak also travels daily from points south of Washington, including Raleigh, Charlotte, Atlanta, cities in Florida, and New Orleans.

Metroliner service—which costs a little more but provides faster transit and roomier, more comfortable seating than regular trains— is available between New York and Washington, D.C., and points in between.

Even faster, roomier, and more expensive than Metroliner service are Amtrak's high-speed **Acela** trains. The trains, which travel as fast as 150 mph, navigate the Northeast Corridor, linking Boston, New York, and Washington, D.C.

Amtrak trains arrive at historic **Union Station,** 50 Massachusetts Ave. NE (© **202/371-9441;** www.unionstationdc.com), a short walk from the Capitol, across the circle from several hotels, and a short cab or Metro ride from downtown. There are always taxis available there.

2

Getting to Know Washington, D.C.

Washington, D.C., is a city of 572,000 residents, 67 square miles, more than 150 embassies, 60-plus museums, at least 100 hotels, roughly 2,000 restaurants, 2 major rivers, 3,700 cherry trees, scores of historic monuments and landmarks, and boundless beauty. And that's just to give you an idea. Read this chapter to learn how to navigate the city before you get out there and go.

1 Orientation

On the one hand, Washington, D.C., is an easy place to get to know. It's a small city, where walking will actually get you places, but also with a model public transportation system that travels throughout D.C.'s neighborhoods and to most tourist spots.

On the other hand, when you do need help, it's hard to find. The city lacks a single, large, comprehensive, and easy-to-find visitor center. Signs to tourist attractions and Metro stations, even street signs, are often missing or frustratingly inadequate.

The District is always in the process of improving the situation, it seems. But in the meantime, you can turn to the following smaller visitor and information centers, helpful publications, and information phone lines.

VISITOR INFORMATION
INFORMATION CENTERS

The Washington, D.C., Visitor Information Center (© 866/ 324-7386 or 202/328-4748; www.dcvisit.com) is inside the immense Ronald Reagan International Trade Center Building, 1300 Pennsylvania Ave. NW. To enter the federal building, you need to show a picture ID. The visitor center lies on the ground floor of the building, a little to your right as you enter from the Wilson Plaza, near the Federal Triangle Metro. From March 15 to Labor Day, the center is open Monday to Friday from 8:30am to 5:30pm, Saturday from 9am to 4pm; from Labor Day to March 15, the center is open Monday to Friday from 9am to 4:30pm.

The **White House Visitor Center,** in the Herbert Hoover Building, Department of Commerce, 1450 Pennsylvania Ave. NW (between 14th and 15th sts.; © **202/208-1631,** or 202/456-7041 for recorded information), is open daily (except for Dec 25, Thanksgiving, and Jan 1) from 7:30am to 4pm.

The **Smithsonian Information Center,** in the "Castle," 1000 Jefferson Dr. SW (© **202/357-2700,** or TTY 202/357-1729; www.si.edu), is open every day (except for Dec 25) from 9am to 5:30pm.

The **American Automobile Association (AAA)** has a large central office near the White House, at 701 15th St. NW, Washington, DC 20005-2111 (© **202/331-3000**). Hours are Monday to Friday from 9am to 5:30pm.

PUBLICATIONS

At the airport, pick up a free copy of *Washington Flyer* magazine (www.fly2dc.com), which a handy planning tool.

Washington has two daily newspapers: the *Washington Post* (www.washingtonpost.com) and the *Washington Times* (www.washingtontimes.com). The Friday "Weekend" section of the *Post* is essential for finding out what's going on, recreation-wise. *City Paper,* published every Thursday and available free at downtown shops and restaurants, covers some of the same material but is a better guide to the club and art gallery scene.

Also on newsstands is *Washingtonian,* a monthly magazine with features, often about the "100 Best" this or that (doctors, restaurants, and so on) in Washington; the magazine also offers a calendar of events, restaurant reviews, and profiles of Washingtonians.

HELPFUL TELEPHONE NUMBERS & WEBSITES

- **National Park Service** (© **202/619-7222;** www.nps.gov/ncro). You reach a real person and not a recording when you call the phone number with questions about the monuments, the National Mall, and national park lands, and activities taking place at these locations. National Park Service information kiosks are located inside the Jefferson, Lincoln, and FDR memorials and near the Vietnam Veterans, Korean War Veterans, and World War II memorials. Park rangers are on hand at the Washington Monument ticket booth at the bottom of the hill, at 15th St. NW and Constitution Ave.; inside the monument; and at the

Ranger Station, located at the southwest point of the monument grounds, across from the Tidal Basin.

- **Dial-A-Park** (© **202/619-7275**). This is a recording of information regarding park-service events and attractions.
- **Dial-A-Museum** (© **202/357-2020;** www.si.edu). This recording offers the locations of the 14 Washington Smithsonian museums and their daily activities.

CITY LAYOUT

The U.S. Capitol marks the center of the city, which is divided into quadrants: **northwest (NW), northeast (NE), southwest (SW),** and **southeast (SE).** Almost all the areas of interest to tourists are in the northwest. If you look at your map, you'll see that some addresses—for instance, the corner of G and 7th streets—appear in all quadrants. Hence you must observe the quadrant designation (NW, NE, SW, or SE) when looking for an address.

MAIN ARTERIES & STREETS   From the Capitol, North Capitol Street and South Capitol Street run north and south, respectively. East Capitol Street divides the city north and south. The area west of the Capitol is not a street at all, but the National Mall, which is bounded on the north by Constitution Avenue and on the south by Independence Avenue.

The primary artery of Washington is **Pennsylvania Avenue,** scene of parades, inaugurations, and other splashy events. Pennsylvania runs northwest in a direct line between the Capitol and the White House—if it weren't for the Treasury Building, the president would have a clear view of the Capitol—before continuing on a northwest angle to Georgetown, where it becomes M Street.

Pennsylvania Avenue in front of the White House, between 15th and 17th streets NW, remains closed to cars for security reasons, but it has been re-made into an attractive pedestrian plaza.

Constitution Avenue, paralleled to the south most of the way by Independence Avenue, runs east-west, flanking the Capitol and the Mall. If you hear Washingtonians talk about the "House" side of the Hill, they're referring to the southern half of the Capitol, the side closest to Independence Avenue and home to Congressional House offices and the House Chamber. Conversely, the Senate side is the northern half of the Capitol, where Senate offices and the Senate Chamber are found, closer to Constitution Avenue.

Washington's longest avenue, **Massachusetts Avenue,** runs parallel to Pennsylvania (a few avenues north). Along the way, you'll find

Washington, D.C., at a Glance

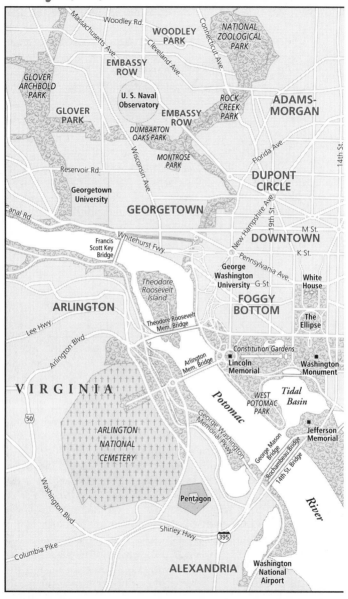

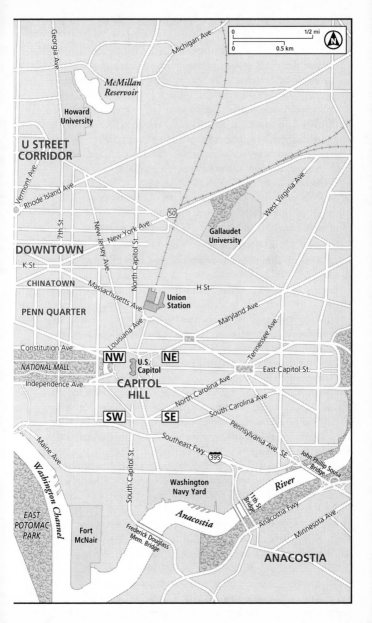

Union Station and then Dupont Circle, which is central to the area known as Embassy Row. Farther out are the Naval Observatory (the vice president's residence is on the premises), Washington National Cathedral, American University, and, eventually, Maryland.

Connecticut Avenue, which runs directly north (the other avenues run southeast-northwest), starts at Lafayette Square, intersects Dupont Circle, and eventually takes you to the National Zoo, to the charming residential neighborhood known as Cleveland Park, and into Chevy Chase, Maryland, where you can pick up the Beltway to head out of town. Downtown Connecticut Avenue, with its posh shops and clusters of restaurants, is a good street to stroll.

Wisconsin Avenue originates in Georgetown; its intersection with M Street forms Georgetown's hub. Antiques shops, trendy boutiques, nightclubs, restaurants, and pubs all vie for attention. Wisconsin Avenue basically parallels Connecticut Avenue.

FINDING AN ADDRESS   Once you understand the city's layout, it's easy to find your way around. As you read this, have a map handy.

Each of the four corners of the District of Columbia is exactly the same distance from the Capitol dome. The White House and most government buildings and important monuments are west of the Capitol (in the northwest and southwest quadrants), as are major hotels and tourist facilities.

Numbered streets run north-south, beginning on either side of the Capitol with First Street. Lettered streets run east-west and are named alphabetically, beginning with A Street. (Don't look for a B, a J, an X, a Y, or a Z St., though.) After W Street, street names of two syllables continue in alphabetical order, followed by street names of three syllables; the more syllables in a name, the farther the street is from the Capitol.

Avenues, named for U.S. states, run at angles across the grid pattern and often intersect at traffic circles. For example, New Hampshire, Connecticut, and Massachusetts avenues intersect at Dupont Circle.

With this in mind, you can easily find an address. On lettered streets, the address tells you exactly where to go. For instance, 1776 K St. NW is between 17th and 18th streets (the first two digits of 1776 tell you that) in the northwest quadrant (NW). *Note:* I Street is often written as "Eye" Street to prevent confusion with 1st Street.

To find an address on numbered streets, you'll probably have to use your fingers. For instance, 623 8th St. SE is between F and G streets (the 6th and 7th letters of the alphabet; the first digit of 623 tells you that) in the southeast quadrant (SE). One thing to remember: You count B as the second letter of the alphabet even though no B Street exists today (Constitution and Independence Aves. were the original B sts.), but since there's no J Street, K becomes the 10th letter, L the 11th, and so on.

THE NEIGHBORHOODS IN BRIEF

Capitol Hill   Everyone's heard of "the Hill," the area crowned by the Capitol. When people speak of Capitol Hill, they refer to a large section of town, extending from the western side of the Capitol to the D.C. Armory going east, bounded by H Street to the north and the Southwest Freeway to the south. It contains not only the chief symbol of the nation's capital, but also the Supreme Court building, the Library of Congress, the Folger Shakespeare Library, Union Station, and the U.S. Botanic Garden. Much of it is a quiet residential neighborhood of tree-lined streets and Victorian homes. There are a number of restaurants in the vicinity and a smattering of hotels, mostly close to Union Station.

The Mall   This lovely, tree-lined stretch of open space between Constitution and Independence avenues, extending for 2½ miles from the Capitol to the Lincoln Memorial, is the hub of tourist attractions. It includes most of the Smithsonian Institution museums and many other visitor attractions. The 300-foot-wide Mall is used by tourists as well as natives—joggers, food vendors, kite-flyers, and picnickers among them. Hotels and restaurants are located on the periphery.

Downtown   The area roughly between 7th and 22nd streets NW going east to west, and P Street and Pennsylvania Avenue going north to south, is a mix of the Federal Triangle's government office buildings, K Street (Lawyer's Row), Connecticut Avenue restaurants and shopping, historic hotels, the city's poshest small hotels, **Chinatown,** and the White House. You'll also find the historic **Penn Quarter,** a part of downtown that continues to flourish since the opening of the MCI Center with trendy restaurants, boutique hotels, and art galleries. (Despite a continuing marketing attempt by the city to promote the name "Penn Quarter," no one I know actually refers to this neighborhood by that title—we tend to say "near the MCI Center" instead, and everyone knows where the MCI Center is.) The total downtown area takes in so many blocks and attractions that I've divided discussions of accommodations and dining into two sections: "Downtown, 16th Street NW and West," and "Downtown, East of 16th Street NW." 16th Street and the White House form a natural point of separation.

U Street Corridor   D.C.'s avant-garde nightlife neighborhood between 12th and 15th streets NW continues to rise from the ashes of nightclubs and theaters frequented decades ago by African Americans. At two renovated establishments, the Lincoln Theater and the Bohemian Caverns jazz club (where Duke Ellington, Louis Armstrong, and Cab Calloway once performed), patrons today can enjoy performances by leading artists. The corridor offers many nightclubs and several restaurants. Go here to party, not to sleep—there are no hotels along this stretch.

Adams-Morgan   This trendy, multiethnic neighborhood is about the size of a postage stamp, and crammed with boutiques, clubs, and restaurants. Everything is located on either 18th Street NW or Columbia Road NW. You won't find any hotels here, although there are several nearby in the Dupont Circle and Woodley Park neighborhoods (see below). Parking during the day is okay, but forget it at night (although a parking garage did open recently on 18th St., which helps things a little). But you can easily walk (be alert—the neighborhood is edgy) to Adams-Morgan from the Dupont Circle or Woodley Park Metro stops, or take a taxi here. Weekend nightlife rivals that of Georgetown and Dupont Circle.

Dupont Circle   My favorite part of town, Dupont Circle is fun day or night. It takes its name from the traffic circle minipark, where Massachusetts, New Hampshire, and Connecticut avenues collide. Washington's famous **Embassy Row** centers on Dupont Circle, and refers to the parade of grand embassy mansions lining Massachusetts Avenue and its side streets. The streets extending out from the circle are lively with all-night bookstores, really good restaurants, wonderful art galleries and art museums, nightspots, movie theaters, and Washingtonians at their loosest. It is also the hub of D.C.'s gay community. There are plenty of hotels.

Foggy Bottom   The area west of the White House and southeast of Georgetown, Foggy Bottom was Washington's early industrial center. Its name comes from the foul fumes emitted in those days by a coal depot and gasworks, but its original name, Funkstown (for owner Jacob Funk), is perhaps even worse. There's nothing foul (and not much funky) about the area today. This is a low-key part of town, enlivened by the presence of the Kennedy Center, George Washington University, small and medium-size hotels, and a mix of restaurants on the main drag, Pennsylvania Avenue, and residential side streets.

Georgetown   This historic community dates from colonial times. It was a thriving tobacco port long before the District of Columbia was formed, and one of its attractions, the Old Stone House, dates from pre-Revolutionary days. Georgetown action centers on M Street and Wisconsin Avenue NW, where you'll find the luxury Four Seasons hotel and less expensive digs, numerous boutiques, chic restaurants, and popular pubs (lots of nightlife here). But get off the main drags and see the quiet, tree-lined streets of restored colonial row houses; stroll through the beautiful gardens of Dumbarton Oaks; and check out the C&O Canal. Georgetown is also home to Georgetown University. Note that the neighborhood gets pretty raucous on the weekends.

Woodley Park   Home to Washington's largest hotel (the Marriott Wardman Park), Woodley Park boasts the National Zoo, many good restaurants, and some antiques stores. Washingtonians are used to seeing conventioneers wandering the neighborhood's pretty residential streets with their name tags still on.

2 Getting Around

Washington is one of the easiest U.S. cities to navigate, thanks to its comprehensive public transportation system of trains and buses. Ours is the second-largest rail transit network and the fifth-largest bus network in the country. But because Washington is of manageable size and marvelous beauty, you may find yourself shunning transportation and choosing to walk.

BY METRORAIL

If you travel by Metrorail during rush hour (Mon–Fri 5:30–9:30am and 3–7pm), you may not be so smitten with the system because delays can be frequent, lines at fare-card machines long, trains over-crowded, and Washingtonians at their rudest. An increasing ridership is overloading the system, maintenance problems are cropping up, and the Washington Metropolitan Transit Authority (WMATA; **www.wmata.com**) is struggling just to keep pace, much less prevent future crises. Among the solutions are the addition of new trains and the installation of passenger information display boxes on station platforms reporting the number of minutes before the arrival of the next train and any delays or irregularities.

Metrorail's system of 86 stations and 106 miles of track includes locations at or near almost every sightseeing attraction and extends to suburban Maryland and northern Virginia. There are five lines in operation—Red, Blue, Orange, Yellow, and Green. The lines connect

Major Metro Stops

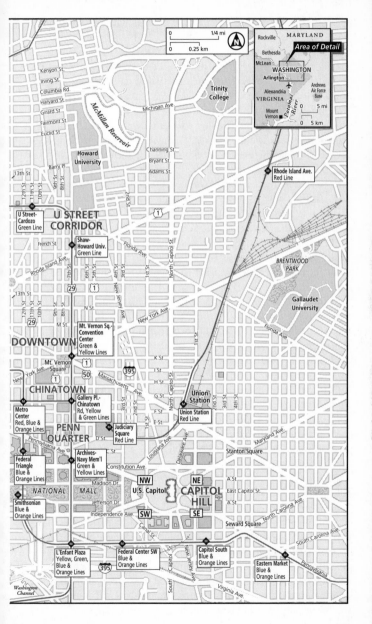

at several points, making transfers easy. All but Yellow and Green Line trains stop at Metro Center; all except Red Line trains stop at L'Enfant Plaza; all but Blue and Orange Line trains stop at Gallery Place/Chinatown. As of 2005, the Blue Line extends further into Prince George's County, Maryland, and a new station is open on New York Avenue, between the Union Station and Rhode Island Avenue stops on the Red line.

Metro stations are indicated by discreet brown columns bearing the station's name and the letter M. Below the M is a colored stripe (or stripes) indicating the line (or lines) that stop there. When using Metro for the first time, go to the kiosk and ask the station manager for a free *Metro System Pocket Guide.* It contains a map of the system, explains how it works, and lists the closest Metro stops to points of interest. The manager can also answer questions about routing or purchase of farecards. You can download a copy of the pocket guide and obtain loads of information, including schedules, from Metro's website (see above).

To enter or exit a Metro station, you need a computerized **farecard,** available at vending machines near the entrance. The machines take nickels, dimes, quarters, and bills from $1 to $20; they can return up to $4.95 in change (coins only). The vending machines labeled PASSES/FARECARDS accept cash and credit cards. At this time, the minimum fare to enter the system is $1.35, which pays for rides to and from any point within 7 miles of boarding during nonpeak hours; during peak hours (Mon–Fri 5:30–9:30am and 3–7pm), $1.35 takes you only 3 miles. The maximum you will pay to the furthest destination is $3.90.

If you are taking several Metro trips during your stay, it's better to put more value on your farecard to avoid having to purchase a new card each time you ride. Up to two children 4 and under can ride free with a paying passenger. Seniors (65 and up) and people with disabilities (with valid proof) ride Metrorail and Metrobus for a reduced fare.

Discount passes, called "One-Day Rail passes," cost $6 per person and allow you unlimited passage for the day, after 9:30am weekdays and all day on weekends and holidays. You can buy them at most stations; at WMATA headquarters, 600 5th St. NW (② **202/637-7000;** www.wmata.com), and at its sales office at Metro Center, 12th and G streets NW; or at retail stores, like Giant or Safeway grocery stores. Other passes are available—check out the website or call the main number for further information.

Tips **Getting to Georgetown**

Metrorail doesn't go to Georgetown, but a special shuttle bus, called the Georgetown Metro Connection, links three Metro stations (Rosslyn, Foggy Bottom, and Dupont Circle) to Georgetown. The shuttle travels between the three stations and Georgetown every 10 minutes Monday to Thursday from 7am to midnight, Friday 7am to 2am, Saturday 8am to 2am, and Sunday 8am to midnight. One-way fares cost $1, or 35¢ with a Metrorail transfer.

When you insert your card in the entrance gate, the time and location are recorded on its magnetic tape, and your card is returned. Don't forget to snatch it up and keep it handy; *you have to reinsert your farecard in the exit gate at your destination,* where the fare will automatically be deducted. The card will be returned if there's any value left on it. If you arrive at a destination and your farecard doesn't have enough value, add what's necessary at the Exitfare machines near the exit gate.

Metro opens weekdays at 5:30am and weekends at 7am, operating until midnight Sunday through Thursday and until 3am on weekends. Call ℂ **202/637-7000** or visit www.wmata.com for holiday hours and information on Metro routes.

BY BUS

The **Metrobus** system encompasses 12,490 stops on its 1,489-square-mile route (including on all major D.C. arteries as well as in the Virginia and Maryland suburbs). You'll know the stops by their red, white, and blue signs. However, the signs tell you only what buses pull into a given stop, not where they go. Plus, the bus schedules posted at bus stops are often out of date, so don't rely on them. For routing information, call ℂ **202/637-7000.** Calls are taken Monday to Thursday from 6am to 10:30pm, Friday 6am to 11:30pm, Saturday 7am to 11:30pm, and Sunday 7am to 10:30pm.

Base fare in the District is $1.25; bus transfers are free and valid for 2 hours from boarding. There may be additional charges for travel into the Maryland and Virginia suburbs. Bus drivers are not equipped to make change, so be sure to carry exact change or tokens.

Most buses operate daily almost around the clock. Service is quite frequent on weekdays, especially during peak hours. On weekends and late at night, service is less frequent.

Up to two children 4 and under ride free with a paying passenger on Metrobus, and there are reduced fares for seniors (✆ **202/ 637-7000**) and people with disabilities (✆ **202/962-1245** or 202/962-1100; see "Travelers with Disabilities" on p. 8 for more transit information).

BY CAR

More than half of all visitors to the District arrive by car; but once you get here, my advice is to park your car and either walk or use Metrorail for getting around. If you must drive, be aware that traffic is always thick during the week, parking spaces are often hard to find, and parking lots are ruinously expensive.

Outside of the city, you'll want a car to get to most attractions in Virginia and Maryland. Within the District, car-rental locations include **Avis,** 1722 M St. NW (✆ 202/467-6585) and 4400 Connecticut Ave. NW (✆ 202/686-5149); **Budget,** Union Station (✆ 202/289-5374); **Enterprise,** 3307 M St. NW (✆ 202/338-0015); **Hertz,** 901 11th St. NW (✆ 202/628-6174); **National** and **Alamo,** Union Station (same location and phone number: ✆ 202/ 842-7454); and **Thrifty,** inside the MCI Center, at 7th and G streets NW (✆ 202/371-0485).

BY TAXI

At the time of this writing, District cabs continue to operate on a zone system instead of using meters, and the cabbies hope to keep it that way. By law, basic rates are posted in each cab. If you take a trip from one point to another within the same zone, you pay just $5.50 (during non–rush hour) regardless of the distance traveled. So it would cost you $5.50 to travel a few blocks from the U.S. Capitol to the National Museum of American History, but the same $5.50 could take you from the Capitol all the way to Dupont Circle. They're both in Zone 1, as are most other tourist attractions: the White House, most of the Smithsonian, the Washington Monument, the FBI, the National Archives, the Supreme Court, the Library of Congress, the Bureau of Engraving and Printing, the Old Post Office, and Ford's Theatre. If your trip takes you into a second zone, the price is $7.60, $9.50 for a third zone, $11.40 for a fourth, and so on. These rates are based on the assumption that you are hailing a cab. If you telephone for a cab, you will be charged an additional $2. During rush hour (defined as 7–9:30am and 4–6:30pm weekdays) you pay a surcharge of $1 per trip, plus a surcharge of $1 when you telephone for a cab, which brings the telephone surcharge to $3.

Other charges might apply, as well: There's a $1 charge for each additional passenger after the first, so a $5.50 Zone 1 fare can become $8.50 for a family of four (although one child under 5 can ride free). Surcharges are also added for luggage (50¢–$2 per piece, depending on size). Try **Diamond Cab Company** (© 202/387-6200) or **Yellow Cab** (© 202/544-1212).

The zone system is not used when your destination is an out-of-District address (such as an airport); in that case, the fare is based on mileage—$2.65 for the first half-mile or part thereof and 80¢ for each additional half-mile or part. You can call © 202/331-1671 to find out the rate between any point in D.C. and an address in Virginia or Maryland. Call © 202/645-6018 to inquire about fares within the District. For more information about D.C. taxicabs than you could ever even guess was available, check out the District of Columbia Taxicab Commission's website, www.dctaxi.dc.gov.

Unique to the city is the practice of allowing drivers to pick up as many passengers as they can comfortably fit, so expect to share (unrelated parties pay the same as they would if they were not sharing). To register a complaint, note the cab driver's name and cab number and file a written complaint either by fax (© 202/889-3604) or mail (Commendations/Complaints, District of Columbia Taxicab Commission, 2041 Martin Luther King Jr. Ave. SE, Room 204, Washington, DC 20020).

FAST FACTS: Washington, D.C.

American Express There's an American Express Travel Service office at 1150 Connecticut Ave. NW (© 202/457-1300).

Area Codes Within the District of Columbia, it's 202. In suburban Virginia, it's 703. In suburban Maryland, it's 301. You must use the area code when dialing any number, even local calls within the District or to nearby Maryland or Virginia suburbs.

Congresspersons To locate a senator or representative, call the Capitol switchboard (© 202/225-3121). Point your Web browser to www.senate.gov and www.house.gov to contact individual senators and representatives by e-mail, find out what bills are being worked on, the calendar for the day, and more.

Drugstores CVS, Washington's major drugstore chain (with more than 40 stores), has two convenient 24-hour locations: 14th Street and Thomas Circle NW, at 1199 Vermont Avenue

NW (© **202/628-0720**), and at Dupont Circle (© **202/785-1466**), both with round-the-clock pharmacies. Check your phone book for other convenient locations.

Hospitals If you don't require immediate ambulance transportation but still need emergency-room treatment, call one of the following hospitals (and be sure to get directions): **Children's Hospital National Medical Center,** 111 Michigan Ave. NW (© **202/884-5000**); **George Washington University Hospital,** 23rd St. NW at Washington Circle (© **202/715-4000**); **Georgetown University Medical Center,** 3800 Reservoir Rd. NW (© **202/784-2000**); or **Howard University Hospital,** 2041 Georgia Ave. NW (© **202/865-6100**).

Hot Lines To reach a 24-hour poison-control hot line, call © **800/222-1222;** to reach a 24-hour crisis line, call © **202/561-7000.**

Internet Access Your hotel should be your first stop, since many hotels now offer free Internet access. Away from the hotel, try **Cyberstop Café,** 1513 17th St. NW (© **202/234-2470;** www.cyberstopcafe.com), where you can get a bite to eat while you surf one of 11 computers for $7 per half-hour, $9 per hour; the cafe is open Monday to Friday from 7am to midnight, Saturday and Sunday 8am to midnight. In Dupont Circle, the bookstore **Kramerbooks and Afterwords,** 1517 Connecticut Ave. NW (© **202/387-1400**), has one computer available for free Internet access, 15-minute limit.

Liquor Laws The legal age for the purchase and consumption of alcoholic beverages is 21. Liquor stores are closed on Sunday. District gourmet grocery stores, mom-and-pop grocery stores, and 7-Eleven convenience stores often sell beer and wine, even on Sunday. Do not carry open containers of alcohol in your car or in any public area that is not zoned for alcohol consumption; police can fine you on the spot.

Maps Free city maps are often available at hotels and throughout town at tourist attractions. You can also contact the **Washington, D.C. Convention and Tourism Corporation,** 901 7th St. NW, fourth floor, Washington, DC 20001 (© **202/789-7000**).

Newspapers & Magazines See "Publications" under "Orientation" (earlier in this chapter).

Police In an emergency, dial ✆ **911.** For a nonemergency, call ✆ **202/727-1010.**

Taxes The sales tax on merchandise is 5.75% in the District, 5% in Maryland, and 4.5% in Virginia. The tax on restaurant meals is 10% in the District, 5% in Maryland, and 4.5% in Virginia. In the District, you pay 14.5% hotel tax. The hotel tax in Maryland varies by county but averages 5% to 8%. The hotel tax in Virginia also varies by county, averaging 9.75%.

Weather Call ✆ **202/936-1212.**

3

Where to Stay

All together, there are more than 100 hotels in the city of Washington. So the first thing you should do is figure out your preferred neighborhood. Most of Washington's hotels lie downtown or near Dupont Circle, with a handful scattered in Georgetown, on Capitol Hill, and northward on Connecticut Avenue. Each of these communities has a distinct personality, which you should consider in choosing a location in which to base yourself. See "The Neighborhoods in Brief" on p. 21 to help you decide which location best suits you.

Within each neighborhood heading, this chapter further organizes hotels based on their lowest high-season rates for double rooms: Very Expensive (from about $250 and up), Expensive (from about $185), Moderate (from about $120), and Inexpensive (anything under $100). But these categories are intended as a general guideline only—rates can rise and fall dramatically, depending on how busy the hotel is. It's often possible to obtain a special package or a better rate.

1 Capitol Hill/The Mall

VERY EXPENSIVE

The Hotel George ⋒⋒ The Hotel George is one of Washington's hippest places to stay. With its facade of stainless steel, limestone, and glass; a lobby done in a sleek white, splashed with red, blue, and black furnishings; posters throughout the hotel depicting a modern-day George Washington, sans wig; and clientele tending toward celebs (everyone from Enrique Iglesias to Gov. Arnold Schwarzenegger), the George is in every way a capital establishment. The oversize guest rooms sport a minimalist look, all creamy white and modern. Fluffy comforters rest on oversize beds; slabs of granite top the desks and bathroom counters; and nature sounds (of the ocean, forest, and wind) emanate from the stereo CD/clock radios. A speaker in the spacious marble bathroom broadcasts TV sounds from the other room; other amenities include cordless phones, umbrellas, and spa robes. All rooms have free high-speed Internet access; eighth-floor rooms also have fax machines, at no extra cost. The hotel has three one-bedroom suites.

Contributing to the hotel's hipness is the presence of its restaurant, **Bistro Bis,** which serves (duh) French bistro food to hungry lobbyists and those they are lobbying. (Capitol Hill is a block away.)

15 E St. NW (at N. Capitol St.), Washington, DC 20001. ℂ **800/576-8331** or 202/347-4200. Fax 202/347-4213. www.hotelgeorge.com. 139 units. Weekdays $285–$350 double; weekends from $149 double; $950 suite. Ask about seasonal and corporate rates. Extra person $25. Children under 16 stay free in parent's room. AE, DC, DISC, MC, V. Parking $24 (2004 rate, may increase year to year),. Metro: Union Station. **Amenities:** Restaurant (French bistro); small 24-hr. fitness center w/steam rooms; cigar-friendly billiards room; 24-hr. concierge; business services; room service (7am–11pm); same-day laundry/dry cleaning; VCR rentals; 4 rooms for guests w/disabilities. *In room:* A/C, TV w/pay movies, 2-line phone w/dataport, mini-bar, coffeemaker, hair dryer, iron, safe, robes.

Mandarin Oriental Washington D.C. ★★★

I took Metro to the Mandarin Oriental, which is easy to do, since the 12th Street exit of the Smithsonian Metro station is only a 5-minute walk from the hotel. The Mandarin does not really cater to Metro-riding guests, however. If you stay at this hotel, you're more likely to arrive by car, limo, taxi, or perhaps yacht (the Washington waterfront is behind the hotel, across a roadway or two, but a pedestrian footbridge connects the complex with the marina and Tidal Basin). My point is that the Mandarin Oriental is fabulously posh, but its location is odd. The hotel is situated at the end of a concrete peninsula, known as the multipurpose Portals complex, which is set to include offices, retail shops, and restaurants. The government building neighborhood is not attractive and at night you will not be where the action is: These streets are not meant for strolling.

Having said all that, I will now tell you that the opening of the Mandarin Oriental in March 2004 upped the ante on luxury in the capital. Once you enter the hotel, you will be swept away. The service is positively sublime, everyone sweetly gracious. Hotel decor richly combines Asian and American traditions. The two-story lobby is a light-filled, glassed-in rotunda, the circular design used here and throughout the hotel to invite good luck. Each guest room is laid out in accordance with the principles of feng shui (for example, the mirror does not face the entry door, to prevent the reflection of good fortune out of the room), and furnishings include lamps of Japanese lantern design; replica pieces from the Smithsonian's Asian art galleries, the Sackler and Freer; and tapestries of hand-woven Thai silk panels. On the thick-mattressed beds are sensuously beautiful linens that make you reach out your hand to touch them.

Washington, D.C., Accommodations

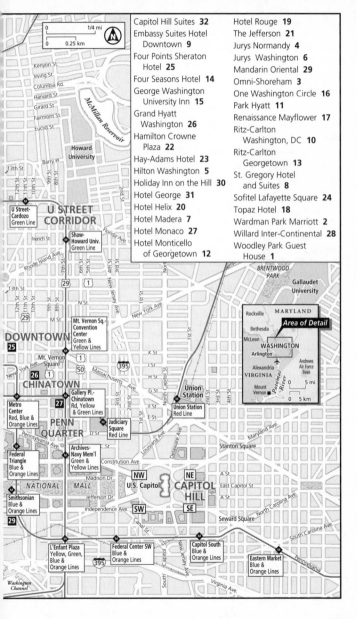

Capitol Hill Suites **32**
Embassy Suites Hotel
  Downtown **9**
Four Points Sheraton
  Hotel **25**
Four Seasons Hotel **14**
George Washington
  University Inn **15**
Grand Hyatt
  Washington **26**
Hamilton Crowne
  Plaza **22**
Hay-Adams Hotel **23**
Hilton Washington **5**
Holiday Inn on the Hill **30**
Hotel George **31**
Hotel Helix **20**
Hotel Madera **7**
Hotel Monaco **27**
Hotel Monticello
  of Georgetown **12**

Hotel Rouge **19**
The Jefferson **21**
Jurys Normandy **4**
Jurys Washington **6**
Mandarin Oriental **29**
Omni-Shoreham **3**
One Washington Circle **16**
Park Hyatt **11**
Renaissance Mayflower **17**
Ritz-Carlton
  Washington, DC **10**
Ritz-Carlton
  Georgetown **13**
St. Gregory Hotel
  and Suites **8**
Sofitel Lafayette Square **24**
Topaz Hotel **18**
Wardman Park Marriott **2**
Willard Inter-Continental **28**
Woodley Park Guest
  House **1**

Finally, the setting that separates the hotel from the rest of the city also helps create a feeling that you are away, but not away. You may not want to roam the neighborhood, but you can walk around the hotel's property, which includes terraces of landscaped gardens and views of the Tidal Basin and marina, the Jefferson Memorial, the Virginia skyline, and District buildings. Guest rooms offer these same views. And when you are on the inside, looking out from the soundproofed, very quiet, and elegant refuge of your room, the landscape seems transformed. Even Interstate 95, seen from this vantage point, appears rather magnificent.

Note: Although too new to review at press time, the hotel's recent additions of a restaurant (CityZen, with chef Eric Ziebold of the West Coast's acclaimed French Laundry) and a 14,000-square-foot spa both promise to be world-class.

1330 Maryland Ave. SW (at 12th St.), Washington, DC 20001. ℂ **866/526-6567** or 202/554-8588. Fax 202/554-8999. www.mandarinoriental.com/washington. 400 units. Weekdays $350–$695 double, $950–$8,000 suite; weekends $295–$525 double, $900–$1,400 suite. Children under 12 stay free in parent's room. For information about special packages, call the hotel directly or check the website. AE, DC, DISC, MC, V. Parking $34. Metro: Smithsonian. **Amenities:** 2 restaurants (French American, Asian-influenced cafe cuisine); 2 bars; fully equipped fitness center; 10,400-sq.-ft. full-service spa w/lap pool; 24-hr. concierge; business center w/full Internet access; 24-hr. room service; same-day laundry/dry cleaning; club levels; several rooms for guests w/disabilities. *In room:* A/C, TV w/pay movies and HDTV, DVD/CD player, 3-line phone w/dataport, high-speed Internet access ($12 per day), minibar, coffeemaker, hair dryer, iron, safe, robes.

EXPENSIVE

Holiday Inn on the Hill 🍴   A major renovation completed in 2003 took the Bing Crosby out of this traditional Holiday Inn, and garnered a "Renovation of the Year Award" from the hotel's umbrella organization, the InterContinental Hotels Group. What you see now is a hotel that's very 21st century—or trying hard to be, anyway. Gone are double beds and family-friendly features, such as the Discovery Zone kids' program. Gone, too, are the prices that made this hotel a great value for families and business folks on a budget (this hotel used to be listed in the "Inexpensive" category). Instead, you'll find guest rooms done in shades of cobalt blue, with zebra wood armoires, glass-topped desks with ergonomic mesh chairs, and a triple-sheeted king- or two queen-size beds. Rooms are standard size, although bathrooms are larger than expected, with a small vanity ledge just outside the bathroom for overflow counter space.

Every guest room offers free high-speed Internet access, and the restaurant and an area of the lobby allow for wireless Internet access.

Some of the hotel's former clientele will be outpriced here, but for others the Capitol Hill location remains unbeatable. Several labor union headquarters are nearby, making the hotel a popular choice among the "labor" folks doing business with one of the unions. And for families, proximity to the Capitol and other sites, as well as certain amenities (such as the fitness center, pool, and "kids 12 and under eat free" restaurant policy), may appeal.

To get the best deals and perks, ask about promotions, the "Great Rates" package, and the "Priority Club" frequent guest membership.

415 New Jersey Ave. NW (between D and E sts.), Washington, DC 20001. ℂ 800/638-1116 or 202/638-1616. Fax 202/638-0707. www.holidayinnonthehill.com. 343 units. $189–$389 double (Mon–Tues are the most expensive). Extra person $20. Children under 19 stay free in parent's room. Ask about special promotions and packages. AE, DC, DISC, MC, V. Parking $22. Metro: Union Station. **Amenities:** Restaurant (American; free for kids 12 and under w/adult); bar; outdoor (unheated) rooftop pool; 24-hr. fitness room; concierge; business center; room service (6am–11pm); same-day laundry/dry cleaning service; 8 rooms for guests w/disabilities (4 w/roll-in shower). *In room:* A/C, TV w/pay movies and Nintendo, 2-line phone w/dataport, coffeemaker, hair dryer, iron.

MODERATE

Capitol Hill Suites 𝕣   A $3 million renovation completed in 2000 at this well-run, all-suite property produced remarkable and lasting results. Bedroom walls are painted cobalt blue, heavy velvet drapes keep out morning sun, lamps and mirrors are from Pottery Barn, desks are long, desk chairs are ergonomically correct, and beds are firm. The lobby, which features an enclosed fireplace, leather chairs, and an antique credenza where self-serve coffee is laid out, is inviting enough to linger. (Sit here long enough and you might spy a congressman or senator—a number of members reserve suites for 100 days at a time.)

The location is another plus: Capitol Hill Suites is the only hotel truly *on* the Hill (on the House side of the Capitol). It stands on a residential street across from the Library of Congress, a short walk from the Capitol and Mall attractions, a food market, and more than 20 restaurants (many of which deliver to the hotel).

The term *suite* denotes the fact that every unit has a kitchenette with coffeemaker, toaster oven, microwave, refrigerator, flatware, and glassware. Most units are efficiencies, with the kitchenette, bed, and sofa all in the same room. The best choices are one-bedroom units, in which the kitchenette and living room are separate from the bedroom. A third option is a "studio double," with two queen-size beds and a kitchenette, but no living room area. Some rooms in each category have pullout sofas.

Kids Family-Friendly Hotels

Embassy Suites Hotel Downtown (p. 52)   You're close to both a Red line and a Blue line Metro station (the zoo is on the Red line; the Smithsonian museums are on the Blue line) and within walking distance of Georgetown. Your kids can sleep on the pullout sofa in the separate living room. You've got some kitchen facilities, but you might not use them because the complimentary breakfast in the atrium is unbelievable, and the restaurant discounts meals for hotel guests (10%–20%) and has a special $4.95 kids' menu. And there's an indoor pool and a free game room.

Hilton Washington (p. 49)   A large heated outdoor pool, three tennis courts, and a goodie bag at check-in—what more does a kid need?

Omni Shoreham Hotel (p. 62)   Adjacent to Rock Creek Park, the Omni is also within walking distance of the zoo and Metro and is equipped with a large outdoor pool and kiddie pool. The hotel gives children a goodie bag at check-in and the concierge has a supply of board games at the ready (no charge to borrow, just remember to return).

Guests, no matter their political leanings, have privileges to dine at the Capitol Hill Club, a members-only club for Republicans, and can charge meals and drinks to their hotel bill.

200 C St. SE (at 2nd St.), Washington, DC 20003. ✆ **800/424-9165** or 202/543-6000. Fax 202/547-2608. www.capitolhillsuites.com. 152 units. $119–$239 double. Weekend and long-term rates may be available. Extra person $20. Rates include continental breakfast. Children under 18 stay free in parent's room. AE, DC, DISC, MC, V. Valet parking $25 plus tax. Metro: Capitol South. **Amenities:** Privileges ($10 per day) at nearby Washington Sports and Health Club; business services; coin-op washer/dryers; same-day laundry/dry cleaning; 8 rooms for guests w/disabilities (all w/roll-in shower). *In room:* A/C, TV w/pay movies, 2-line phone w/dataport, high-speed Internet access (about $10 per day), fridge, coffeemaker, hair dryer, iron.

2 Downtown, East of 16th Street NW
VERY EXPENSIVE
Grand Hyatt Washington ✿   Until the D.C. Convention Center's on-site hotel, with its 1,000-plus rooms, opens in 2007, the Grand Hyatt is the largest hotel near the convention center.

The Grand Hyatt has a lot of other things going on besides its room count of 900. The vast lobby is in an atrium 12 stories high and enclosed by a glass, mansard-style roof. A baby grand piano floats on its own island in the 7,000-square-foot "lagoon"; waterfalls, catwalks, 22-foot-high trees, and an array of bars and restaurants on the periphery will keep you permanently entertained. Should you get bored, head to the nearby nightspots and restaurants, or hop on Metro, to which the Hyatt has direct access. The hotel lies between Capitol Hill and the White House, 2 blocks from the MCI Center, and about 3 blocks from the new D.C. Convention Center, at 801 Mount Vernon Place NW.

Guest rooms and corridors underwent a complete renovation in 2003. Features include new shower heads and light-colored marble in the bathrooms; a fresh contemporary look of dark, hardwood furniture and hues of blue and gold in the guest rooms; and updated carpeting everywhere. Nearly half of the rooms offer high-speed Internet access, for a rate of $9.95 per 24 hours. Among the potpourri of special plans and packages available is one for business travelers: Pay an extra $20 and you stay in an eighth- or ninth-floor room equipped with a large desk, fax machine, computer hookup, and coffeemaker; have access to printers and other office supplies on the floor; and are entitled to complimentary continental breakfast and access to the health club. Always ask about seasonal and special offers, and check the website for the best deals.

1000 H St. NW, Washington, DC 20001. ✆ **800/233-1234** or 202/582-1234. Fax 202/628-1641. www.grandwashington.hyatt.com. 900 units. Weekdays $350 double; weekends $125–$139 double; $360–$2,200 suite. Extra person $25. Children under 18 stay free in parent's room. Ask about special promotions and packages. AE, DC, DISC, MC, V. Valet parking $26; self-parking $20. Metro: Metro Center. **Amenities:** 4 restaurants (Italian/Asian, Continental, deli); 3 bars; health club w/whirlpool, lap pool, steam and sauna rooms, aerobics, and spa services (hotel guests pay $11 for club use); concierge; courtesy car to nearby destinations available on a first-come, first-served basis; business center; room service (6am–1am); in-room and health-club massage; same-day dry cleaning; concierge-level rooms; 24 rooms for guests w/disabilities (8 w/roll-in shower). *In room:* A/C, TV w/pay movies, 2-line phone w/dataport, minibar, coffeemaker, hair dryer, iron.

Hotel Monaco Washington D.C. ✦✦✦   Let's cut to the chase: This is where I'd stay if I were a visitor to D.C. The Monaco has been winning awards and great notice ever since it opened in 2002. Museum-like in appearance, the Monaco occupies a four-story, all-marble mid-19th-century building, half of which was designed by Robert Mills, the architect for the Washington Monument, the other half designed by Thomas Walter, one of the architects for the

U.S. Capitol. The two halves connect seamlessly, enclosing an interior, landscaped courtyard. Jutting into the courtyard from the F Street side of the hotel is its marvelous restaurant, **Poste,** which got off to a rough start but has finally established itself as a top spot for dining. The hotel takes up an entire block, between 7th and 8th streets, and E and F streets. Superlatives are in order: The hotel is truly magnificent.

Constructed originally as the General Post Office, and later used to house the Tariff Commission, the building is a designated National Historic Landmark, and it remains a federal building. The Kimpton Hotel & Restaurant Group, LLC, has leased the building for 60 years, performing an extensive renovation, which retains many original features, as required by its historic status, that blend creatively with the hotel's humming, hip, upscale decor. So you've got 19th-century columns uplit by Italian chrome-and-alabaster torchieres in the lobby, a grand spiral staircase at each of the four corners, and high vaulted ceilings along corridors lit with whimsical, lanternlike red lamps.

The spacious guest rooms, similarly, combine the historic and the hip. The vaulted ceilings are high (12–18 ft.) and windows are long, hung with charcoal-and-white patterned drapes. Eclectic furnishings include neoclassical armoires and three-legged desks. The color scheme successfully marries creamy yellow walls with periwinkle blue lounge chairs and orange damask pillows. Interior rooms overlook the courtyard and the restaurant; you'll see the charming arched passageway through which horse and carriage came a century ago. Exterior rooms view the MCI Center and the Smithsonian's National Portrait Gallery on the north side, and downtown sights on the south side. This is a great location: When you stay at the Monaco, you're not just downtown, you're part of the scene.

700 F St. NW (at 7th St.), Washington, DC 20004. (©) **800/649-1202** or 202/628-7177. Fax 202/628-7277. www.monaco-dc.com. 184 units. Weekdays $239–$349 double. $439–$849 suite; weekends $149–$349 double, $349–$699 suite. Extra person $20. Children under 18 stay free in parent's room. Rates include complimentary Starbucks coffee in morning and wine receptions in evening. AE, DC, DISC, MC, V. Parking $27. Pets get VIP treatment, with their own registration cards at check-in, maps of neighborhood fire hydrants and parks, and gourmet puppy and kitty treats. Metro: Gallery Place. **Amenities:** Restaurant (modern American); bar; spacious fitness center w/flat-screen TVs; 24-hr. concierge; full-service business center; 24-hr. room service; same-day laundry/dry cleaning; 9 rooms for guests w/disabilities (4 w/roll-in shower). *In room:* A/C, TV w/pay movies and Nintendo, CD player, 2-line phone w/dataport and high-speed Internet access, minibar, hair dryer, iron, safe, robes.

Sofitel Lafayette Square Washington DC 𝒶𝒶 The Hay-Adams (p. 45) faces some competition since the 2002 opening of this luxury hotel, which, like the Hay-Adams, borders Lafayette Square and is just minutes from the White House. The Hay-Adams offers White House views and the Sofitel does not, it's true, but the Sofitel's other appealing features may make up for that.

This handsome, 12-story limestone building was erected in the early 20th century, and its distinctive facade includes decorative bronze corner panels, bas-relief sculptural panels at ground-floor level, and a 12th-floor balcony that travels the length of both the H and 15th street sides of the structure (decorative, not accessible, alas). Inside, hotel staff members dressed in designer uniforms greet you with *"Bonjour!"*—small hints that a French company (Accor Hotels) owns the Sofitel. French designer Pierre-Yves Rochon styled the interior; a Michelin three-star chef is behind the contemporary French cuisine served in Café 15, the hotel's restaurant; and the gift shop sells such specialty items as French plates and porcelain dolls. The Sofitel also has a super bar, Le Bar, which also serves lunch.

Due to its corner location and large windows, guest rooms are bright with natural light; second- and third-floor rooms facing 15th or H street bring in more light still, because their windows extend nearly from floor to ceiling. Each room sports elegantly modern decor that includes a long desk, a creamy duvet with a colorful throw on a king-size bed (about 17 rooms have two double beds instead of kings), a much-marbled bathroom with tub separate from the shower stall, fresh flowers, and original artwork, including dramatic photographs of Washington landmarks. The 11th floor has been designed with visiting heads of state in mind, and can be easily secured. In each of the 17 suites, the bedroom is separate from the living room.

806 15th St. NW (at H St.), Washington, DC 20005. ℂ **202/737-8800.** Fax 202/730-8500. www.sofitel.com. 237 units. Weekdays $235–$480 double; weekends, call for rates, which can start as low as $139 double; from $495 suite. For lowest rates at any time, call directly to the hotel and ask about specials or packages or check out the website. Extra person $20. Children under 12 stay free in parent's room. AE, DC, DISC, MC, V. Parking $26. Pets allowed with prior approval. Metro: McPherson Square, Farragut West, or Farragut North. **Amenities:** Restaurant; bar; library w/books about D.C. and Paris; 24-hr. state-of-the art fitness center; 24-hr. concierge; 24-hr. business services; 24-hr. room service; same-day laundry/dry cleaning; 8 rooms for guests w/disabilities (all w/roll-in shower). *In room:* A/C, TV w/pay movies and Nintendo, CD player, 2-line phone w/dataport and high-speed Internet access ($9.95 per day), minibar, hair dryer, iron, safe, robes.

Willard InterContinental Washington 𝒶𝒶𝒶 If you're lucky enough to stay here, you'll be a stone's throw from the White House and the Smithsonian museums, in the heart of downtown near plenty of excellent restaurants, down the block from the National Theatre, and down the avenue from the Capitol. The Willard is among the best hotels in the city and, naturally, one of the most expensive. Heads of state favor the Willard (the hotel offers one floor as "Secret Service-cleared"), as do visitors from other countries (the gift shop sells newspapers from around the world; some are available free) and movie directors (who like to shoot scenes in the famously ornate lobby and restaurant).

A renovation completed in late 2000 spruced up the guest rooms' handsome, if staid, decor, which is heavy on reproduction Federal- and Edwardian-style furnishings. More recently, the hotel installed wireless Internet service throughout the hotel, including all of the guest rooms. The rooms with the best views are the oval suites over-looking Pennsylvania Avenue to the Capitol and the rooms fronting Pennsylvania Avenue. Rooms facing the courtyard are the quietest. Best of all is the "Jenny Lind" suite, perched in the curve of the 12th floor's southeast corner; its round bull's-eye window captures glimpses of the Washington Monument.

The Willard's designation as a National Historic Landmark in 1974 and magnificent restoration in the 1980s helped revitalize Pennsylvania Avenue and this part of town. Stop in at the Round Robin Bar for a mint julep (introduced here), and listen to bartender and manager Jim Hewes spin tales about the history of the 1901 Willard and its predecessor, the City Hotel, built on this site in 1815.

Always inquire about off-season and weekend packages, when rates are sometimes halved and come with one of several compli-mentary options, sometimes an upgrade to a suite, valet parking, or a second room at half-price.

1401 Pennsylvania Ave. NW (at 14th St.), Washington, DC 20004. © **800/827-1747** or 202/628-9100. Fax 202/637-7326. www.washington.interconti.com. 341 units. Weekdays $480 double, weekends from $209; $850–$4,200 suite. Ask about special promotions and packages. AE, DC, DISC, MC, V. Parking $25. Metro: Metro Center. Small pets allowed. **Amenities:** Restaurant (modern French-American); cafe; bar; modest-size but state-of-the-art fitness center; children's programs; concierge; business center; 24-hr. room service; babysitting; same-day laundry/dry cleaning; currency exchange; airline/train ticketing. *In room:* A/C, TV, 2-line phone w/dataport and complimentary wireless Internet access, minibar, hair dryer, iron, safe, robes.

EXPENSIVE

Hamilton Crowne Plaza Washington DC ⟨ꝁ⟩   A much needed renovation in 2002 updated the appearance and amenities in the guest rooms, adding handy items like CD players and wireless Internet access (the latter for $9.95 per day), handsome features such as royal blue robes and dark wood armoires and headboards, and comfortable accommodations like the seven-layer bed. Not much they could do about the size of the rooms, though, so those with king-size beds feel a bit tight; those with two double beds seem a little roomier. Rooms on the K Street side overlook Franklin Park, which is pleasant, and those on the upper floors offer views of the city skyline. In keeping with the times, the hotel has a designated "women's floor," accessible only to those with a special elevator key. This is a well-placed hotel, sort of central between the two sections of downtown: the K Street side and the section that's fast being revitalized around the MCI Center. The hotel's restaurant is popular with office workers at weekday lunch, thanks to a generous $15 buffet of soups, salads, and rotisserie items.

1001 14th St. NW (at K St.), Washington, DC 20005. © **800/2-CROWNE** or 202/682-0111. Fax 202/682-9525. www.hamiltoncrowneplazawashingtondc.com. 318 units. Weekdays $119–$325 double, $300–$600 suite; look for much lower rates on weekends. Extra person $20. Children under 18 stay free in parent's room. AE, DC, DISC, MC, V. Parking $24. Metro: McPherson Square. **Amenities:** Restaurant (American); bar; 24 hr. fitness room; concierge; 24-hr. business center; room service (6am–midnight); same-day laundry/dry cleaning (not on weekends); club level. *In room:* A/C, TV w/pay movies, 2-line speaker phone w/dataport, wireless high-speed Internet access ($10 per day), CD player/clock radio, coffeemaker, hair dryer, iron, safe, robes.

MODERATE

Four Points by Sheraton Washington, D.C. Downtown ⚡ *Value*
This former Days Inn has been totally transformed into a contemporary property that offers all the latest gizmos, from complimentary high-speed Internet access in all the rooms, and wireless Internet access in the lobby and meeting rooms, to a 650-square-foot fitness center. A massive renovation undertaken by a new owner essentially gutted the old building, but the location is still as terrific as ever (close to the D.C. Convention Center, MCI Center, and downtown). The rates are reasonable and hotel amenities spectacular, which make this a good choice for both business and leisure visitors.

Five types of rooms are available: units with two double beds, with one queen-size bed, or with one king-size bed; junior suites; or one-bedroom suites. In 2003, the hotel put "Heavenly Beds" (custom-designed, multilayered, pillow-top mattresses) in all of the rooms. Corner rooms (there are only about 10) are a little more spacious than others, which are of standard size. While guest rooms offer city views, the rooftop pool and lounge boast a sweeping vista of the city that includes the Capitol. Under separate ownership from the hotel is a recommended restaurant, Corduroy.

1201 K St. NW (at 12th St.), Washington, DC 20005. ✆ **888/481-7191** or 202/289-7600. Fax 202/349-2215. www.fourpointswashingtondc.com. 265 units. In season $149–$275 double; off season $99–$245 double; from $400 suite. Extra person $20. Children under 18 stay free in parent's room. AE, DC, DISC, MC, V. Parking $26. Metro: McPherson Square or Metro Center. **Amenities:** Restaurant (seasonal American); bar; indoor heated pool on rooftop; fitness center; business center; room service (6am–midnight); same-day laundry/dry cleaning; executive-level rooms; 8 rooms for guests w/disabilities (3 w/roll-in shower). *In room:* A/C, TV w/pay movies, 2-line phone w/dataport and high-speed Internet access, minibar, coffeemaker, hair dryer, iron, safe, robes.

Hotel Helix ✦   The Helix doesn't so much invite you in, as intrigue you in. Those giant, peacock blue English lawn chairs and the Magritte-like painting out front are just the beginning. Your steps across a mosaic-tiled vestibule trigger an automatic swoosh of curtains, parting to let you inside the hotel. The small lobby is spare, its main furnishings the illuminated "pods," or podiums with flat computer screens for check in. It's hard to tell who are staff and who are guests, which is intentional—"takes away barriers," says my hotel guide, Danielle. The guest rooms have a minimalist quality to them, too, which is an odd thing to say about a decor that uses such startling colors: cherry red and royal blue ottomans, striped green settees, bright orange vanities in bathrooms, metallic-sheen walls, lime-green honor bar/armoires. But rooms are uncluttered and roomy, due to a design that puts the platform bed behind sheer drapes in an alcove (in the king deluxe rooms), leaving the two-person settee, a triangular desk, and the 22-inch flat-screen TV on its stainless steel stand out in the open. Deluxe rooms, without alcoves, feel a little less spacious but otherwise look the same. Roomiest are the 18 suites, with a separate bedroom and, in the living room, slate blue sectional sofas. Every guest room has a five-disc CD changer, complimentary wireless Internet access, and Web TV (for a charge).

1430 Rhode Island Ave. NW (between 14th and 15th sts.), Washington, DC 20006. ✆ **866/508-0658** or 202/462-9001. Fax 202/332-3519. www.hotelhelix.com. 178 units. $119–$239 double; specialty rooms: add $40 to double rate; suites: add $125 to double rate. Best rates usually Sun–Mon. Extra person $20. Children under 18 stay free in parent's room. Rates include "bubbly hour" (champagne) in evening. AE, DC, DISC, MC, V. Parking $22 plus tax. Pets welcome. Metro: McPherson Square. **Amenities:** Bar/cafe; exercise room w/treadmill, recumbent bike, weight system; room service (during breakfast and dinner hours); same-day laundry/dry cleaning; 9 rooms for guests w/disabilities (5 w/roll-in shower). *In room:* A/C; TV w/pay movies, Nintendo, and Web access (for a fee); free wireless Internet access; 2-line phones w/dataport and high-speed Internet access; minibar; hair dryer; iron.

3 Downtown, 16th Street NW & West

VERY EXPENSIVE

Hay-Adams ★★   An extensive $18 million renovation completed in spring 2002 was the Hay-Adams's first major refurbishment in its 75-year history. Some improvements, such as the new heating and air-conditioning system and structural changes that make the hotel accessible to guests with disabilities, were long overdue. Other improvements, such as the modernized kitchen, are invisible to guests. Whether or not you've stayed at the Hay-Adams before, you'll appreciate the hotel's elegant decor of sage green, off-white, beige, and gold tones; the CD players; high-speed and wireless Internet access; custom European linens; new furnishings (the hotel donated its old furniture to local homeless shelters); and thermostats in each room.

But the best of the Hay-Adams remains much the same: The hotel still offers the best views in town. Reserve a room on the sixth through eighth floors on the H Street side of the hotel (or as low as the second floor in winter, when the trees are bare), pull back the curtains from the windows, and *voilà!*—you get a full-frontal view of Lafayette Square, the White House, and the Washington Monument in the background. (You'll pay more for rooms with these views.) The view from rooms facing 16th Street isn't bad, either: Windows overlook the yellow-painted exterior of St. John's Episcopal Church, built in 1815 and known as the "church of the presidents."

The Hay-Adams is one in the triumvirate of exclusive hotels built by Harry Wardman in the 1920s (the Jefferson and the St. Regis are the other two). Its architecture is Italian Renaissance and much of the original features, such as ornate plaster moldings and ornamental fireplaces, the walnut-paneled lobby, and high-ceilinged guest rooms, are still in place. The hotel has about 13 one-bedroom suites (the living room and bedroom are separate) and seven junior suites (living room and bedroom are together in one space). Stop in at the Off the Record bar for casual fare at lunch and dinner and the occasional sighting of a big name in the media or administration.

1 Lafayette Sq. (at 16th and H sts. NW), Washington, DC 20006. © **800/853-6807** or 202/638-6600. Fax 202/638-2716. www.hayadams.com. 145 units. Weekdays $385–$595 double, weekends $269–$489 double; from $785 junior suite, from $1,250 1-bedroom suite. Extra person $30. Children under 18 stay free in parent's room. AE, DC, DISC, MC, V. Valet parking $28. Metro: Farragut West or McPherson Square. Pets under 25 lb. accepted. **Amenities:** Restaurant (American); bar; access to local health club ($15 per day); 24-hr. concierge; complimentary morning car service; secretarial and business services; 24-hr. business center; 24-hr. room

service; same-day laundry/dry cleaning, 9 rooms for guests w/disabilities (3 w/roll-in shower). *In room:* A/C, TV w/pay movies, 2-line phone w/dataport, wireless Internet access, minibar, hair dryer, iron, safe, robes.

The Jefferson, a Loews Hotel 🍴🍴 Opened in 1923 just 4 blocks from the White House, the Jefferson is one of the city's three most exclusive hotels (along with the Hay-Adams and the St. Regis). Those looking for an intimate hotel, with excellent service, a good restaurant, sophisticated but comfortable accommodations, inviting public rooms (should you want to hang out), and proximity to attractions and restaurants (should you not want to hang out) will find that the Jefferson satisfies on all scores. About one-third of the lodgings are suites: junior, and one- and two-bedroom. The hotel's largest standard rooms are located in the "carriage house," an attached town house with its own elevator, which you reach by passing through the pub/lounge in the main building. Guest rooms are individually decorated with antiques and lovely fabrics, evoking a European feel. A fine art collection, including original documents signed by Thomas Jefferson, graces the public areas as well as the guest rooms. A renovation in 2004 restored antiques, added sleeper sofas to all of the suites, and installed wireless Internet access in the public areas.

Many local foodies like to dine at the hotel's acclaimed **Restaurant at the Jefferson** 🍴🍴. And the paneled pub/lounge is another popular stopping place for Washingtonians; here you can sink into a red leather chair and enjoy a marvelous high tea or cocktails.

1200 16th St. NW (at M St.), Washington, DC 20036. ℭ **800/235-6397** or 202/347-2200. Fax 202/331-7982. www.loewsjefferson.com. 100 units. Weekdays from $339 double, $439–$1,500 suite; weekends from $199 double, from $299 suite. Extra person $25. Children under 12 stay free in parent's room. AE, DC, DISC, MC, V. Parking $28. Metro: Farragut North. Pets welcomed and pampered. **Amenities:** Restaurant (American); bar/lounge (serving high tea 3–5pm); 24-hr. fitness room w/mainly cardio machines; access to health club (w/pool) at the University Club across the street ($20 per visit); children's program (care package at check-in); 24-hr. concierge; 24-hr. room service; 24-hr. butler service; in-room massage; baby-sitting; same-day laundry/dry cleaning; 1 room for guests w/disabilities (w/roll-in shower); video and CD rentals. *In room:* A/C, TV w/pay movies and VCR, CD player, 2-line phone w/dataport and high-speed Internet access ($11 fee), minibar, hair dryer, safe, robes.

Renaissance Mayflower 🍴 Superbly located in the heart of downtown, the Mayflower has been the hotel of choice for guests as varied as Kurt Russell and Wynton Marsalis. The lobby, which extends an entire block from Connecticut Avenue to 17th Street, is always bustling—chaotic at check-in and checkout times—because Washingtonians tend to use it as a shortcut in their travels.

The Mayflower is steeped in history: When it opened in 1925, it was the site of Calvin Coolidge's inaugural ball (although Coolidge didn't attend—he was mourning his son's death from blood poisoning). President-elect FDR and family lived in room nos. 776 and 781 while waiting to move into the White House, and this is where he penned the words, "The only thing we have to fear is fear itself." A major restoration in the 1980s uncovered large skylights and renewed the lobby's pink marble bas-relief frieze and spectacular promenade.

In 2004 the hotel completed a $9 million, top-to-bottom renovation that transformed the guest rooms into individual refuges of pretty elegance: Silvery green bed coverings, embroidered drapes, silk wall coverings, pillow-top mattresses, and sink-into armchairs are some of the finer touches. Certain gracious appointments remain: Each guest room still has its own marble foyer, high ceiling, mahogany reproduction furnishings (Queen Anne, Sheraton, Chippendale, and Hepplewhite) and an Italian marble bathroom. All rooms now have high-speed Internet access for a charge of $9.95 per 24 hours. The Mayflower now has a club level on the eighth floor, as well as 74 executive suites.

In the hotel's lovely Café Promenade, lawyers and lobbyists continue to gather for weekday power breakfasts, and a full English tea is served Monday through Saturday afternoons. The clubby, mahogany-paneled Town and Country Lounge is the setting for light buffet lunches and complimentary hors d'oeuvres during cocktail hour. Bartender Sambonn Lek has quite a following, as much for his conversation as for his magic tricks, so the place is jumping.

1127 Connecticut Ave. NW (between L and M sts.), Washington, DC 20036. © 800/468-3571 or 202/347-3000. Fax 202/776-9182. www.renaissancehotels. com/WASSH. 657 units. Weekdays $199–$399 double; from $329 suite; weekends $109–$209 double; from $259 suite. Rates include complimentary coffee service with wakeup call. No charge for extra person in room. AE, DC, DISC, MC, V. Parking $26. Metro: Farragut North. **Amenities:** Restaurant (Mediterranean); lobby lounge; bar; fitness center; concierge; 24-hr. business center; 24-hr. room service; same-day laundry/dry cleaning; club level; 15 rooms for guests w/disabilities. *In room:* A/C, TV w/pay movies, 2-line phone w/dataport and high-speed Internet access, hair dryer, iron, robes.

MODERATE

Hotel Rouge Ⓐ High-energy rock music dances out onto the sidewalk. A red awning extends from the entrance. A guest with sleepy eyes and brilliant blue hair sits diffidently upon the white tufted leather sofa in the small lobby. Casually dressed patrons come and go, while an older couple roosts at a table just inside the doorway of the adjoining Bar Rouge sipping martinis. Shades of red are everywhere: in the staff's funky shiny shirts, in the accent pillows on the retro furniture, and in the artwork. This used to be a Quality Hotel: It's come a long way, baby.

The Kimpton Hotel & Restaurant Group, LLC (known for its offbeat but upscale boutique accommodations), has transformed five old D.C. buildings into cleverly crafted and sexy hotels. In the case of Rouge, this means that your guest room will have deep crimson drapes at the window; a floor-to-ceiling red "pleather" headboard for your comfortable, white-with-red-piping duvet-covered bed; and, in the dressing room, an Orange Crush–colored dresser, whose built-in minibar holds all sorts of red items, such as Hot Tamales candies, red wax lips, and Red Bull. Guest rooms in most boutique hotels are notoriously cramped; not so here, where the rooms are spacious enough to easily accommodate several armchairs and a large ottoman (in shades of red and gold); a number of funky little lamps; a huge, mahogany framed mirror leaning against a wall; and a 10-foot-long mahogany desk. The Rouge has no suites but does offer 15 specialty guest rooms, including "Chill Rooms," which have DVD players and a Sony PlayStation; "Chat Rooms," which have computers and printers; and "Chow Rooms," which have a microwave and refrigerator. All guest rooms, specialty or otherwise, are equipped for high-speed Internet access. The hotel embraces the theme of adventure, inviting guests to partake of a complimentary bloody mary in the lobby on weekends from 10am to 11am. Weeknights from 5 to 6pm, the hotel serves complimentary red wine and red beer. If that aperitif whets your appetite, you can head to the **Bar Rouge,** settle into one of the thronelike armchairs and slurp a "Brigitte Bardot Martini" (orange vodka, citron, Grand Marnier, and orange juice) or some other exotic concoction, with a plate of seductive bar food to go with it.

1315 16th St. NW (at Massachusetts Ave. NW and Scott Circle), Washington, DC 20036. ⓒ **800/368-5689** or 202/232-8000. Fax 202/667-9827. www.rougehotel. com. 137 units. Weekdays $159–$269 double, weekends $129–$219 double. Add $40 to reserve a specialty room. Best rates available on the website or by calling the toll-free number and asking for promotional price. Extra person $20. Rates include complimentary bloody marys and cold pizza weekend mornings 10–11am and complimentary wine and beer weeknights 5–6pm. Children under 18 stay free in parent's room. AE, DC, DISC, MC, V. Parking $22. Metro: Dupont Circle. Pets are pampered here. **Amenities:** Bar/restaurant (American w/a French twist); modest-size fitness center w/treadmill and stationary bikes; 24-hr. concierge; business center; room service (7am–11pm); same-day laundry/dry cleaning; 6 rooms for guests w/disabilities (1 w/roll-in shower). *In room:* A/C, 27-in. flat-screen TV w/pay movies, CD player, 2-line cordless phone w/dataport and high-speed Internet access, minibar, coffeemaker (w/Starbucks coffee), hair dryer, iron, robes.

4 Adams-Morgan

Note: The hotels listed here are situated just north of Dupont Circle, more at the mouth of Adams-Morgan than within its actual boundaries.

EXPENSIVE

Hilton Washington *Kids* This sprawling hotel, built in 1965, occupies 7 acres and calls itself a "resort"—mostly on the basis of having landscaped gardens, tennis courts, and an Olympic-style pool on its premises, unusual amenities for a D.C. hotel. The Hilton caters to corporate groups, some of whom may have families in tow (during the summer, the reception desk gives families a complimentary gift and lends them board games—ask for the "Vacation Station" perk), and is accustomed to coordinating meetings for thousands of attendees. Its vast conference facilities include one of the largest hotel ballrooms on the East Coast (it accommodates nearly 4,000). By contrast, guest rooms are on the small side. A renovation of all guest rooms completed in 2003 installed elegant dark wood furnishings in every room. High-speed Internet access is available in all guest rooms for $10 per 24 hours. From the fifth floor up, pool-side, you'll have panoramic views of Washington. The hotel's health club has been thoroughly renovated and expanded and now offers extensive spa services.

The designated concierge level rooms usually go for about $30 more than the standard room rate. The hotel has 52 suites, in all kinds of configurations, from the junior executive (in which parlor and bedroom are combined) to the huge Presidential suite.

The Hilton puts you within an easy stroll of embassies, great restaurants, museums, and the charming neighborhoods of Adams-Morgan and Woodley Park (all up the hill), and Dupont Circle (down the hill).

1919 Connecticut Ave. NW (at T St.), Washington, DC 20009. © **800/HILTONS** or 202/483-3000. Fax 202/232-0438. www.Washington.Hilton.com. 1,119 units. Weekdays $169–$374 double, weekends (and some weekdays and holidays) $119–$314 double; $500–$1,800 suite. Find deals on the website or by calling the toll-free number. Extra person $25. Children 18 and under stay free in parent's room. AE, DC, DISC, MC, V. Self-parking $21. Metro: Dupont Circle. **Amenities:** 2 restaurants (both American); deli; pub; 2 bars (the pub and lobby bar occasionally feature a pianist); Olympic-style heated outdoor pool; 3 lighted tennis courts; extensive health-club facilities; concierge; transportation/sightseeing desk; comprehensive business center; lobby shops; room service (until 2am); same-day laundry/dry cleaning; concierge-level rooms; 28 rooms for guests w/disabilities (8 w/roll-in shower). *In room:* A/C, TV w/pay movies; 2-line phone w/dataport, coffeemaker, hair dryer, iron.

INEXPENSIVE

Jurys Normandy Inn 🍴 *(Finds)*   This gracious hotel is a gem—a small gem, but a gem nonetheless. Situated in a neighborhood of architecturally impressive embassies, the hotel hosts many embassy-bound guests. You may discover this for yourself on a Tuesday evening, when guests gather in the charming Tea Room to enjoy complimentary wine and cheese served from the antique oak sideboard. This is also where you'll find a daily continental breakfast (for about $6.50), complimentary coffee and tea after 10am, and cookies after 3pm. You can lounge or watch TV in the conservatory or, in nice weather, you can move outside to the garden patio.

The six-floor Normandy has small but pretty guest rooms (all remodeled in 2003) with twin and queen-size beds. Furnishings are tapestry-upholstered mahogany and cherrywood in 18th-century style, and pretty floral-print bedspreads cover firm beds. Rooms facing Wyoming Avenue overlook the tree-lined street, while other rooms mostly offer views of apartment buildings. The Normandy is an easy walk from both Adams-Morgan and Dupont Circle, where many restaurants and shops await you. All rooms offer complimentary high-speed Internet access.

2118 Wyoming Ave. NW (at Connecticut Ave.), Washington, DC 20008. ℂ **800/ 424-3729** or 202/483-1350. Fax 202/387-8241. www.jurysdoyle.com. 75 units. $89–$185 double. Extra person $10. Children under 12 stay free in parent's room. AE, DC, DISC, MC, V. Parking $15 plus tax Metro: Dupont Circle. **Amenities:** Access to the neighboring Courtyard by Marriott Northwest's pool and exercise room; room service at breakfast; coin-op washer/dryers; same-day laundry/dry cleaning (Mon–Sat); 4 rooms for guests w/disabilities (1 w/roll-in shower). *In room:* A/C, TV, 2-line phone w/dataport, mini-fridge, coffeemaker, hair dryer, iron, safe.

5 Dupont Circle

EXPENSIVE

St. Gregory Luxury Hotel and Suites 🍴🍴   The St. Gregory, open since 2000, is an affordable luxury property with marble floors and chandeliers. The hotel is well situated at the corner of 21st and M streets, not far from Georgetown, Dupont Circle, Foggy Bottom, and the White House, and with many good restaurants within a literal stone's throw.

Most of the guest rooms are one-bedroom suites, with a separate living room and bedroom and a pullout sofa in the living room. For privacy and views, choose one of the 16 "sky" suites on the ninth floor, each with terrace and city overlooks. Of the 100 suites, 85 have fully appointed kitchens, including a microwave, oven, and full-size refrigerator (the other 15 suites have no kitchen). In the remaining 54 units are either a king-size or two double beds. Decor throughout the hotel is an attractive mélange of olive green and gold, with un-hotellike lamps, mirror frames, and fabrics. Three whole floors of the hotel are reserved for club-level rooms. All rooms offer high-speed Internet access for $9.95 per 24 hours.

The St. Gregory offers special rates to long-term and government guests, and to those from the diplomatic community. If you don't fall into one of those categories, check the hotel's website for great deals such as the often available "One Dollar Clearance Sale": You pay a set price—this can fluctuate, sometimes $159, sometimes $209—the first night and only $1 for the second night for Friday and Saturday or Saturday and Sunday stays. To book this discount, you must call the hotel's toll-free number.

2033 M St. NW (at 21st St.), Washington, DC 20036. (©) 800/829-5034 or 202/530-3600. Fax 202/466-6770. www.stgregoryhotelwdc.com. 154 units. Weekdays $189–$269 double or suite, weekends $149–$249 double or suite. Extra person $20. Children under 16 stay free in parent's room. Ask about discounts, long-term stays, and packages. AE, DC, MC, V. Parking $22 weekdays, $15 weekends. Metro: Dupont Circle or Farragut North. **Amenities:** Restaurant and coffee bar (American) w/seasonal sidewalk seating; state-of-the-art fitness center, as well as access ($20 fee) to the nearby and larger Sports Club/LA (p. 56); concierge; tour desk; business center; room service (6:30am–10:30pm); massage; babysitting; coin-op laundry room; same-day laundry/dry cleaning; concierge-level rooms; 6 rooms for guests w/disabilities (2 w/roll-in shower). *In room:* A/C, TV w/pay movies, CD player, 2-line phone w/dataport, fridge, coffeemaker, hair dryer, iron.

Topaz Hotel ⟨⟩   Like the Hotel Rouge, the Topaz is an upscale boutique hotel for those who think young. This hotel seems tamer than the Rouge, but it still has a buzz about it, a pleasant, interesting sort of buzz. The reception area, lobby, and bar flow together, so if you arrive in the evening, you may feel like you've arrived at a party: **The Topaz Bar** and the Bar Rouge have fast become favorite hangouts for the after-work crowd. At the Topaz, they're liking drinks called "Blue Nirvana" (champagne mixed with vodka and blueberry liqueur) and "Pop" (6-oz. single servings of Pommery champagne), the better-than-bar-food cuisine with an Asian accent, and the decor of velvety settees, zebra-patterned ottomans, and a lighting system that fades in and out.

Upstairs are guest rooms appealingly and whimsically decorated with striped lime green wallpaper; a polka-dot padded headboard for the down-comforter-covered bed; a bright blue, curved-back settee; a big, round mirror set in a sunburst frame; a light green and yellow armoire with fabric panels; and a red with gold star–patterned cushioned chair. The rooms are unusually large (in its former life as the Canterbury Hotel, these were "junior suites" and held kitchenettes), and each has an alcove where the desk is placed, and a separate dressing room that holds a dressing table and cube-shaped ottoman. The Topaz pursues a sort of New Age wellness motif; do note the spill of smooth stones arranged just so upon your bed ("Through time people have carried special stones called totems to bring them energy and empowerment . . ." reads a little card accompanying the stones.) You also have the option to book a specialty room: one of four "energy" guest rooms, which include a piece of exercise equipment (either a treadmill or a stationary bike), and fitness magazines; or one of three "yoga" rooms, which come with an exercise mat, an instructional tape, padded pillows, special towels, and yoga magazines. Wireless Internet access is available in all guest rooms.

The Topaz lies on a quiet residential street, whose front-of-the-house windows overlook picturesque town houses.

1733 N St. NW (right next to the Tabard Inn, between 17th and 18th sts.), Washington, DC 20036. © **800/424-2950** or 202/393-3000. Fax 202/785-9581. www.topazhotel.com. 99 units. Weekdays $209–$279 double; $280 specialty room; weekends $139 double; $169 specialty room. Find a much lower rate by calling the hotel or booking a reservation online. Extra person $20. Children under 16 stay free in parent's room. Rates include complimentary morning energy potions. AE, DC, DISC, MC, V. Parking $24. Pets welcome. Metro: Dupont Circle. **Amenities:** Bar/restaurant (innovative American w/Asian influence); access to nearby health club ($5 per guest); 24-hr. concierge; 24-hour business center; room service (7am–11pm); same-day laundry/dry cleaning; 5 rooms for guests w/disabilities (2 w/roll-in shower). *In room:* A/C, TV w/pay movies, 2-line cordless phone w/dataport, wireless Internet access, minibar, teapot w/exotic teas, hair dryer, iron, safe, robes.

MODERATE

Embassy Suites Hotel Downtown *Value* *Kids*   This hotel offers unbelievable value and a convenient location within walking distance of Foggy Bottom, Georgetown, and Dupont Circle. You enter into a tropical and glassy eight-story atrium with two waterfalls constantly running. This is where you'll enjoy an ample complimentary breakfast—not your standard cold croissant and coffee, but stations from which you can choose omelets made to order, waffles, bacon, fresh fruit, juices, bagels, and pastries. Tables are scattered in alcoves throughout the atrium to allow for privacy. Each evening, the atrium is the setting for complimentary beverages (including cocktails) and light cold snacks. The hotel's restaurant offers discounts to hotel guests and a children's menu for $5.

By February 2005, the hotel will have completed a $4.5 million renovation to give the entire property an "urban-modern, but not chi-chi" look: Dark marble replaces light marble, guest room sofas will be covered in maroon tapestry fabric, and wireless Internet access will be available throughout the hotel (guests pay $9.95 per 24 hr. for a computer access card, if needed).

The accommodations remain, as always, nicer than your average hotel room, with better amenities. Every unit is a two-room suite, with a living room that closes off completely from the rest of the suite. The living room holds a queen-size sofa bed, TV, easy chair, and large table with four comfortable chairs around it. The bedroom lies at the back of the suite, overlooking either a quiet courtyard of brick walkways or the street. A king-size bed or two double beds, TV, sink, easy chair, and chest of drawers furnish this space. Between the living room and the bedroom are the bathroom, a small closet, and a kitchenette. It's worth requesting one of the eighth- or ninth-floor suites with views of Georgetown and beyond, as far as Washington National Cathedral (the hotel will note your request, but won't be able to guarantee you such a suite). For the roomiest quarters, ask for an "executive corner suite," the slightly larger, slightly more expensive suites situated in the corners of the hotel.

1250 22nd St. NW (between M and N sts.), Washington, DC 20037. ℂ 800/ **EMBASSY** or 202/857-3388. Fax 202/293-3173. www.embassysuitesdcmetro.com. 318 suites. $149–$309 double. Rates include full breakfast and evening reception. Ask for AAA discounts or check the website for best rates. Extra person $25 weekdays. Children 18 under stay free in parent's room. AE, DC, DISC, MC, V. Parking $20. Metro: Foggy Bottom. **Amenities:** Restaurant (northern Italian); state-of-the-art fitness center w/indoor pool, whirlpool, and sauna; game room; concierge; business center (w/free Internet access on 3 computers); room service (11am–11pm); coin-op washer/dryers; same-day laundry/dry cleaning; 8 rooms for guests w/disabilities (2 w/roll-in shower). *In room:* A/C, TV w/pay movies, 2-line phone w/dataport, kitchenette w/fridge and microwave, coffeemaker, hair dryer, iron.

Hotel Madera ⭐   The Hotel Madera fancies itself as a kind of *pied-à-terre*, or home away from home, for travelers. But it would be a mistake to think that means the hotel is homey in the traditional sense. This is a boutique hotel, whose sisters, the hotels Rouge, Topaz, Helix, and Monaco, have all made separate splashes in our fair city. The Madera, likewise, caters to those with avant-garde tastes. The registration desk in the small lobby is covered in leather; a hammered copper mobile of abstract leaflike shapes dangles overhead. The guest rooms are large (this used to be an apartment building), measuring an average 340 square feet. Those on the New Hampshire Avenue side have balconies that offer city views. Rooms at the back of the house on the 6th through 10th floors don't have balconies, but do have pretty good views of Rock Creek Park,

Georgetown, and the Washington National Cathedral. All rooms are comfortable and furnished with sofas and bed benches, and with beds whose wild-looking headboards are giant dark wood panels inset with a patch of vibrant blue padded mohair. Other fey touches: pillows covered in animal print or satiny fabrics, grass-clothlike wall coverings, and black granite with chrome bathroom vanities. Every guest room has complimentary high-speed Internet access. The "specialty" rooms (a feature of all Kimpton Group hotels) at the Madera include a Nosh Room (studio with kitch-enette and grocery shopping service), Flash Room (with personal computer and printer), Strength (with a Nautilus machine) and Cardio (with either a treadmill, exercise bike, or elliptical steps) rooms, and a Screening Room (equipped with a second TV, DVD player, and a library of DVDs).

The Madera has an excellent restaurant, **Firefly** (p. 89).

1310 New Hampshire Ave. NW (between N and O sts.), Washington, DC 20036. ℭ **800/368-5691** or 202/296-7600. Fax 202/293-2476. www.hotelmadera.com. 82 units. $159–$259 double; add $40 to the going rate for a specialty room. For best rates, call the hotel or go its website. Extra person $20. Children under 16 stay free in parent's room. Rates include evening wine hour. AE, DC, DISC, MC, V. Parking $24. Pets welcome. Metro: Dupont Circle. **Amenities:** Bar/restaurant (American bistro); access to the posh Sports Club/LA health club at the nearby Ritz-Carlton ($15 per guest per day; p. 56); 24-hr. concierge; business center; room service (during restaurant hours); same-day laundry/dry cleaning; 6 rooms for guests w/disabilities (all w/roll-in shower). *In room:* A/C, TV w/pay movies, 2-line cordless phone w/dataport and free Internet access, minibar, coffeemaker w/Starbucks coffee, hair dryer, iron, safe, robes.

Jurys Washington Hotel ⓐ *(Value* This hotel gets high marks for convenience (it's located right on Dupont Circle), service, and com-fort. Open since 2000, the hotel is favored by business groups espe-cially, who like its reasonable rates. Each of the large rooms is furnished with two double beds with firm mattresses, an armoire with TV, a desk, a wet-bar alcove, and a tiny but attractive bathroom. Decor is Art Deco-ish, with lots of light wood furniture. All guest rooms offer complimentary high-speed Internet access. Despite its prime location in a sometimes raucous neighborhood, the hotel's rooms are insulated from the noise. Rooms on higher floors offer the best views of the city and of Dupont Circle. An Irish management company owns this hotel (along with two other properties in Washington, D.C.), and the comfortable and attractive hotel pub, Biddy Mulligan's, proudly features a bar imported from the Emerald Isle. Its American restaurant, **Dupont Grille,** opened in spring 2003, and it is a welcome addition to the hotel and the neighborhood.

1500 New Hampshire Ave. NW (across from Dupont Circle), Washington, DC 20036. © 866/JD-HOTELS or 202/483-6000. Fax 202/238-3265. www.jurysdoyle.com. 314 units. $89–$245 double; from $600 suite. Check the website for guaranteed lowest rates. Extra person $15. Children 17 and under stay free in parent's room. AE, DC, DISC, MC, V. Parking $20. Metro: Dupont Circle. **Amenities:** Restaurant (American); bar; exercise room; 24-hr. concierge; business center; same-day laundry/dry cleaning; room service (6:30am–midnight); 11 rooms for guests w/disabilities (4 w/roll-in shower). *In room:* A/C, TV w/pay movies, 2-line phone w/dataport, minibar, coffeemaker, hair dryer, iron, safe.

6 Foggy Bottom/West End

VERY EXPENSIVE

Park Hyatt Washington 🎔🎔 This luxury hotel, last renovated in 1998, features large guest rooms with goose-down duvets on the beds, modern furniture, wall coverings, and fabrics. For a fee, high-speed Internet access is available in all the guest rooms. Specially commissioned artwork hangs throughout the hotel. More than half of the rooms are suites (meaning the parlor and bedroom are separate), and the remaining rooms are deluxe kings. The suites also have dressing rooms with full vanities. Each bathroom has a TV, a radio, and a telephone, along with the usual amenities. The 17-year-old 10-story hotel hosts big names, royal families (who use the Presidential Suite, with its fireplace and grand piano), lobbyists, and tourists. Rooms are handsome and service is superb. A major renovation scheduled for completion in 2005 will re-design the look of the sleeping rooms.

The bright and lovely **Melrose** dining room offers four-star cuisine with an emphasis on seafood; the amiable chef, Brian McBride, pops into the dining room personally from time to time to make sure all is well. Adjoining the Melrose is a bar, where there's swing dancing to live jazz every weekends.

1201 24th St. NW (at M St.), Washington, DC 20037. © **800/778-7477** or 202/789-1234. Fax 202/419-6795. www.parkhyattwashington.com. 223 units. Weekdays $320–$450 double; weekends $215–$289 double. For the lowest rate, visit the website. Extra person $25 on weekdays. Children 18 and under stay free in parent's room. AE, DC, DISC, MC, V. Valet parking $25. Metro: Foggy Bottom or Dupont Circle. Pets allowed. **Amenities:** Restaurant (American); bar/lounge (w/live entertainment Fri–Sat); health club w/indoor pool, whirlpool, and sauna and steam rooms; spa w/hair and skin salon; concierge; business center; 24-hr. room service; in-room massage; same-day laundry/dry cleaning; 10 rooms for guests w/disabilities (3 w/roll-in shower). *In room:* A/C, TV w/pay movies, 2-line phone w/dataport, minibar, hair dryer, iron, safe, robes.

The Ritz-Carlton Washington D.C. 🎔🎔🎔 This Ritz-Carlton, which opened in 2000, stands in the upper echelon of D.C.'s very best hotels. From the cadre of doormen and valet attendants who greet you when you arrive, to the graceful young women in long dresses who swan around you serving cocktails in the bar and lounge, the Ritz staff is always looking after you.

The hotel is built around a multitiered Japanese garden and courtyard with reflecting pools and cascading waterfall; guest rooms on the inside of the complex overlook the waterfall or terraced garden, while guest rooms on the outside perimeter view landmarks and cityscapes. The woman who showed me to my terrace-view room inadvertently, but appropriately, kept referring to the hotel as the "Rich-Carlton." My standard room was very large, and richly furnished with a firm king-size bed covered in a duvet and a bedspread, decorative inlaid wooden furniture, a comfy armchair and ottoman, and very pretty artwork. The marble bathroom was immense, with long counter space, separate bathtub and shower stall, and the toilet in its own room behind a louvered door. The clock radio doubles as a CD player, and the phone features a button for summoning the "technology butler" (a complimentary, 24/7 service for guests with computer questions). Other nice touches in the rooms include an umbrella, windows that open, and an outlet for recharging laptops. Don't make the same mistake that I did when I passed up the evening turndown—the maid places a warm, freshly baked brownie upon your pillow instead of the usual mint. Among the different versions of suites available, most are "executives," which include a sitting room and separate bedroom.

Guests enjoy free use of the hotel's fitness center, the two-level, 100,000-square-foot **Sports Club/LA,** which officially leaves all other hotel health clubs in the dust with its state-of-the-art weight-training equipment and free weights, two regulation-size basketball courts and four squash courts, an indoor heated swimming pool and an aquatics pool with a sun deck, exercise classes, personal trainers, the full-service Splash Spa and Roche Salon, and its own restaurant and cafe.

The Ritz's bar and lounge are also exceptionally inviting, with lots of plush upholstered couches and armchairs, a fire blazing in the fireplace in winter, and a pianist playing every day. Afternoon tea is served in the lounge daily.

1150 22nd St. NW (at M St.), Washington, DC 20037. ☎ **800/241-3333** or 202/835-0500. Fax 202/835-1588. www.ritzcarlton.com. 300 units. $450 double; from $595 suite. No charge for extra person in the room. Ask about discount packages. AE, DC, DISC, MC, V. Valet parking $28. Metro: Foggy Bottom or Dupont Circle. Pets accepted (no fee). **Amenities:** Restaurant (American); lounge; best health club and spa in the city; 24-hr. concierge; business center (weekdays); 24-hr. fax and currency-exchange services; salon; 24-hr. room service; in-room massage; babysitting; same-day laundry/dry cleaning w/1-hr. pressing; club level w/5 complimentary food presentations throughout the day (including a chef station each morning to prepare individual requests); 10 rooms for guests w/disabilities (6 w/roll-in shower). *In room:* A/C, TV w/pay movies, 2-line phone w/high-speed Internet access ($10 per day), minibar/fridge, hair dryer, iron, safe, robes.

EXPENSIVE

George Washington University Inn

Rumor has it that this whitewashed brick inn, another former apartment building, used to be a favorite spot for clandestine trysts for high-society types. These days you're more likely to see Kennedy Center performers and visiting professors. The university purchased the hotel (formerly known as the Inn at Foggy Bottom) in 1994 and renovated it. The most recent refurbishment, in 2001, replaced linens, drapes, and the like in the guest rooms. Free high-speed Internet access was added in 2004.

Rooms are a little larger and corridors are a tad narrower than those in a typical hotel, and each room includes a roomy dressing chamber. More than one-third of the units are one-bedroom suites. These are especially spacious, with living rooms that hold a sleeper sofa and a TV hidden in an armoire (there's another in the bedroom). The suites, plus the 16 efficiencies, have kitchens. The spaciousness and the kitchen facilities make this a popular choice for families and for long-term guests.

This is a fairly safe and lovely neighborhood, within easy walking distance to Georgetown, the Kennedy Center, and downtown. But keep an eye peeled—you have to pass through wrought-iron gates into a kind of cul-de-sac to find the inn.

Off the lobby is the restaurant, **Nectar** (p. 94), which opened in spring 2003.

If it's not full, the inn may be willing to offer reduced rates. Mention your affiliation with George Washington University, if you have one, to receive a special "GWU" rate.

824 New Hampshire Ave. NW (between H and I sts.), Washington, DC 20037. ℃ **800/426-4455** or 202/337-6620. Fax 202/298-7499. www.gwuinn.com. 95 units. Weekdays $139–$249 double, $159–$269 efficiency, $179–$289 1-bedroom suite; weekends $119–$189 double; $139–$209 efficiency, $159–$229 1-bedroom suite. Children under 12 stay free in parent's room. AE, DC, MC, V. Limited parking $18. Metro: Foggy Bottom. **Amenities:** Restaurant (upscale contemporary American); complimentary passes to nearby fitness center; room service; coin-op washer/dryers; same-day laundry/dry cleaning; 5 rooms for guests w/disabilities (1 w/roll-in shower). *In room:* A/C, TV w/pay movies and Nintendo, CD player, 2-line phone w/dataport and complimentary high-speed Internet access, fridge, coffeemaker, microwave, hair dryer, iron, safe, robes.

MODERATE

One Washington Circle Hotel ⟨★⟩   Built in 1960, this building was converted into a hotel in 1976, making it the city's first all-suite hotel property. The George Washington University purchased the hotel in 2001 (see its other property, the George Washington University Inn, above), closed the place down and totally renovated it, reopening in 2002. One Washington Circle gleams now, from its double-paned windows to its contemporary new furniture. Five types of suites are available, ranging in size from 390 to 710 square feet. The one-bedroom suites have a sofa bed and dining area; all rooms are spacious and have walkout balconies, some overlooking the Circle and its centerpiece, the statue of George Washington. But keep in mind that across the Circle is George Washington University Hospital's emergency room entrance, which is busy with ambulance traffic; even with the installation of those double-paned windows, you may still hear sirens, so ask for a suite on the L Street side if you desire a quieter room. Ninety percent of the suites have full kitchens, each with an oven, a microwave, and a refrigerator.

Clientele is mostly corporate, but families like the outdoor pool, in-house restaurant, prime location near Georgetown and Metro, and the full kitchen. Be sure to mention a GWU affiliation if you have one. The well-reviewed **Circle Bistro,** serves bistro food with a Mediterranean influence.

1 Washington Circle NW (between 22nd and 23rd sts. NW), Washington, DC 20037. ✆ 800/424-9671 or 202/872-1680. Fax 202/887-4989. www.thecirclehotel.com. 151 units. Smallest suites: weekdays $149–$209, weekends $129–$189; largest suites: weekdays $169–$229, weekends $149–$209. Call hotel to get best rates. Extra person: $20. Children under 12 stay free in parent's room. AE, DC, MC, V. Parking $20. Metro: Foggy Bottom. **Amenities:** Restaurant (traditional bistro w/Mediterranean flair), bar; on-site fitness center, outdoor pool; concierge; room service (7am–midnight weekends, 7am–11pm weekdays); coin-op washer/dryers; same-day laundry/dry cleaning; 5 rooms for guests w/disabilities (1 w/roll-in shower). *In room:* A/C, TV w/pay movies and Nintendo, complimentary high-speed Internet access, CD player, 2-line cordless phone, full kitchen (in 90% of suites; w/oven, fridge, and microwave), coffeemaker, hair dryer, iron.

7 Georgetown

VERY EXPENSIVE

Four Seasons Hotel ⟨★★★⟩   A renovation was slated to wind up in early 2005, bringing big changes to this Four Seasons, including the gutting of all of the guest rooms in the hotel's main building. In the end, guest rooms will be fewer, but much larger, and will feature the design of world-famous interior designer Pierre Yves Rochon, who renovated the landmark Four Seasons Georges V Hotel in Paris. The new decor will include custom-designed furniture and color schemes of either celadon or purple.

The hotel's lobby and lower levels, which hold the restaurant, conference room, spa and exercise center, will stay open throughout the renovation, as will the hotel's auxiliary building of 25 rooms and 35 suites. Certain Four Seasons features always hold true: The hotel continues to attract the rich, the famous, and the powerful people used to being catered to. Staff members are trained to know the names, preferences, and even allergies of guests, and repeat clientele rely on this discreet attention.

The hotel sits at the mouth of Georgetown, backing up against Rock Creek Park and the C&O Canal. The auxiliary building's guest rooms offer state-of-the-art business amenities (each is soundproof and has an office equipped with a fax machine, at least three telephones with two-line speakers, portable telephones, and headsets for private TV listening). Three of the suites have kitchenettes. Original avant-garde artwork from the personal collection of owner William Louis-Dreyfus (yes, Julia's dad) hangs in every room and public space. Transmitters installed throughout the hotel allow you wireless connection to the Internet on your laptop, wherever you go in the hotel. The Four Seasons is always devising new ways to pamper its guests; in 2003 the hotel initiated its "On the Road to Room Service," which allows guests who have been picked up by the hotel's car service to place a room service order from the limo and have the meal delivered to their guest room moments after they arrive.

2800 Pennsylvania Ave. NW (which becomes M St. a block farther along), Washington, DC 20007. ℭ **800/332-3442** or 202/342-0444. Fax 202/944-2076. www.fourseasons.com. 257 units. Weekdays $455–$615 double, $695–$5,150 suite; weekends from $295 double, from $550 suite. Extra person $40. Children under 16 stay free in parent's room. AE, DC, MC, V. Parking $26, plus tax. Metro: Foggy Bottom. Pets up to 15 lb. allowed. **Amenities:** Formal restaurant (regional American); lounge (for afternoon tea and cocktails); extensive state-of-the-art fitness club and spa w/personal trainers, lap pool, Vichy shower, hydrotherapy, and synchronized massage (2 people work on you at the same time); bike rentals; children's program (various goodies provided, but no organized activities); 24-hr. concierge; complimentary sedan service weekdays within the District; business center; salon; 24-hr. room service; in-room massage; babysitting; same-day laundry/dry cleaning; 7 rooms for guests w/disabilities (4 w/roll-in shower). *In room:* A/C, TV w/pay movies and Web access, high-speed Internet access, high-tech CD player, minibar, hair dryer, iron, safe, robes.

The Ritz-Carlton Georgetown ⭐⭐ Staff at area hotels have taken to calling this hotel the "Baby Ritz," to distinguish it from the

other, larger Ritz on 22nd Street. The moniker is the only cute thing about the hotel, however. The Georgetown Ritz is a sophisticated property, exclusively small (only 86 rooms), and designed to feel like a refuge in the middle of wild and woolly Georgetown. The hotel opened in April 2003, after years of construction, which I observed in stages through the windows of nearby Interiano hair salon, on the second floor of 1025 31st St., every time I went for a haircut. Look for the 130-foot-high smokestack to guide you to the hotel, which is built on the site of a historic incinerator and incorporates the smoke-stack into the design. In fact, you can have a meeting at the bottom of the smokestack, which, obviously, is inoperative. The lobby, whose brick walls are original to the incinerator, always smells of a recently lit fire, even on a summer day. (There's a large fireplace at one end of the lobby.) The restaurant is called "Fahrenheit," the bar is called "Degrees," and the signature drink is the "Fahrenheit 5 Martini." To get to your room, you have to go down one level from the lobby and travel along a wide, cavelike corridor with vaulted brick ceiling to a special elevator. You must have a key card to operate the elevator, so anyone visiting you at the hotel must either be escorted by a staff person or be met by you. Rooms are very large, decorated in serious colors of moss green, gold, and a burnt red, with lots of dark wood furniture and accents. Ritz-Carlton hotels have the best bathrooms, and this property is no exception: spacious, marble vanities; separate tub and shower; and fancy wood shelving.

3100 South St. NW (at 31st. St., between K and M sts.), Washington, DC 20007. ℃ **800/241-3333** or 202/912-4100. Fax 202/912-4199. www.ritzcarlton.com. 86 units. Weekdays from $425 double; weekends from $285 double. Suites from $579. No charge for extra person in the room. Check the website or call the toll-free number for weekend packages and specials. AE, DC, DISC, MC, V. Valet parking $28. Metro: Foggy Bottom, with Georgetown shuttle bus connection. Small (under 30 lb.) pets accepted (no fee). **Amenities:** Restaurant (seasonal American); lounge; fitness room (complimentary) and spa; 24-hr. concierge; fax and some currency-exchange services; 24-hr. room service; in-room massage; babysitting; same-day laundry/dry cleaning; 1-hr. pressing; 3 rooms for guests w/disabilities (all w/roll-in shower). *In room:* A/C, TV w/pay movies and Web access, CD player, 2-line phone w/high-speed Internet access (about $10 per 24 hr.), minibar, hair dryer, iron, safe, robes.

MODERATE

Hotel Monticello of Georgetown ☆ *Value*   This hotel gets a lot of repeat business from both corporate and leisure travelers, who appreciate the intimacy of a small hotel, including personalized service from a staff who greets you by name and protects your pri-vacy. It's also a favorite choice for families celebrating weddings or graduations (both Georgetown and George Washington universities

are close by); they sometimes book several suites, or maybe a whole floor. A major renovation in 2000 gutted the whole building and created a more upscale setting (this used to be the Georgetown Dutch Inn). Rooms now bring in much more light, thanks to layout and design changes, better use of windows, and the placement of French doors with frosted glass between rooms. You'll notice that the top sheet on your bed is monogrammed, the sofa in the living room folds out, and those are Hermès bath products in the marble bathrooms. Wireless Internet access is available in all guest rooms, at no extra charge.

Accommodations are medium-size one- and two-bedroom apartment-like suites. Six of the suites are studios, in which the living room and bedroom are joined, and nine of them are duplex penthouses with one-and-a-half bathrooms. Every suite has a wet bar with a microwave and refrigerator. The duplex penthouses have full kitchens. In addition to continental breakfast in the morning, fresh fruit, coffee, and herbal tea are available in the lobby all day.

The hotel is in the heart of Georgetown, surrounded by shops and restaurants. The C&O Canal towpath, just down the block, is ideal for jogging and cycling, though you should be wary at night.

1075 Thomas Jefferson St. NW (just below M St.), Washington, DC 20007. © 800/388-2410 or 202/337-0900. Fax 202/333-6526. www.monticellohotel.com. 47 suites. Weekdays peak season $149–$189; off season $129–$149; weekends $109–$129. Call for promotional rates and discounts and to find out penthouse suite rates. Extra person $20. Rates include continental breakfast. Children under 14 stay free in parent's room. AE, DC, DISC, MC, V. Limited parking $10 (small to midsize cars only—no SUVs). Metro: Foggy Bottom, with a 20-min. walk, or take the Georgetown Shuttle. Bus: 32, 34, and 36 to all major Washington tourist attractions. **Amenities:** Free access to nearby fitness center; business center; in-room massage; babysitting; same-day laundry/dry cleaning except Sun; 2 rooms for guests w/disabilities. *In room:* A/C, TV, 2-line phone w/dataport, complimentary wireless Internet access, kitchenette w/microwave, fridge, coffeemaker, hair dryer, iron.

8 Woodley Park

VERY EXPENSIVE

Wardman Park Marriott Hotel ⓖ   This is Washington's biggest hotel, resting on 16 acres just down the street from the National Zoo and several good restaurants. Its size and location (the Woodley Park–Zoo Metro station is literally at its doorstep) make it a good choice for conventions, tour groups, and individual travelers. (*Warning:* You can get lost here, and I have.) Built in 1918, it is also one of Washington's oldest hotels. A massive $100 million renovation completed in 1999 replaced bed and bath linens, carpeting, and wall coverings in all the guest rooms; upgraded the ballroom and meeting rooms; restructured the outdoor pools; revamped the restaurants; and topped the lobby with a soaring four-story dome. More recently, the hotel remodeled all of the guest room bathrooms, replacing walls, floors, and fixtures. The hotel has also added outdoor seating to Harry's Bar and an outdoor cafe to its Starbucks, set in the center of beds of blooming flowers. Wireless Internet access is available in the Lobby Lounge, Starbucks, and the atrium.

From the outside, the hotel resembles a college campus: There's an old part, whose entrance is draped by stately trees, and a new part, preceded by a great green lawn. The oldest section is the nicest. The 86-year-old red-brick Tower houses 205 guest rooms, each featuring high ceilings, ornate crown moldings, and an assortment of antique French and English furnishings. This was once an apartment building whose residents included presidents Hoover, Eisenhower, and Johnson, as well as actors such as Douglas Fairbanks, Jr., and authors such as Gore Vidal.

The hotel has 125 suites in all, ranging in size from one to three bedrooms. Best are the 54 suites in the Wardman Tower, many of which have balconies overlooking the gardens. The size of the hotel enables it to accommodate requests for different setups: two double beds, king-size beds, and so on. All rooms offer high-speed Internet access for $9.95 per day.

2660 Woodley Rd. NW (at Connecticut Ave. NW), Washington, DC 20008. ℂ 800/228-9290 or 202/328-2000. Fax 202/234-0015. www.marriotthotels.com/wasdt. 1,349 units. Weekdays $289 double, weekends $119–$289 double; $350–$2,500 suite. Children under 18 stay free in parent's room. AE, DC, DISC, MC, V. Valet parking $22, self-parking $19. Metro: Woodley Park–Zoo. Pets under 20 lb. permitted, but charges may apply; call for details. **Amenities:** 2 restaurants (American, Mediterranean); pub (serves meals); deli/pastry shop (offers to-go gourmet dinners, which you can heat up in the shop's microwave); lobby bar; Starbucks; 2 outdoor heated pools w/sun deck; well-equipped fitness center; concierge; business center; salon; room service (6am–1am); in-room massage; babysitting; coin-op washer/dryers; same-day laundry/dry cleaning; concierge-level rooms; 32 rooms for guests w/disabilities (10 w/roll-in shower). *In room:* A/C, TV w/pay movies, 2-line phone w/dataport and high-speed Internet access ($10 per day), coffeemaker, hair dryer, iron.

EXPENSIVE

Omni Shoreham Hotel 🅡 (Kids)   This is Woodley Park's *other* really big hotel, although with 836 rooms, the Omni Shoreham is still 500 short of the behemoth Marriott Wardman Park. And it's all the more appealing for it because it's not quite so overwhelming as the Marriott. Its design—wide corridors, vaulted ceilings and archways, and arrangements of pretty sofas and armchairs in the lobby and public spaces—endows the Shoreham with the air of a grand hotel. A massive $80 million renovation completed in 2000 installed a new air-conditioning system; restructured the pool; upgraded the already excellent fitness center health spa; and restored a traditional, elegant look to guest rooms and the lobby. The spacious rooms remain twice the size of your average hotel room, and every guest room is equipped with free wireless high-speed Internet access, added in 2003. Most of the 52 suites are junior suites, with the sitting room and bedroom combined. The hotel sits on 11 acres overlooking Rock Creek Park; park-side rooms are a little smaller but offer spectacular views.

With its 22 meeting rooms and seven ballrooms (some of which open to terraces overlooking the park!), the hotel is popular as a meeting and convention venue. Leisure travelers, especially families, appreciate the Shoreham for its large outdoor swimming pool; its proximity to the National Zoo, excellent restaurants, and the Woodley Park–Zoo Metro station; and the immediate access to biking, hiking, and jogging paths through Rock Creek Park. Children receive a goodie bag at check-in that includes coloring books, puzzles, playing cards, postcards, and candy. You can walk to the more hip neighborhoods of Adams-Morgan and Dupont Circle from the hotel; the stroll to Dupont Circle, taking you over the bridge that spans Rock Creek Park, is especially nice (and safe at night, too).

Built in 1930, the Shoreham has been the scene of inaugural balls for every president since FDR. Do you believe in ghosts? Ask about room no. 870, the haunted suite (available for $3,000 a night).

2500 Calvert St. NW (near Connecticut Ave.), Washington, DC 20008. © **800/ 843-6664** or 202/234-0700. Fax 202/265-7972. www.omnihotels.com. 836 units. $179–$309 double; from $350–$3,000 suite. Call for best rates. Extra person $20. Children under 18 stay free in parent's room. AE, DC, DISC, MC, V. Valet parking $26; self-parking $22. Metro: Woodley Park–Zoo. **Amenities:** Restaurant (Continental; terrace overlooks Rock Creek Park); gourmet carryout; bar/lounge (serves light fare and has live music Thurs–Sat nights); fitness center and spa w/heated outdoor pool, separate kids' pool, and whirlpool; children's gifts; concierge; travel/sightseeing desk; business center; shops; 24-hr. room service; massage; same-day laundry/dry cleaning; 41 rooms for guests w/disabilities (7 w/roll-in shower). *In room:* A/C, TV w/pay movies and Nintendo, 2-line phone w/dataport, free wireless Internet access, coffeemaker, hair dryer, iron, robes.

INEXPENSIVE

Woodley Park Guest House   This charming, 18-room B&B offers clean, comfortable, and cozy lodging, inexpensive rates, super location, and a personable staff. How's that for a recommendation?

Special features of the guesthouse include a tree-shaded front porch; exposed brick walls; beautiful antiques, and breathtaking original art (the innkeepers only buy works from artists who have stayed at the guesthouse, so the art is diffuse rather than profuse, and each piece quite different). Rooms have two twins, one double, or one queen-size bed, each covered with a pretty chenille spread or quilt. An intimate alternative to the grand 1,349-room Marriott Wardman Park hotel directly across the street, the guesthouse nevertheless benefits from its proximity to the big hotel because it's able to offer lodgers quick access to airport shuttles and taxis and views of the Wardman Park's beautifully landscaped gardens. Meanwhile, the Woodley Park–Zoo Metro stop is literally cater-cornered to the inn, Connecticut Avenue and its good restaurants 1 block away, and Rock Creek Park and the National Zoo only a few minutes further.

2647 Woodley Rd. NW (at Connecticut Ave. NW), Washington, DC 20008. ⓒ **866/667-0218** or 202/667-0218. Fax 202/667-1080. www.woodleypark guesthouse.com. 18 units, 11 with private bathroom (all with shower only). 7 with shared bath. $80–$90 double with shared bathroom, $100–$160 double with private bathroom. Rates include continental breakfast. AE, MC, V. On-site parking $10. Metro: Woodley Park–Zoo. No children under 12. **Amenities:** Laundry and ironing service; wireless Internet access for $7 per day (your laptop must be equipped w/access card). *In room:* A/C, phone w/voice mail and dataport.

4

Where to Dine

Washington, D.C., generally, is not the kind of city where you can find a good meal in any restaurant you turn in to. And yet, it can happen. Take your chances, if you dare, and see what you discover. But if you'd prefer to make your dining experience more of a sure thing, here's the best the capital has to offer.

1 Capitol Hill

For information on eating at the Capitol, see "Dining at Sightseeing Attractions" on p. 68.

VERY EXPENSIVE

Charlie Palmer Steak ✦ STEAKHOUSE   Nothing intimate about Charlie Palmer. It's a place to see and be seen—in big groups, preferably. The ceilings are high and the rooms expansive. The bar and lounge are made for circulating. The most provocative feature is the glass-walled wine storage area, which is suspended over a shallow pool of water; the inventory stocks 10,000 bottles of exclusively American wines, representing nearly every state. Guests survey the wine list via the eWinebook, a kind of Palm Pilot that allows you to scroll through the selections. Three sommeliers are on hand for face-to-face communication. Other touches include a large mural of a nondescript landscape that covers the far wall of the dining room, and deep couches and overstuffed chairs. The restaurant advertises that it overlooks the Capitol, but views are seasonal: In winter, you'll see more of the Capitol than you do in summer, when only the Capitol dome and the grounds are visible. Best views are from the rooftop terrace, which is open only for private parties. About a third of the menu's main courses are beef entrees, like the excellent grilled beef filet mignon, with roasted-shallot-and-cabernet sauce. But Charlie Palmer Steak, despite its name, also serves "progressive American" fish and fowl dishes, such as smoked squab

Capitol Hill, Downtown & Foggy Bottom Dining

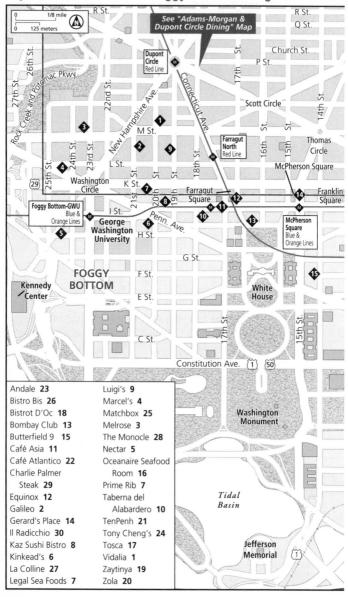

See "Adams-Morgan & Dupont Circle Dining" Map

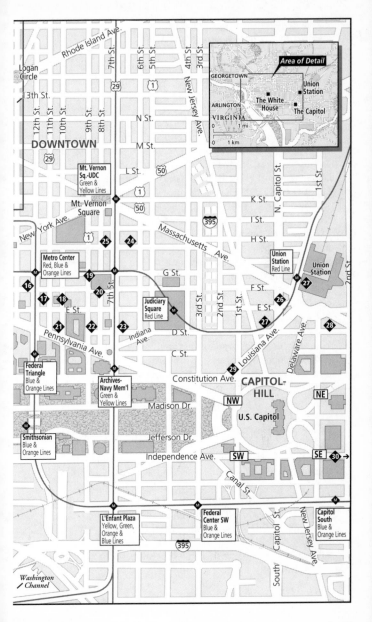

Dining at Sightseeing Attractions

With so many great places to eat in Washington, I have a hard time recommending those at sightseeing attractions. Most are overpriced and too crowded, even if they are convenient. But a few places stand out for their admirable cuisine, noteworthy setting, or both.

Two restaurants within the Capitol building itself may be open to the public, with certain conditions. The **House of Representatives Restaurant** (also called the Members' Dining Room) in Room H118, at the South end of the Capitol (② **202/225-6300**), is open when the House is in session (weekdays 8am–2:30pm). Tuesday through Thursday from 11am to 1:45pm, you may lunch here only as the guest of a Member. Monday and Friday—and any weekday for breakfast or between 1:45pm and 2:30pm—you may dine here unaccompanied by a Member. The food is all-American and prices are reasonable: everything from a cup of soup for $1.50; to entree salads for $8.50; to the favorite, the crab cake platter, for $19. The **Senate Dining Room** (② **202/ 224-4100**) is open only when the Senate is in session, and you may lunch here weekdays between 1:30pm and 2:30pm. You must dress appropriately: jacket and tie for men, no jeans or sloppy appearance for men or women. You must also present a letter from your senator confirming his or her invitation to you. Be sure to call and ask about other requirements. The menu features American cuisine and "comfort food," such as meatloaf, grilled salmon, crab Louis (a kind of crab salad), and lots of sandwiches; prices range from $9 to $22.

You are always welcome (after you've gone through security, of course) in the eateries located in the Capitol office buildings across the street from the Capitol. You'll be surrounded by Hill staffers, who head to places like the immense, full-service **Rayburn House Office Building Cafeteria** (② **202/225-7109**), which is in the basement of the building, at First Street and Independence Avenue SW. Adjoining the cafeteria is a carryout that sells pizza and

sandwiches. At the **Longworth Building Cafeteria,** Independence Avenue and South Capitol Street SE (📞 202/
225-0878), you can grab a bite from a fairly nice food court.
By far the best deal for visitors is the **Dirksen Senate Office
Building South Buffet Room,** First and C streets NE (📞 202/
224-4249). Just $11 per adult ($8.50 per child under 10) buys
a buffet that includes a carving station and eight other hot
entrees, a nonalcoholic drink, and dessert. The dining room
is often crowded but accepts reservations for parties of
more than five. Other options include the Russell Carryout,
in the basement of the Russell Building, and the Cannon
Carryout, in the basement of the Cannon Building. All of
these eateries are open weekdays only. The carryouts stay
open until late afternoon, while the other dining rooms
close at 2:30pm.

In the same neighborhood, two institutions offering
great deals and fair views (of famous sights or people) at
weekday breakfast and lunch are the **Library of Congress**'s
cafeteria and its more formal Montpelier Room (📞 202/
707-8300), where the options usually cost under $10 per
person; and the **Supreme Court**'s cafeteria (📞 202/479-
3246), where you'll likely spy a justice or two enjoying the
midday meal.

Among museum restaurants, the ones that shine are the
six-story Atrium Cafe in the **National Museum of Natural
History** (📞 202/357-2700); and the **National Gallery of Art**'s
Sculpture Garden Pavilion Café (📞 202/289-3360); Garden
Café (📞 202/216-2480); and Terrace Café (📞 202/216-5966),
which is open only Saturday and Sunday from 11am to 3pm
for jazz brunch.

Finally, the newly renovated **Kennedy Center**'s Roof
Terrace Restaurant and KC Café (📞 202/416-8555 for both)
offer convenient gourmet dining in glamorous settings.
These two restaurants take in dramatic views from immense
windows that present a sweeping panorama of the
Potomac River and Washington landmarks.

with chipotle glaze and seared diver sea scallops with potato crème fraiche foam.

101 Constitution Ave. NW, at Louisiana Ave. ✆ 202/547-8100. www.charlie palmer.com. Reservations recommended. Lunch main courses $13–$23; dinner main courses $19–$38. AE, DC, MC, V. Mon–Fri 11:30am–2:30pm and 5:30–10pm; Sat 5–10:30pm. Metro: Union Station.

EXPENSIVE

Bistro Bis ⭐⭐ FRENCH BISTRO   The chic Hotel George is the home of this excellent French restaurant, whose owner-chef, Jeff Buben, and his wife, Sallie, also run Vidalia (p. 82). You can sit at tables in the bar area (which always seem loud, even when it's not that crowded), on the balcony overlooking the bar, or at leather banquettes in the main dining room, where you can watch Buben and staff at work in the glass-fronted kitchen. (In warm weather, there's a sidewalk cafe.) The menu covers French classics like bouillabaisse, pistou, and steak *frites* (steak with fries), as well as Buben's own take on grilled salmon (with oyster mushrooms and braised lentils); pan-seared red snapper; and seared scallops provençale with tomatoes, garlic, olives, and eggplant custard. Many items, including the salmon and the steak *frites,* appear on both the lunch and dinner menus but are considerably cheaper at lunch. The restaurant has been popular from the day it opened, with hungry movers and shakers intermingling with ordinary folk who just love good food. The wine list is mostly French and American.

15 E St. NW. ✆ 202/661-2700. www.bistrobis.com. Reservations recommended. Breakfast $6.75–$12; lunch main courses $13–$23; dinner main courses $20–$32. AE, DC, DISC, MC, V. Daily 7–10am, 11:30am–2:30pm, and 5:30–10:30pm. Metro: Union Station.

La Colline ⭐⭐ FRENCH   This is the perfect spot for that breakfast fundraiser. Hill people like La Colline for its convenience to the Senate side of the Capitol; the great bar; the four private rooms; the high-backed leather booths that allow for discreet conversations; and, last but not least, the food. You'll always get a good meal here. The regular menu offers an extensive list of French standards, including salade niçoise, terrine of foie gras, and fish—poached, grilled, or sautéed. Almost as long is the list of daily specials—the soft-shell crab is superb here in season, and so is the gratin of crayfish. Trout and salmon are smoked in-house—try them. The wine list concentrates on French and California wines; by-the-glass choices change with the season to complement the menu. Don't let the dessert cart roll past you; the apple pie is a winner—as is the restaurant, which has been in business for 23 years.

400 N. Capitol St. NW. ✆ 202/737-0400. www.restaurant.com/lacolline. Reservations recommended. Breakfast $5–$8.75; lunch main courses $12–$19; dinner main courses $12–$24. AE, DC, MC, V. Mon–Fri 7am–10pm, Sat 6–10pm. Metro: Union Station.

The Monocle ✹ *Finds* AMERICAN   A Capitol Hill institution, the Monocle has been around since 1960. This is a men-in-suits place, where the litter of briefcases resting against the too-close-together tables can make for treacherous navigating. But you might want to take a look at whose briefcase it is you're stumbling over, for its proximity to both the Supreme Court and the Capitol guarantees that the Monocle is the haunt of Supreme Court justices and members of Congress. At lunch you'll want to order either the hamburger, which is excellent; the tasty federal salad (field greens and tomatoes tossed with balsamic vinaigrette); the penne pasta with tomato-basil sauce and olives; or the white-bean soup, whenever it's on the menu. At dinner, consider the baked oysters or the pork-rib chop with pommery mustard sauce. Or you can do what my friend and Monocle regular, Bob Harris, does, and order Nick's Dish, which is a rib-eye steak served with a side of pasta and butter; named after the affable owner, Nick's Dish is not found on the menu. Don't bother with the crab cakes. Service is old style, all male.

107 D St. NE. ✆ 202/546-4488. www.themonocle.com. Reservations recommended. Lunch main courses $9–$18; dinner main courses $15–$29. AE, DC, MC, V. Mon–Fri 11:30am–midnight. Closed 2 weeks before Labor Day. Metro: Union Station.

INEXPENSIVE

Il Radicchio *Value* ITALIAN   What a great idea: Order a replenishable bowl of spaghetti for the table at a set price of $6.95, and each of you chooses your own sauce from a long list, at prices that range from $1.95 to $4. Most are standards, like the puttanesca with black olives, capers, garlic, anchovies, and tomato. Or try the radicchio, sausage, red wine, and tomato sauce. It's a great deal.

The kitchen prepares daily specials, such as a sautéed fresh trout with sautéed green beans and garlic and tomato sauce, as well as sandwiches and an assortment of wood-baked pizzas, with a choice of at least 20 toppings.

Ingredients are fresh and flavorful, the service quick and solicitous. The restaurant gets a lot of overworked Hill staffers, who appreciate Il Radicchio's heartening food and low prices.

223 Pennsylvania Ave. SE. ℂ **202/547-5114.** www.robertodonna.com. Reservations not accepted. Main courses $7.95–$19. AE, DC, DISC, MC, V. Mon–Thurs 11am–2:30pm and 4:30–10pm; Fri–Sat 11:30am–11pm; Sun 5–10pm. Metro: Capitol South.

2 Downtown, East of 16th Street NW
VERY EXPENSIVE

Butterfield 9 ★★★ NEW AMERICAN   This remains a favorite restaurant of my husband, and he eats at fine establishments nearly every day. In the spring of 2001, less than a year after opening, Butterfield 9 was chosen by *Condé Nast Traveler* magazine as one of the top 100 new restaurants in the world. We recently enjoyed a tossed salad with baby artichoke hearts; risotto with shrimp, crab, peas, and carrots; venison with a pistachio bread pudding; and the horseradish-crusted halibut with leek fondue.

The highlight of Butterfield 9's classy decor is a series of large, stylized black-and-white prints of handsome men and women dressed in 1930s, 1940s, and 1950s fashions. Butterfield 9 is the latest venture of restaurateur Amarjeet (Umbi) Singh, owner of New Heights (p. 100). A bar menu of about nine items priced from $5 to $13 is available all day, featuring the soup of the day, a cheese plate with fresh fruit, fried oysters, duck spring rolls, and gnocchi.

600 14th St. NW. ℂ **202/BU9-8810.** www.butterfield9.com. Reservations recommended. Lunch main courses $14–$22; dinner main courses $18–$36. AE, DC, DISC, MC, V. Mon–Fri 11:30am–2:30pm; Sun–Thurs 5:30–10pm; Fri–Sat 5:30–11pm. Metro: Metro Center.

Gerard's Place ★★★ FRENCH   Gerard Pangaud is the only Michelin two-star chef working in this country. His restaurant has been here for quite some time now, and his popularity shows no signs of abating. Although Pangaud changes his menu every 2 weeks, he can be counted on to combine exquisite taste sensations, such as Jerusalem artichokes with foie gras and truffles, curried eggplant soup, cod with sautéed endives, or fricassee of monkfish in a red wine sauce. Every once in a while you'll see his famous lobster with ginger, lime, and sauterne on the menu (for $53); if you do, order it, for it's justly famous. The dining room itself is small, seating only 50 at a time, and rather underwhelming in design. This is a quiet restaurant, not a place to get rowdy. You're here for the food and quiet conversation. And although Gerard's Place is also very expensive, the restaurant bows to your budget by offering a three-course fixed-price weekday lunch for $30; on Monday nights it waives the corkage fee (usually $25), so feel free to bring your own bottle of wine.

915 15th St. NW. ℭ 202/737-4445. www.restaurant.com/gerardsplace. Reservations recommended. Lunch and dinner main courses $23–$50; fixed-price menu $85. AE, MC, V. Mon–Fri 11:30am–2pm; Mon–Thurs 5:30–9pm; Fri–Sat 5:30–9:30pm. Metro: McPherson Square.

EXPENSIVE

Bistrot D'Oc ✺✺ FRENCH   Fans of Bernard and Thasanee Grenier, who for 20 years owned the French restaurant, La Miche, in the Maryland suburb of Bethesda, have followed the family to this French bistro, which the Greniers opened in the spring of 2003. Business has been brisk at Bistrot D'Oc from the start, and we were among the first to delight in the hangar steak and pommes frites; mussels in cream sauce; bouillabaisse; and a special salad of haricots verts, avocado, and tomato with a mustard vinaigrette. The cuisine represents the tastes of Bernard's native Languedoc, in southwestern France, and the red-and-yellow washed walls call to mind the colors seen in that part of the country. An extensive wine list includes selections from the Languedoc region.

518 10th St. NW (between E and F sts. NW). ℭ 202/393-5444. Reservations recommended. Lunch main courses $13–$18, dinner main courses $13–$22. AE, DC, DISC, MC, V. Mon–Thurs 11:30am–2:30pm and 5:30–10pm, Fri 11:30am–2:30pm and 5:30–11pm, Sat 11:30am–4:30pm (brunch) and 5:30–11pm, Sun 11:30am–4:30pm (brunch) and 4:30–8:30pm. Metro: Metro Center.

Café Atlántico ✺✺ *Finds* LATIN AMERICAN   This place rocks all week long, but especially on weekend nights, it's a favorite hot spot in Washington's still-burgeoning downtown. The colorful three-tiered restaurant throbs with Latin, calypso, and reggae music, and everyone is having a fiesta—including, it seems, the waiters. If the place is packed, try to snag a seat at the second-level bar, where you can watch the genial bartender mix the potent drinks for which Café Atlantico is famous: the *caipirinha,* made of lime, sugar, and *cachacha* (sugar-cane liqueur); the *mojito,* a rum and crushed mint cocktail; or the passion-fruit cocktail, a concoction of passion-fruit juice, ginger, and jalapeño mixed with mandarin orange-flavored vodka. But take a gander at the remarkable, award-winning wine list, too—it boasts 110 selections, mostly from South America, with many bottles priced under $30.

Seated at the bar or table, you'll watch as your waiter makes fresh guacamole right before your eyes. As for the main dishes, you can't get a more elaborate meal for the price. Check out the ceviche; duck confit; and seared scallops with coconut crispy rice and ginger, squid, and squid ink oil (though the menu changes, you're sure to find these or their equivalent listed). Tropical side dishes and pungent sauces produce a burst of color on the plate.

For adventurous gourmands: Make a reservation at the Minibar at Café Atlántico, where chef José Andrés concocts a $65-per-person prix-fixe menu of 30 to 40 small dishes—from foie gras in a cocoon of cotton candy to pineapple raviolis—for six people per seating Tuesday to Saturday at 6pm and 8:30pm.

405 8th St. NW. © 202/393-0812. www.cafeatlantico.com. Reservations recommended. Lunch main courses $9–$15; dinner main courses $18–$24; pretheater menu $22 (5–6:30pm); Latino dim sum: you can choose a la carte ($2–$9 each) items, or pay $25 for a vegetarian all-you-can-eat meal, or $35 for a deluxe version (Sat 11:30am–2:30pm). AE, DC, DISC, MC, V. Mon–Thurs 11:30am–2:30pm and 5–10pm; Fri 11:30am–2:30pm and 5–11pm; Sat brunch 11:30am–2pm and 5–11pm; Sun brunch 11:30am–2pm and 5–10pm. The bar stays open late on weekends. Metro: Archives–Navy Memorial and Gallery Place/MCI Center.

Oceanaire Seafood Room ⋒ SEAFOOD   The Oceanaire is a good spot for a lively party, with its red leather booths, Art Deco-ish decor, long bar, and festive atmosphere. It would be hard to get romantic or serious about business here—there's just too much to distract you, like the sight of mile-high desserts en route to another table. Oceanaire serves big portions of everything (including cocktails, another reason to bring a bunch of friends here). On a menu that proclaims, "Fresh fish flown in daily from around the world!" you'll read intriguing names of fish on offer that day: grilled Hawaiian Opah moonfish, Tasmanian steelhead trout, Ecuadorian mahimahi, and so on. The waitstaff excels at explaining the tastes and textures of everything on the menu, so don't hesitate to ask. Two of the best entrees are not hard to figure at all: the crab cakes, which are almost all lump crabmeat; and the fisherman's platter, a fresh, fried selection of oysters, scallops, shrimp, and other seafood, with hot matchstick fries alongside it all. The dozen varieties of oysters are fresh and plump, but if you want to start with a salad, consider the BLT, which is like eating a bacon-lettuce-tomato sandwich without the toast.

1201 F St. NW. © 202/347-2277. www.theoceanaire.com. Reservations recommended. Lunch and dinner main courses $9.95–$40. AE, DISC, MC, V. Mon–Thurs 11:30am–10pm; Fri 11:30am–11pm; Sat 5–11pm; Sun 5–9pm. Metro: Metro Center.

TenPenh ⋒⋒ ASIAN FUSION   We'd heard that the service was excellent here, and in its early days this proved to be true: Our waiter actually split a glass of wine for me and my friend when we both wanted a little more but not an entire additional glass. The same waiter checked out someone we thought was Rob Lowe in the bar, reporting back to us, alas, that it was not he. But service is not what it used to be, or so it seemed when we dined here recently and waited quite a while for dinner to arrive. The atmosphere is still lively, however, and the food is still stellar. This is one of those restaurants that has a separate loungy, hard-to-leave bar, but the dining room itself is inviting, with soft lighting, comfortable booths, and an open kitchen. In this, his second restaurant (DC Coast is his other), Jeff Tunks presents translations of dishes he's discovered in travels throughout Asia: smoked salmon and crisp wonton napoleon (which actually has too much salmon), five-spice pecan-crusted halibut, Chinese style smoked lobster, wok-seared calamari, and dumplings filled with chopped pork and crab. We finished with a trio of crème brûlée, the best of which was the coffee-crème.

1001 Pennsylvania Ave. NW (at 10th St.). (?) **202/393-4500**. www.tenpenh.com. Reservations recommended. Lunch main courses $13–$18; dinner main courses $13–$28. AE, DISC, MC, V. Mon–Fri 11:30am–2:30pm; Mon–Thurs 5:30–10:30pm; Fri–Sat 5:30–11pm. Metro: Archives–Navy Memorial.

Tosca ✪✪✪ NORTHERN ITALIAN   Washington probably has more Italian restaurants than any other kind of ethnic eatery, yet this central part of downtown has almost no Italian fare. In fact, since it opened in the spring of 2001, Tosca remains the standout fine *ristorante italiano* between Capitol Hill and the western edge of downtown, a range of at least 20 blocks. Tosca's interior design of pale pastels in the thick carpeting and heavy drapes creates a hushed atmosphere, a suitable foil to the rich food.

The menu, meanwhile, emphasizes the cooking of chef Cesare Lanfranconi's native Lake Como region of Italy. A good example of a traditional pasta dish is the *scapinasch,* a ravioli of aged ricotta and raisins (or sometimes it's made with amaretto cookies) with butter and sage sauce. Lanfranconi's take on a rack of veal is to marinate and grill the meat, serving it with Yukon gold and roasted garlic potato purée and local asparagus timbale. Tosca has something for everyone, including simply grilled fish accompanied by organic vegetables for the health conscious, tiramisu and citrus cannoli for those with a sweet tooth. No wonder the restaurant is always full. Remarkably, even when there's a crowd, Tosca doesn't get too noisy—the restaurant's designers kept the acoustics in mind.

1112 F St. NW. (?) **202/367-1990**. www.toscadc.com. Reservations recommended. Lunch main courses $9–$18; dinner main courses $16–$34. AE, DC, MC, V. Mon–Thurs 11:30am–2:30pm and 5:30–10:30pm; Fri 11:30am–2:30pm and 5:30–11pm; Sat 5:30–11pm; Sun 5:30–10:30pm. Metro: Metro Center.

MODERATE

Andale ✪ MEXICAN   Chef Allison Swope's vision of Mexican cuisine and restauranting is uniquely her own. During a visit to the

Yucatán peninsula a couple of years ago, Swope was so taken with the cuisine of Oaxaca, Mexico, that upon her return to Washington she set about transforming her "robust American" restaurant, The Mark, into the inventive Mexican Andale (*ándale* means go!"). The menu features dishes that combine authentic regional Mexican cuisine with fresh and often non-traditional ingredients, such as sushi-grade tuna marinated with achiote, garlic, Mexican oregano, and sour orange juice. The leg of lamb roasted in avocado leaves and presented in a soupy sauce of lamb broth, thickened with garbanzo beans, carrots, and potato, is a standout. Not to miss: the smoky, spicy salsa picante appetizer and the Mexican-style doughnuts with dipping chocolate for dessert. The bar offers 35 brands of tequila and concocts an excellent margarita.

Opt for seating in the storefront window for optimum people-watching (Andale is in the middle of downtown) or in the main dining room, where Mexican artwork now hangs. Every Monday after 5pm, you can order a bottle of wine or champagne for half-price with the order of an entree.

401 7th St. NW. (✆ **202/783-3133**. www.andaledc.com. Reservations recommended. Lunch main courses $7–$14; dinner main courses $9–$22. AE, DC, DISC, MC, V. Mon 11:30am–3pm and 5–9pm; Tues–Thurs 11:30am–3pm and 5–10pm; Fri–Sat 11:30am–3pm and 5–11pm. Mon–Fri bar stays open but no food is served, 3–5pm. Metro: Gallery Place or Archives/Navy Memorial.

Zaytinya ✿✿✿ GREEK/TURKISH/LEBANESE Honest, I would have liked Zaytinya even if my waiter, Isa, hadn't told me I had beautiful eyes. Isa also has beautiful eyes, by the way. All right, down to business. *Condé Nast Traveler* magazine's May 2003 issue named Zaytinya as one of the top 75 new restaurants in the world (the restaurant opened in Oct 2002). Executive chef José Andrés (see Café Atlántico on p. 73) is behind it all. Zaytinya is a big restaurant, and it stays busy all the time. The place takes reservations only at lunch and for pretheater dinners, 5 to 6:30pm, which is why the restaurant hands out beepers if there's a long wait for a table.

Zaytinya was hopping on the Sunday night we were there, but fortunately we didn't have a wait. Once seated, we received a basket of hot and billowy thin shells of pita bread, along with a saucer of olive oil swirled with pomegranate syrup. Isa guided us through the menu, explaining that the wine list was almost entirely Greek, that Zaytinya is Turkish for "olive oil," and pointing out which mezze dishes he would recommend. Although the dinner menu lists several entrees, what you want to do here is order lots of little dishes. We savored the zucchini-cheese cakes, which came with a caper-and-yogurt sauce;

Family-Friendly Restaurants

Nearly every restaurant welcomes families these days, starting, most likely, with the one in your hotel. Chinese restaurants are always a safe bet, and so are these:

Legal Sea Foods (p. 83) Believe it or not, this seafood restaurant has won awards for its kids' menu. It features the usual macaroni and cheese and hot dogs, but also kids' portions of steamed lobster; fried popcorn shrimp; a small fisherman's platter of shrimp, scallops, and clams; and other items, each of which comes with fresh fruit and a choice of baked potato, mashed potatoes, or french fries. Prices range from $3.95 for the hot dog to $16 for the 1-pound lobster (you can also order a ½-lb. lobster for $8.95).

Famous Luigi's Pizzeria Restaurant (p. 84) Introduce your kids to pre-Domino's pizza. Luigi's, which has been around since 1943, serves the real thing: big, thick, ungreasy pizza with fresh toppings. Sit at tables covered in red-checked cloths that have probably withstood countless spilled drinks and splotches of tomato sauce in their time. The restaurant gets noisy, so chances are that loud ones in your party will blend right in.

Old Glory Barbecue (p. 99) A loud, laid-back place where the waiters are friendly without being patronizing. Go early because the restaurant becomes more of a bar as the evening progresses. There is a children's menu, but you may not need it—the barbecue, burgers, fries, and desserts are so good that everyone can order from the main menu.

the carrot-apricot-pine-nut fritters, served with pistachio sauce; sardines; a marinated salmon; *fattoush,* or salad of tomatoes and cucumbers mixed with pomegranate reduction, sumac, and olive oil, with crispy pita bread croutons; and shrimp with tomatoes, onions, ouzo, and kefalofraviera cheese. Many of these flavors were new to my palette, but I found everything to be wonderfully delicious. For dessert, we ordered a Turkish coffee chocolate cake, and the more exotic Medjool dates roasted in Vinsanto (a kind of dessert wine), rolled in crushed orange shortbread, with olive oil ice cream. The dates were our favorite. Isa was quite proud of us.

701 9th St. NW (at G St.). © **202/638-0800**. www.zaytinya.com. Reservations at lunch and pretheater dinner 5–6:30pm. Mezze items $3.75–$8. Main dinner courses $13–$17. AE, DC, DISC, MC, V. Sun–Mon 11:30am–10pm; Tues–Thurs 11:30am–11:30pm; Fri–Sat 11:30am–midnight. Metro: Gallery Place/Chinatown (9th St. exit).

Zola AMERICAN A lot of people liked Zola right from the start, when it opened in 2002, but I wasn't one of them. But ever since chef Frank Morales took over the kitchen, I've been totally won over. I've had a simple ham and gouda sandwich at lunch and loved it, and I've had seared scallops that tasted delicately sweet, a perfectly done duck breast, and an artichoke-and-goat-cheese tart for dinner, and they were each divine. And then there was dessert; the creamsicle is "mandarin orange and vanilla cream layered atop a 'Nilla wafer crust with bitter chocolate sauce"—another hit. Zola is also a cleverly designed restaurant, trading on its location next to the International Spy Museum for a decor that includes backlit panels of coded KGB documents, and a center-pivoted swinging wall/door that's like something straight out of the TV show *Get Smart*. We very much liked the red velvet booths in the dining room and the long curving bar where there are plenty of little ledges to rest your drink. Zola, in its superb downtown location, has become a popular place for the young and single to hang. Servers are friendly.

800 F St. NW (at 8th St.). © **202/654-0999**. www.zoladc.com. Reservations recommended. Lunch main courses $7–$17; dinner main courses $7–$24. AE, DC, DISC, MC, V. Mon–Thurs 11:30am–11pm; Fri 11:30am–midnight; Sat 5pm–midnight; Sun 5–9pm. Metro: Gallery Place/Chinatown.

INEXPENSIVE

Matchbox PIZZA/ITALIAN This restaurant occupies three floors of a skinny town house in Chinatown, an odd place to find a pizzeria, maybe, but welcome, nonetheless. Matchbox opened in the spring of 2003 and a year later had grown so popular that it won the 2004 Restaurant Association of Metropolitan Washington Award for best new restaurant. The key thing here is the wood-fired brick oven, which bakes the thin pizza crust at temperatures as high as 900°F (482°C). You can choose a regularly featured pizza, like the "prosciutto white," which is topped with prosciutto, kalamata olives, fresh garlic, ricotta, fresh mozzarella, and extra virgin olive oil; or you can request your own set of toppings, from smoked bacon to artichoke hearts. Matchbox is actually a cut above a pizzeria, for it also serves super salads, appetizers, sandwiches, and entrees; its full bar on the first floor is quite the social scene.

713 H St. NW. ⓒ 202/289-4441. www.matchbox.com. Pizzas and sandwiches $8–$17; main courses at lunch and dinner $13-$21. AE, MC, V. Mon–Sat 11:30am–10pm. Metro: Gallery Place/Chinatown.

Tony Cheng's Seafood Restaurant ⓐ CHINESE/SEAFOOD
Most of the restaurants in Chinatown look seedy, no matter how good the food might be. Tony Cheng's is the most presentable of Chinatown's eateries, and also a good choice if you like Cantonese specialties and spicy Szechuan and Hunan cuisine. The restaurant is located on the second floor, above Tony Cheng's Mongolian Restaurant, which is related but not the same eatery. Tony Cheng's Seafood Restaurant has been here for 28 years and has earned a reputation for its Cantonese roast duck; lobster or Dungeness crab, stir-fried and served with either ginger and scallions or black bean sauce; or Szechuan crispy beef, to name just a few. Dim sum is available at lunch weekdays, as well as on the weekend, but you order items off the menu during the week.

619 H St. NW (between 6th and 7th sts.). ⓒ 202/371-8669. Reservations recommended. Lunch main courses $5–$13, dinner main courses $7–$29. AE, MC, V. Daily 11am–11pm. Metro: Gallery Place/Chinatown.

3 Downtown, 16th Street NW & West
VERY EXPENSIVE
Galileo ⓐⓐⓐ NEAPOLITAN ITALIAN   Food critics mention Galileo as one of the best Italian restaurants in the country and Roberto Donna as one of the nation's best chefs. The likable Donna opened the white-walled grottolike Galileo in 1984; since then, he has opened other restaurants in the area, including Il Radicchio (p. 71) on Capitol Hill. He's also written a cookbook and has established himself as an integral part of Washington culture.

Donna cures his own ham for salami and prosciutto, and his sausages, pastas, mozzarella, marmalades, and breads are all made in-house. Galileo has long featured the cuisine of Donna's native Piedmont region, an area in northern Italy influenced by neighboring France and Switzerland—think truffles, hazelnuts, porcini mushrooms, and veal. Lately, Donna is preparing Neapolitan cuisine, dishes traditional to Naples, in Italy's southern Campania region. Examples include roasted rack of lamb served with a porcini mushroom tart in a black olive sauce; homemade ravioli filled with buffalo ricotta, ham, and mozzarella in a meat ragu; and Mediterranean dorade fish baked in foil with mussels. Whether your menu features Neapolitan or Piedmontese dishes, you will have the choice of ordering a la carte or from three fixed-price menus: $65 for four courses, $75 for five courses, and $85 for six courses. The cellar boasts more than 400 vintages of Italian wine. The atmosphere is relaxed; some diners are dressed in jeans, others in suits. Waiters can be supercilious, though.

But wait—there's more. For the ultimate dining experience, book a seat in Donna's **Laboratorio del Galileo** ✮✮✮ (✆ **202/331-0880**), a private dining area and kitchen enclosed by glass, where Donna prepares the 12- to 14-course tasting menu ($98 weekdays, $110 weekends) and entertains you and 29 other lucky diners.

Galileo also has a terrace for warm-weather dining. And last but not least, if you're intrigued but can't afford a dinner here, reserve a seat at the bar for lunch and enjoy something stupendous, say lasagna Bolognese or a bowl of fusilli tossed with asparagus, provolone, and prosciutto, for only $4 to $12.

1110 21st St. NW. ✆ **202/293-7191**. www.robertodonna.com. Reservations recommended. Lunch main courses $14–$20; dinner main courses $24–$40. AE, DC, DISC, MC, V. Mon–Fri 11:30am–2pm and 5:30–10pm; Sat 5:30–10:30pm; Sun 5:30–10pm. Metro: Foggy Bottom.

The Prime Rib ✮✮ STEAK/SEAFOOD The Prime Rib has plenty of competition now, but it makes no difference. Beef lovers still consider this The Place. It's got a definite men's club feel about it, with brass-trimmed black walls, leopard-skin carpeting, and comfortable black leather chairs and banquettes. Waiters are in black tie, and a pianist at the baby grand plays show tunes and Irving Berlin classics at lunch; at dinner, a bass player joins the pianist.

The meat is from the best grain-fed steers and has been aged 4 to 5 weeks. Steaks and cuts of roast beef are thick, tender, and juicy. In case you had any doubt, The Prime Rib's prime rib is the best item on the menu: juicy and thick, top-quality meat. For less carnivorous diners, there are about a dozen seafood entrees, including an excellent crab imperial. Mashed potatoes are done right, as are the fried potato skins, but I recommend the hot cottage fries.

2020 K St. NW. ✆ **202/466-8811**. www.theprimerib.com. Reservations recommended. Jacket and tie required for men. Lunch main courses $11–$26; dinner main courses $20–$38. AE, DC, MC, V. Mon–Thurs 11:30am–3pm and 5–11pm; Fri 11:30am–3pm and 5–11:30pm; Sat 5–11:30pm. Metro: Farragut West.

Taberna del Alabardero ✮✮ *Finds* SPANISH Dress up to visit this truly elegant restaurant, where you receive the royal treatment from the Spanish staff, who are accustomed to attending to the real thing—Spain's King Juan Carlos and Queen Sofía have dined here. Not long ago, the Spanish government named the Taberna del Alabardero the best Spanish restaurant outside Spain. The Taberna is also a favorite of dignitaries attending meetings at the nearby World Bank and International Monetary Fund.

The dining room is ornate, with red tufted banquettes, green satin stretched across chairs, and gilded cherubs placed at ceiling corners. Order a plate of tapas to start: lightly fried calamari, shrimp in garlic and olive oil, artichokes sautéed with thin smoky Serrano ham, and marinated mushrooms. Although the a la carte menu changes with the seasons, several paellas (the menu says each feeds two, but you can ask for a single serving) are always available. The lobster and seafood paella served on saffron rice is rich and flavorful. (Ask to have the lobster shelled; otherwise, you do the cracking.) Another signature dish is the stuffed squid sauced in its own ink. The wine list features 250 Spanish wines.

This is the only Taberna del Alabardero outside of Spain, where there are five locations. All are owned and operated by Father Luis de Lezama, who opened his first tavern outside the palace gates in Madrid in 1974 as a place to train delinquent boys for employment.

1776 I St. NW (entrance on 18th St. NW). © 202/429-2200. Reservations recommended. Jacket and tie for men suggested. Lunch main courses $18–$24; dinner main courses $26–$37. AE, DC, DISC, MC, V. Mon–Thurs 11:30am–2:30pm and 5:30–10:30pm; Fri 11:30am–2:30pm and 5:30–11pm; Sat 5:30–11pm. Metro: Farragut West.

EXPENSIVE

Equinox 🌟🌟 NEW AMERICAN Everyone seems to love Equinox. It's not splashy in any way, just a pretty, comfortable restaurant that serves creatively delicious American food. Even if you aren't vegetarian, you'll eat all your vegetables here because as much care is taken with the garnishes as with the entree itself. And every entree comes with a garnish or two, like the leek fondue or the forest mushrooms with applewood bacon, or the white bean ragout. You can order additional side dishes; consider the macaroni and cheese: Vermont cheddar, Parmesan, and black truffle reduction. The home runs, of course, are the entrees, and the menu is short and to the point: crab cakes made with lump crab mixed with capers, brioche bread crumbs, mayonnaise, and lemon-butter sauce; barbecued wild King salmon with roasted sweet corn; and two or three other dishes, that's it. Equinox has two tasting menus, a $65 four-course and $85 six-course, available at dinner most nights.

818 Connecticut Ave. NW. © 202/331-8118. www.equinoxrestaurant.com. Reservations recommended. Lunch main courses $16–$27; dinner main courses $30–$33. AE, DC, DISC, MC, V. Mon–Thurs 11:30am–2pm and 5:30–10pm; Fri 11:30am–2pm and 5:30–10:30pm; Sat 5:30–10:30pm; Sun 5–9pm. Metro: Farragut West.

Vidalia ✿✿ REGIONAL AMERICAN/SOUTHERN   If you're hesitant to dine at a restaurant that's down a flight of steps from the street, your doubts will vanish as soon as you enter Vidalia's tiered dining room. There's a party going on down here. In fact, Vidalia is so popular, you may have to wait a short time in the newly remodeled wine bar—even if you arrive on time for your reservation. But the bar is fun, too, and gives you a jump-start on getting into the mood of the place. And if you don't have a dinner reservation, you might want to check out the bar menu, whose items include deviled eggs and rabbit rillettes at prices that range from $4.50 to $12.

Executive chef Peter Smith recently revamped the menu to bring a taste of New Orleans to owner/chef Jeff Buben's already Southern cuisine. The new menu features dishes such as pan-roasted loin of monkfish with crayfish rice fritters, tasso ham, and étouffée sauce; and rockfish filet with succotash and turnip greens. A signature entree remains the scrumptious sautéed shrimp on a mound of creamed grits and caramelized onions in a thyme-and-shrimp cream sauce. Corn bread and biscuits with apple butter are served at every meal. Vidalia is known for its lemon chess pie, which tastes like pure sugar; I prefer the pecan pie. A carefully chosen wine list highlights American vintages and offers 30 wines by the glass.

1990 M St. NW. ✆ 202/659-1990. www.vidaliadc.com. Reservations recommended. Lunch main courses $13–$22; dinner main courses $23–$30. AE, DC, DISC, MC, V. Mon–Thurs 11:30am–2:30pm and 5:30–10pm; Fri 11:30am–2:30pm and 5:30–10:30pm; Sat 5:30–10:30pm; Sun–5:30–10pm. Closed Sun July 4th to Labor Day. Metro: Dupont Circle.

MODERATE

Bombay Club ✿ *(Finds* INDIAN   The Bombay Club is a pleasure, sure to please patrons who know their Indian food as well as those who've never tried it: Dishes present an easy introduction to Indian food for the uninitiated and are sensitive to varying tolerances for spiciness. I'm a wimp in the "heat" department, my husband's the opposite, and we're both happy here.

The spiciest item on the menu is the fiery green chile chicken ("not for the fainthearted," the menu warns—this is the one my husband orders a lot). Most popular are the tandoori salmon and the delicately prepared lobster malabar (that last one is my personal favorite). These two and the other tandoori dishes—such as the chicken marinated in a yogurt, ginger, and garlic dressing—are specialties, as is the vegetarian fare—try the black lentils cooked overnight on a slow fire. The Bombay Club is known for its vegetarian offerings (at least nine items are on the menu) and for its

Sunday champagne brunch, which offers a buffet of fresh juices, fresh baked breads, and assorted Indian dishes. Patrons are as fond of the service as the cuisine: Waiters seem straight out of *Jewel in the Crown,* attending to your every whim. This is one place where you can linger over a meal as long as you like. Slow-moving ceiling fans and wicker furniture accentuate the colonial British ambience.

815 Connecticut Ave. NW. ℂ **202/659-3727.** www.bombayclubdc.com. Reservations recommended. Main courses $7.50–$22; Sun brunch $19. AE, DC, MC, V. Mon–Thurs 11:30am–2:30pm and 6–10:30pm; Fri 11:30am–2:30pm and 6–11pm; Sat 6–11pm; Sun 11:30am–2:30pm (brunch) and 5:30–9pm. Metro: Farragut West.

Legal Sea Foods 🏃 *Kids* SEAFOOD This famous family-run Boston-based seafood empire, whose motto is "If it's not fresh, it's not Legal," made its Washington debut in 1995. The softly lit dining room is plush, with terrazzo marble floors and rich cherrywood paneling. Sporting events, especially Boston games, are aired on a TV over the handsome marble raw bar, and you can usually pick up a copy of the *Boston Globe* near the entrance. As for the food, not only is everything fresh, but it's also from certified-safe waters.

Legal's buttery-rich clam chowder is a classic. Other worthy appetizers include garlicky golden-brown farm-raised mussels au gratin and fluffy pan-fried Maryland lump crab cakes served with mustard sauce and greens tossed with asparagus. You can have one of eight or so varieties of grilled fresh fish or opt for one of Legal's specialty dishes, like the Portuguese fisherman's stew, in which cod, mussels, clams, and chorizo are prepared in a saffron-tomato broth. Top it off with a slice of Boston cream pie. Wine lovers will be happy to know that Legal's wine list has received recognition from *Wine Spectator* magazine; parents will be glad that Legal's award-winning kid's menu offers not just macaroni and cheese, but also steamed lobster, popcorn shrimp, and other items, each of which comes with fresh fruit and a choice of baked potato, mashed potatoes, or french fries. At lunch, oyster po'boys and the lobster roll are real treats.

You'll find another Legal Sea Foods at National Airport (ℂ 703/413-9810); a third location is at 704 7th St. NW (ℂ 202/347-0007), across from the MCI Center.

2020 K St. NW. ℂ **202/496-1111.** www.legalseafoods.com. Reservations recommended, especially at lunch. Lunch main courses $9–$16; sandwiches $9–$17; dinner main courses $12–$30. AE, DC, DISC, MC, V. Mon–Thurs 11am–10pm; Fri 11am–10:30pm; Sat 4–10:30pm. Metro: Farragut North or Farragut West.

INEXPENSIVE

Café Asia ASIAN FUSION It's easy to miss Café Asia, nestled as it is between hair salons and offices on I St. right near the White

House. Inside is a different story. The decor and menu both stand out in really interesting ways. The restaurant has three levels to it, set within an atrium. From street level, walk downstairs to the main dining room, where furniture looks like it's made for child's play: The circular and rectangular pieces in orange, yellow, and white are set closer to the ground than normal. My friend Bill, who is a little over 6 feet tall, said he was not uncomfortable, though. Upstairs is more of a lounge area, overlooking the lower level; one more flight up is reserved mostly for private parties.

The menu here is pan-Asian: Chinese, Indonesian, Japanese, Thai. Our waitress steered my 12-year-old to the Indonesian fried rice, which she said was "more interesting than Chinese"; this turned out to mean it's spicier (it's got chiles in it, for one thing). So if you like Americanized, or tamed down, Asian food, you might be happy with the teriyaki and satays. You have many more choices if you want to sample exotic food. I tried the nasi uduk, an Indonesian coconut rice platter with spicy beef, crispy anchovies, pickled vegetables, emping (acorn chips), chicken satay, and spicy prawn sauce; I enjoyed it very much, although I was reaching for the water glass after every swallow. My husband and Bill were crazy about the ikan pepes, which is Indonesian grilled fish filet with spicy turmeric sauce, fresh basil, and lemon grass, wrapped in banana leaves. Café Asia also serves delicious sushi.

1720 I St. NW. ① 202/659-2696. www.cafeasia.com. Reservations accepted. Lunch and dinner main courses $7–$14. AE, DC. DISC, MC, V. Mon–Thurs 11:30am–11pm; Fri 11:30am–midnight; Sat noon–midnight; Sun noon–11pm. Metro: Farragut West.

Famous Luigi's Pizzeria Restaurant *Kids* ITALIAN Before there was Domino's or Pizza Hut or Papa John's, there was Luigi's. Make that *way* before—Luigi's opened in 1943. People who grew up in Washington consider Luigi's an essential part of their childhood. I've been here a couple of times with my daughters and they like to reminisce about the place as if it were Italy we'd visited. Whether you go at lunch or dinner, you can expect to be among a sea of office folks. At night, the restaurant's atmosphere changes a little, as office workers come in groups to unwind, have a drink, or get a bite; but this isn't a bar, so it doesn't get rowdy. The menu is long, listing all kinds of pastas, sandwiches, grilled dishes, and pizzas (with 44 toppings to choose from). Come here for a little local color, and to please everyone in the family.

1132 19th St. NW (between L and M sts.). ① 202/331-7574. www.famous luigis.com. Main courses $5–$17. AE, DC, DISC, MC, V. Mon–Sat 11am–midnight; Sun noon–midnight. Metro: Dupont Circle or Farragut North.

4 U Street Corridor

INEXPENSIVE

Ben's Chili Bowl *(Finds)* AMERICAN   Ben's is a veritable institution, a mom-and-pop place, where everything looks, tastes, and probably even costs the same as when the restaurant opened in 1958. Ben's has won national recognition, too, most recently when it was chosen by the 2004 James Beard Foundation Awards as an "America's Classic," one of four restaurants in the country so named for being "renowned for their timeless appeal."

The most expensive item on the menu is the double turkey burger sub for $6.25. Formica counters, red bar stools, and a jukebox that plays Motown and reggae tunes—that's Ben's. Ben's continues as a gathering place for black Washington and visitors like Bill Cosby, who's a longtime customer (a chili dog is named after him). Everyone's welcome, though, even the late-nighters who come streaming out of nearby nightclubs at 2 or 3am on the weekend. Of course, the chili, cheese fries, and half-smokes are great, but so are breakfast items. Try the salmon cakes, grits, scrapple, or blueberry pancakes (6–11am only).

1213 U St. NW. © **202/667-0909.** www.benschilibowl.com. Reservations not accepted. Main courses $2.50–$6.50. No credit cards. Mon–Thurs 6am–2am; Fri–Sat 6am–4am; Sun noon–8pm. Metro: U St.–Cardozo.

5 Adams-Morgan

EXPENSIVE

Cashion's Eat Place *(★★)* *(Finds)* AMERICAN   Cashion's has all the pleasures of a neighborhood restaurant—easy, warm, comfortable—combined with cuisine that is out of this world. Owner/chef Ann Cashion continues to rack up culinary awards as easily as she pleases her patrons; in 2004, Cashion was named "Best Chef/MidAtlantic" by the James Beard Foundation. Her menu changes daily, always featuring about eight entrees, split between seafood and meat: rabbit stuffed with ham and truffles; fritto misto of whole jumbo shrimp and black sea bass filet, served with onion rings and house-made tartar sauce; pork loin with garlic sauce; fried sweetbreads on a bed of sautéed spinach; and so on. The side dishes that accompany each entree, such as lemon cannelloni bean purée or radish and sprout salad, are equally as appealing. Desserts, like coconut layer cake with huckleberries, or chocolate cinnamon mousse, are worth saving room for. Sunday brunch is popular, too; you can choose from breakfast fare (challah French toast, spinach and Gruyère omelets) or heartier items (grilled rainbow trout, croque-monsieurs).

The charming dining room curves around a slightly raised bar. In warm weather, the glass-fronted Cashion's opens invitingly to the sidewalk, where you can also dine. Tables at the back offer a view of the small kitchen, where Cashion and her staff work away. In winter, ask for a table away from the front door, which lets in a blast of cold air with each new arrival.

1819 Columbia Rd. NW. © **202/797-1819.** Reservations recommended. Brunch $8.95–$12; dinner main courses $17–$26. MC, V. Tues 5:30–10pm; Wed–Sat 5:30–11pm; Sun 11:30am–2:30pm and 5:30–10pm.

MODERATE

Lauriol Plaza ✸ MEXICAN/SPANISH/LATIN AMERICAN
This place is gigantic—it seats 330—but it's immensely popular—often named as the city's best Mexican restaurant—so you may still have to wait for a table. Lauriol Plaza looks like a factory from the outside, but inside it's stunning. You have a choice of sitting at sidewalk tables, on the rooftop deck, or in the two-tiered dining room with its large mural of a fiesta on one wall and windows covering another. We had good, though warm, margaritas; the standout carne asada fajitas; and tasty *camarones diablo* (six broiled jumbo shrimp seasoned with spices). Anything mesquite grilled is sure to please. Servings are as large as the restaurant. Sunday brunch, also recommended, is served from 11am to 3pm. With so many people dining here, Lauriol Plaza is a good place to people-watch.

1835 18th St. NW. © **202/387-0035.** www.lauriolplaza.com. Reservations not accepted. Main courses $8–$17. AE, DC, DISC, MC, V. Sun 11am–11pm; Mon–Thurs 11:30am–11pm; Fri–Sat 11:30am–midnight. Metro: Dupont Circle.

INEXPENSIVE

Meskerem ETHIOPIAN Washington has a number of Ethiopian restaurants, but this is probably the best. It's certainly the most attractive; the three-level high-ceilinged dining room (sunny by day, candlelit at night) has an oval skylight girded by a painted sunburst and walls hung with African art and musical instruments. On the mezzanine level, you sit at *messobs* (basket tables) on low, carved Ethiopian chairs or upholstered leather poufs. Ethiopian music enhances the ambience.

Diners share large platters of food, which they scoop up with a sourdough crepelike pancake called *injera* (no silverware here). You'll notice a lot of *watt* dishes, which refers to the traditional Ethiopian stew (made with your choice of beef, chicken, lamb, or

Adams-Morgan & Dupont Circle Dining

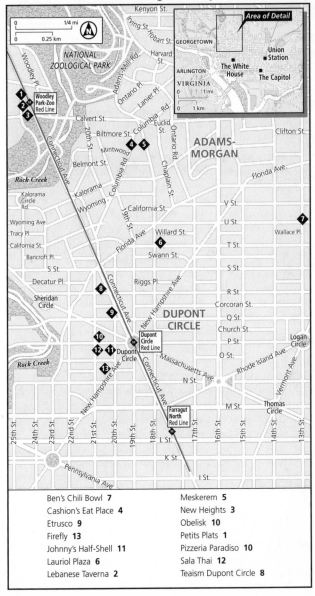

Ben's Chili Bowl **7**

Cashion's Eat Place **4**

Etrusco **9**

Firefly **13**

Johnny's Half-Shell **11**

Lauriol Plaza **6**

Lebanese Taverna **2**

Meskerem **5**

New Heights **3**

Obelisk **10**

Petits Plats **1**

Pizzeria Paradiso **10**

Sala Thai **12**

Teaism Dupont Circle **8**

vegetables), in varying degrees of hot and spicy; the *alicha watts* are milder and more delicately flavored. You might also share an entree—perhaps *yegeb kay watt* (succulent lamb in thick, hot *berbere* sauce)—along with a platter of five vegetarian dishes served with tomato and potato salads. Some combination platters comprise an array of beef, chicken, lamb, and vegetables. There's a full bar; the wine list includes Ethiopian wine and beer.

2434 18th St. NW. ✆ **202/462-4100.** www.meskeremonline.com. Reservations recommended. Lunch and dinner main courses $7–$13. AE, DC, MC, V. Daily noon–midnight; bar open until 3am Fri–Sat.

6 Dupont Circle

VERY EXPENSIVE

Obelisk 🌶🌶🌶 ITALIAN   Obelisk is the most consistently excellent restaurant in the city. Service and food are simply the best. In this pleasantly spare room that seats only 36, the walls are decorated with 19th-century French botanical prints and Italian lithographs. Here, owner/chef Peter Pastan presents his small fixed-price menus of sophisticated Italian cuisine, using the freshest possible ingredients. Each night diners are offered two or three choices for each of five courses. Dinner might begin with fried soft-shell crab with artichoke salad and onion rings, followed by squash blossom ravioli with pesto, and then an artfully arranged dish of pan-cooked grouper with artichokes and thyme, or grilled venison tenderloin with morels and green garlic . . . or whatever Pastan has been inspired to create. Dessert is a choice of cheese or baked specialties, such as pear spice cake. Breads and desserts are all baked in-house and are divine. Pastan's carefully crafted wine list represents varied regions of Italy, as well as California vintages. The fixed-price menu is a deal, but the cost of wine and coffees can easily double the price per person.

2029 P St. NW. ✆ **202/872-1180.** Reservations recommended. Fixed-price 5-course dinner $60. DC, MC, V. Tues–Sat 6–10pm. Metro: Dupont Circle.

EXPENSIVE

Etrusco 🌶🌶 ITALIAN   Etrusco is just the sort of place you'd hope to stumble upon as a stranger in town. It's pretty, with a sophisticated but relaxed atmosphere, and the food is excellent. From the outdoor terrace, you descend a short flight of steps to the exquisite dining room, which resembles a trattoria with ochre and burnt sienna walls, arched skylight, and tile floor.

On the menu you'll find warm baby octopus salad, *ribollita* (minestrone thickened with bread and Parmesan cheese), pappardelle with shredded duck, grilled scallops, crumb-coated grilled tuna, and the more traditional veal scaloppini and osso buco. It's all very, very good. End with "Grandfather's cake," a light chocolate pie.

1606 20th St. NW. © 202/667-0047. Reservations recommended. Main courses $14–$30. AE, DC, MC. V. Mon–Sat 5:30–10:30pm. Metro: Dupont Circle.

Firefly ☆ CONTEMPORARY AMERICAN

This is an intimate restaurant and popular, which makes for a rollicking experience but also a crowded one—you can feel squeezed in here. A floor-to-ceiling "firefly tree" hung with lanterns heightens this feeling. The food is quite good. We enjoyed the potato gnocchi with smoked trout and sage brown butter and the grilled New York steak with housemade fries, watercress, and Smithfield ham. If fries don't come with your meal, it's worth ordering them as a side, as they're excellent and arrive hot and salty in a paper cone set in its own stand. At lunch, consider the grilled salmon BLT or the Amish chicken Cobb salad. We had the caramelized apple tart for dessert, which was no good at all, and not even served warm. Firefly lies within the Hotel Madera, but has a separate entrance.

In the Hotel Madera, 1310 New Hampshire Ave. NW. © 202/861-1310. www. firefly-dc.com. Reservations recommended. Brunch main courses $7.50–$14; lunch main courses $10–$17, dinner main courses $12–$23. AE, DC, DISC, MC, V. Mon–Thurs 7–10:30am, 11:30am–2:30pm, and 5:30–10pm; Fri 10:30am, 11:30am–2:30pm, and 5:30–11pm; Sat 10am–2:30pm and 5:30–11pm; Sun 10am–2:30pm and 5:30–10pm. Metro: Dupont Circle.

Johnny's Half Shell ☆ *Finds* SEAFOOD

Whenever a friend visits from out of town and I haven't gotten around to making a restaurant reservation, we usually end up at Johnny's. It's easy, fun, and comfortable; it's open continuously from lunch through the afternoon to closing; it takes no reservations, so you can usually walk right in and get something fresh from the sea (though weekend nights after 8:30pm, you'll probably have at least a 20-min. wait); and it feels like a hometown restaurant, a rare thing in a city whose residents tend to originate from many other hometowns. Johnny's owners, Ann Cashion and John Fulchino, own another very popular restaurant, Cashion's Eat Place (p. 85) in Adams-Morgan. The restaurant is small, with a decor that features an aquarium behind the long bar, booths along one paneled wall, a tile floor, and a partly open kitchen. The professional yet friendly waiters seem to enjoy themselves.

It's reassuring, too, that the menu seldom changes because everything is reliably good, from the farm-raised chicken with old-fashioned Eastern Shore slippery dumplings, garden peas, and button mushrooms, to the crabmeat imperial with a salad of *haricots verts,* tomatoes, and shallots. I recently opted for that crab imperial, which was almost as good as the one my mom used to make. On another visit, I enjoyed the delicious fried oyster po'boy sandwich, while my friend Sue went for the Maryland crab cakes with coleslaw and french fries; we both devoured every morsel. If the sautéed soft-shell crabs with Old Bay and basil beurre blanc and corn pudding are on the menu, get them. My daughter Cait likes the barbecued shrimp appetizer with Asiago cheese grits. Oysters and Wellfleet clams on the half shell are always available, of course. The short wine list includes a few selections by the glass; there are four beers on tap. Desserts are simple but perfect, including homemade ice cream; a choice of hazelnut, almond, pecan, or chocolate tart; and chocolate angel food cake with caramel sauce.

2002 P St. NW. ✆ **202/296-2021.** Reservations not accepted. Lunch main courses $6.95–$20; dinner main courses $16–$22. AE, MC, V. Mon–Thurs 11:30am–10:30pm; Fri–Sat 11:30am–11pm (weekdays, between 3 and 5pm, a light fare menu of soups and salads is available); Sun 5–10pm. Metro: Dupont Circle.

INEXPENSIVE

Pizzeria Paradiso ✿ ITALIAN   This is still the best pizza place in the city, no contest. Peter Pastan, master chef/owner of Obelisk (located right next door and reviewed just above), owns this classy, often crowded, 16-table pizzeria. An oak-burning oven at one end of the charming room produces exceptionally doughy but light pizza crusts. As you wait, you can munch on mixed olives and gaze up at the ceiling painted to suggest blue sky peeking through ancient stone walls. Pizzas range from the plain Paradiso, which offers chunks of tomatoes covered in melted mozzarella, to the robust Siciliano, a blend of nine ingredients including eggplant and red onion. Or you can choose your own toppings from a list of 29. As popular as the pizzas are the *panini* (sandwiches) of homemade focaccia stuffed with marinated roasted lamb and vegetables and other fillings, and the salads, such as tuna and white bean. Good desserts, but a limited wine list. Pizzeria Paradiso has finally opened another location, at 3282 M St. NW (✆ 202/337-1245), in Georgetown, right next door to Dean & Deluca. This location is larger, has a full bar, and a private party room.

2029 P St. NW. ✆ **202/223-1245.** Reservations not accepted. Pizzas $9.50–$17; sandwiches and salads $4.50–$7.95. DC, MC, V. Mon–Sat 11:30am–11pm, Sun noon–10pm. Metro: Dupont Circle.

Sala Thai THAI   At lunch, you'll see a lot of diners sitting alone and reading newspapers, happy to escape the office. At dinner, the restaurant is filled with groups and couples, plus the occasional family. Among the 53 items to recommend on the menu are no. 41, *nua kra ting tone,* which is spicy beef with onion, garlic, and parsley sauce ("not found at any other Thai restaurant in Washington," said my Thai waitress, sporting multicolored streaks in her hair); and, no. 26, *ka prow,* which is an even spicier dish of either beef, chicken, or pork sautéed with basil leaves and chiles. The restaurant lies downstairs from the street; with no windows to watch what's happening on P Street—but you're really here for the food, which is excellent and cheap. Even conventional pad thai doesn't disappoint. Pay attention if your waiter cautions you about the level of spiciness of a dish you order—for some dishes (like no. 38, stir-fried sliced pork in red curry sauce with peppers), you'll need an asbestos tongue.

2016 P St. NW. ℂ 202/872-1144. www.salathaidc.com. Reservations accepted for 5 or more. Lunch main courses $6.95–$11; dinner main courses $7.95–$17. AE, DC, DISC, MC, V. Mon–Thurs 11:30am–3pm and 4–10:30pm; Fri 11:30am–11pm; Sat noon–11pm; Sun noon–10:30pm. Metro: Dupont Circle.

Teaism Dupont Circle *(Finds* ASIAN FUSION Occupying a turn-of-the-20th-century neoclassical building on a tree-lined street, Teaism has a lovely rustic interior. A display kitchen and tandoor oven dominate the sunny downstairs room, which offers counter seating along a wall of French windows, open in warm weather. Upstairs seating is on banquettes and small Asian stools at hand-crafted mahogany tables.

The impressive tea list comprises close to 30 aromatic blends, most of them from India, China, and Japan. On the menu is light Asian fare served on stainless-steel plates or in lacquer lunch boxes (Japanese "bento boxes," which hold a delicious meal of, for example, teriyaki salmon, cucumber-ginger salad, a scoop of rice with seasoning, and fresh fruit—all $8). Dishes include Thai chicken curry with sticky rice, ostrich burger with Asian slaw, and a Portobello and goat cheese sandwich. Baked goods, coconut rice pudding, and lime shortbread cookies are among desserts. At breakfast, you might try ginger scones or cilantro eggs and sausage with fresh tandoor-baked onion nan bread. Everything's available for takeout. Teapots, cups, and other gift items are for sale. *Note:* Teaism has two other locations, both convenient for sightseeing. **Teaism Lafayette Square,** 800 Connecticut Ave. NW (ℂ 202/835-2233), is across from the White House; it's open weekdays from 7:30am to 5:30pm and serves afternoon tea. **Teaism Penn Quarter** *(Finds,* 400 Eighth St. NW (ℂ 202/638-6010), which is near the MCI Center, the

National Gallery, and nightspots, is the only branch that serves beer, wine, and cocktails. Teaism Penn Quarter is open daily, serving all three meals and afternoon tea, and brunch on Saturday and Sunday; its happy hour on Thursday and Friday, from 5:30 to 7:30pm, features free hors d'oeuvres (with purchased drink—try the mango or ginger margaritas) like curries and Asian noodle salads.

2009 R St. NW (between Connecticut and 21st sts.). **②** **202/667-3827.** All menu items $1.50–$8. AE, MC, V. Mon–Thurs 8am–10pm; Fri 8am–11pm; Sat 9am–11pm; Sun 9am–10pm. Metro: Dupont Circle.

7 Foggy Bottom/West End
VERY EXPENSIVE

Marcel's *⚔⚔* FRENCH   When you walk through the front door, look straight ahead into the exhibition kitchen—chances are you'll be staring directly into the eyes of owner/chef Robert Wiedmaier. He is firmly at the helm here, creating French dishes that include nods to his Belgian training: duck breast with baby turnips, rose lentils, and Calvados sauce; or venison with ragout of winter mushrooms and Madeira sauce. Desserts usually include seasonal tarts, such as spring pear tart with raspberry coulis.

Marcel's, named after Wiedmaier's young son, occupies the space that once was home to the restaurant Provence, and Wiedmaier has kept that restaurant's country French decor, including panels of rough-hewn stone framed by rustic shutters and antique hutches displaying Provençal pottery. Stone walls and floors don't do much to buffer all the bustle, however, so you can expect to have a very noisy time of it. To the right of the exhibition kitchen is a spacious bar area. Marcel's offers seating on the patio—right on Pennsylvania Avenue—in warm weather, and live jazz nightly year-round.

2401 Pennsylvania Ave. NW. **②** **202/296-1166.** www.marcelsdc.com. Reservations recommended. Dinner main courses $26–$39; pretheater dinner 5:30–7pm (including round-trip limo to Kennedy Center) $48. AE, MC, V. Mon–Thurs 5:30–10pm; Fri–Sat 5:30–11pm; Sun 5:30–9:30pm. Metro: Foggy Bottom.

Melrose *⚔⚔* AMERICAN   Situated in an upscale hotel, this pretty restaurant offers fine cuisine presented with friendly flourishes. In nice weather, dine outdoors on the beautifully landscaped, sunken terrace whose greenery and towering fountain protect you from traffic noises. The glass-walled dining room overlooks the terrace and is decorated in accents of marble and brass, with more greenery and grand bouquets of fresh flowers.

Brian McBride is the beguiling executive chef who sometimes emerges from the kitchen to find out how you like the angel-hair pasta with mascarpone and lobster, or his pan-seared diver scallops with parsnip purée, or his breast of pheasant stuffed with pistachio mousseline. McBride is known for his use of seafood, which makes up at least half of the entrees and nearly all of the appetizers. Specialties of the house include shrimp ravioli with sweet corn, black pepper, tomato, and lemongrass beurre blanc and Melrose crab cakes with grilled vegetables in a rémoulade sauce. Desserts, like the raspberry crème brûlée or the chocolate bread pudding with chocolate sorbet, are excellent. The wine list offers about 25 wines by the glass. Sunday night, the restaurant dispenses with corkage fees; feel free to bring your own bottle. Saturday night (and sometimes Fri night) from 7 to 11pm, a quartet plays jazz, swing, and big-band tunes; lots of people get up and dance.

In the Park Hyatt Washington hotel, 1201 24th St. NW. (C) **202/955-3899.** Reservations recommended. Breakfast $9–$19; lunch main courses $18–$34; dinner main courses $20–$38; pretheater dinner $35; Sun brunch $55 ($60 with house champagne, $68 with premium champagne). AE, DC, DISC, MC, V. Mon–Fri 6:30–11am, 11:30am–2:30pm, and 5:30–10:30pm; Sat–Sun 7–11am, 11:30am–2:30pm, and 5:30–10:30pm; light fare served daily 2:30–5:30pm. Metro: Foggy Bottom.

EXPENSIVE

Kinkead's 🌟🌟🌟 AMERICAN/SEAFOOD   When a restaurant has been as roundly praised as Kinkead's, you start to think no place can be *that* good—but Kinkead's really is. After a brief closure in early 2004 for a remodeling of the dining room (purple walls, but otherwise nothing drastic) and a revamping of the menu, Kinkead's re-opened with even more pleasing items on the menu, like the lobster potpie. But most of the favorite dishes are still here: the fried Ipswich clams; cod topped with crab imperial; clam chowder; and pepita-crusted salmon with shrimp, crab, and chiles. And chef Kinkead continues to pile on appetizing garnishes—that crab-crowned cod, for instance, comes with sweet potato purée and ham-laced spoon bread.

Award-winning chef/owner Bob Kinkead is the star at this three-tier, 220-seat restaurant. He wears a headset and orchestrates his kitchen staff in full view of the upstairs dining room, where booths and tables neatly fill the nooks and alcoves of the town house. At street level is a scattering of tables overlooking the restaurant's lower level, the more casual bar and cafe, where a jazz group or pianist performs nearly every evening. *Beware:* If the waiter tries to seat you in the "atrium," you'll be stuck at a table mall-side just outside the doors of the restaurant—yuck.

Kinkead's menu (which changes daily for lunch and again for dinner) features primarily seafood, but always includes at least one beef and one poultry entree. The wine list comprises more than 300 selections, and you can trust expert sommelier Michael Flynn to lead you to one you'll enjoy. You can't go wrong with the desserts either, like the chocolate dacquoise with cappuccino sauce. If you're hungry but not ravenous in the late afternoon, stop in for some delicious light fare: fish and chips, lobster roll, soups, and salads.

2000 Pennsylvania Ave. NW. ✆ 202/296-7700. www.kinkead.com. Reservations recommended. Lunch main courses $15–$25; dinner main courses $26–$35; light fare $6–$23. AE, DC, DISC, MC, V. Sun–Thurs 11:30am–2:30pm and 5:30–10pm; Fri–Sat 11:30am–2:30pm and 5:30–10:30pm; light fare served daily 2:30–5:30pm. Metro: Foggy Bottom.

Nectar ⭐⭐ AMERICAN   This tiny place, seating 42, opened in April 2003. Nectar has some intriguing features: Its short menu offers as many appetizers as entrees—six of each. The modest but unusual wine list offers every wine by the glass, half-bottle, or bottle, with prices per glass ranging from $7 to $100, and per bottle ranging from $29 to $450. The decor combines elegant—gilded mirrors and golden sponge-painted walls—with unpretentious: Pipes are exposed, though painted. Three friends and I agreed that our meals were winners. For appetizers we chose a fresh and minty pea soup, salad greens topped with sesame dressing, and fresh asparagus; for entrees, we selected veal cheeks with butternut squash purée and Masala spices, pheasant on a bed of ramps, and scallops sautéed with *haricots verts,* chorizo, dried fruit, pistachio, and curry spices. Everything was cooked perfectly and flavored nicely. We found fault only with the service, which was a little slow. Our server was an earnest young chap, though, and had spent summers in Maine, where we like to go too, so we forgave him.

In the George Washington University Inn, 824 New Hampshire Ave. NW. ✆ 202/ 298-8085. www.nectardc.com. Reservations recommended. Dinner main courses $25–$28. AE, DC, DISC, MC, V. Tues–Thurs 5–10pm, Fri–Sat 5–11pm. Metro: Foggy Bottom.

MODERATE

Kaz Sushi Bistro JAPANESE   Amiable chef/owner Kazuhiro ("Kaz") Okochi opened his own place after having worked at Sushi-Ko for many years. This is said to be the best place for sushi in the Washington area, and aficionados vie for one of the six chairs at the bar to watch Kaz and his staff do their thing, preparing salmon roe, sea urchin, tuna, and many other fish for sushi. Besides sushi, Kaz is known for his napoleon of sea trout and wonton skins, and for his bento boxes, offering exquisite tastings of pan-seared salmon, spicy broiled mussels, and the like. Kaz is one of few chefs in the area trained to handle tora fugu, the blowfish, which can be poisonous if not cleaned properly. The blowfish, if available, is served in winter. This is also the place to come for premium sakes.

1915 I St. NW. 🕐 202/530-5500. Reservations recommended. www.kazsushi.com. Sushi a la carte $3.25–$6.50; lunch main courses $9.25–$17; dinner main courses $12–$45. AE, DC, DISC, MC, V. Mon–Fri 11:30am–2pm; Mon–Sat 6–10pm. Metro: Farragut West.

8 Georgetown

Michel Richard Citronelle 👌👌👌 INNOVATIVE FRENCH   If Citronelle's ebullient chef/owner Michel Richard is in the kitchen (and you know when he is because the dining room views the open kitchen), diners in the know decline the menu and ask simply for whatever it is Richard wants to make. Whether you go that route, or choose from the fixed-price or tasting menus, you're in for a (very expensive) treat. Emerging from the bustling kitchen are appetizers like the fricassee of escargots or an eggshell filled with caviar, sweetbreads, porcinis, and crunchy pistachios; and entrees like the crispy lentil-coated salmon or squab leg confit with macaroni gratin and black truffles. But each presentation is a work of art, with swirls of colorful sauce surrounding the main event. If you are passionate about food, you may want to consider dining at the chef's table, which is in the kitchen, so you can watch Richard at work ($250 per person, with a minimum of six people, is the stated price, but that's to give you a ballpark idea; call to inquire about more exact information).

Citronelle's decor is also breathtaking and includes a wall that changes colors, a state-of-the-art wine cellar (a glass-enclosed room that encircles the dining room, displaying its 8,000 bottles and a collection of 18th- and 19th-c. corkscrews), and a Provençal color scheme of mellow yellow and raspberry red.

The dessert of choice: Michel Richard's richly layered chocolate "bar" with sauce noisette (hazelnut sauce). Citronelle's extensive wine list offers about 20 premium by-the-glass selections, but with all those bottles staring out at you from the wine cellar, you may want to spring for one.

In the Latham Hotel, 3000 M St. NW. 🕐 202/625-2150. www.citronelledc.com. Reservations required. Jacket required, tie optional for men at dinner. Fixed-price 6-course dinner $85, fixed-price 9-course dinner $125. AE, DC, MC, V. Sun–Wed 6–9pm, Thurs–Sat 6–9:30pm. Closed Sun July–Aug.

1789 *ƙƙ* AMERICAN   In my corduroy skirt and wool sweater, I felt I'd dressed too casually, when I dined here last. The staff never made me feel uncomfortable; it was a quick look around the room that did it, for fellow female diners (of all ages) were dressed in lacy tops, short flouncy dresses, or fancy long skirts.

So put on your best duds for the 1789. The formal but cozy restaurant is housed in a Federal town house near Georgetown University. The best of the five intimate dining rooms is the John Carroll Room, where the walls are hung with equestrian and historical prints and old city maps, a log fire blazes in the hearth, and a gorgeous flower arrangement tops a hunting-themed oak sideboard. Throughout, silk-shaded brass oil lamps provide romantic lighting.

Noted chef Ris Lacoste varies her menus daily. Appetizers might include lobster tart on puffed pastry with mushrooms, leeks, and tarragon, or grilled quail with barley and mushrooms. Typical entrees range from osso buco with risotto Milanese; to ginger-glazed sea scallops with pea shoots, mango, and curried pistachio rice; to roast rack of Colorado lamb with creamy feta potatoes au gratin in red pepper purée–infused Merlot sauce. Finish with the decadent hot fudge sundae.

The pretheater menu includes appetizer, entree, dessert, and coffee.

1226 36th St. NW. *©* **202/965-1789.** www.1789restaurant.com. Reservations recommended. Jacket required for men. Main courses $18–$38; fixed-price pretheater menu (Mon–Fri 6–6:45pm; Sat–Sun 5:30–6:45pm) $30. AE, DC, DISC, MC, V. Mon–Thurs 6–10pm; Fri 6–11pm; Sat 5:30–11pm; Sun 5:30–10pm.

EXPENSIVE

Café Milano *ƙ* ITALIAN   The beautiful people factor rises exponentially here as the night wears on. Café Milano has long been a magnet for Washington's famous and attractive, and their visitors. In fact, the restaurant plays up its reputation, staging occasional "fashion brunches," where models strut their stuff while you dine. But this restaurant/nightclub/bar also serves very good food. Salads are big, pasta servings are small, and fish and meat entrees are just the right size. We had the endive, radicchio, and arugula salad topped with thin sheets of Parmesan cheese; a *panzanella* salad of tomatoes, potatoes, red onion, celery, and cucumber basking in basil and olive oil; *cappellacci* (round ravioli) pockets of spinach and ricotta in cream sauce; sautéed sea bass on a bed of vegetables with lemon chive sauce; and the Santa Babila pizza, which has tomatoes, fresh mozzarella, oregano, and basil on a light pizza crust. All were delicious. At Café Milano, it's the nonsmokers who are relegated to the

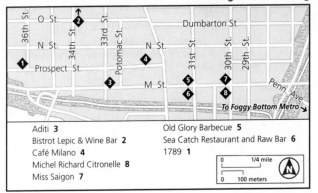

Aditi **3**

Bistrot Lepic & Wine Bar **2**

Café Milano **4**

Michel Richard Citronelle **8**

Miss Saigon **7**

Old Glory Barbecue **5**

Sea Catch Restaurant and Raw Bar **6**

1789 **1**

back room, while the smoking section takes over the main part of the restaurant and bar, which opens through the glass front to the sidewalk cafe. A bevy of good-humored waiters takes care of you.

3251 Prospect St. NW. © **202/333-6183.** www.cafemilano.net. Reservations recommended. Lunch main courses $12–$25; dinner main courses $14–$37. Sun–Wed 11:30am–11pm (bar menu served until midnight); Thurs–Sat 11:30am–midnight (bar menu served until 1am).

Sea Catch Restaurant and Raw Bar *Finds* SEAFOOD If you're walking around Georgetown and the crowds are starting to get to you, duck into the brick passageway that lies to the right of a little coffee bar and Mr. Smith's bar on M Street (at 31st St.) and follow it back to the little plaza, where you will find the entrance to the Sea Catch, a true refuge. (Or else you can walk south on 31st St. from M St., and turn right, into the plaza.) Since 1988, the Sea Catch has perched on the bank of the C&O Canal, with an awning-covered wooden deck where you can watch ducks, punters, and mule-drawn barges glide by while you dine. The innlike main dining room has a working fireplace and rough-hewn fieldstone walls from Georgetown quarries. There's also a handsome white Carrara-marble raw bar and a deluxe brasserie. Classic jazz recordings play in the background.

Nothing at the Sea Catch is fried or breaded. For openers, plump farm-raised oysters, clams, house-smoked fish, and other raw-bar offerings merit consideration. Daily fresh fish and seafood specials may include big, fluffy jumbo lump crab cakes served with julienne vegetables in a remoulade sauce or grilled marinated squid with fennel and basil aioli. The kitchen willingly prepares dishes to your specifications, including live lobster from the tanks. An extensive wine list highlights French, Italian, and American selections. Fresh-baked desserts usually include excellent pumpkin pie with pecans.

1054 31st St. NW. ☎ 202/337-8855. www.seacatchrestaurant.com. Reservations recommended. Lunch main courses $7.25–$18; dinner main courses $18–$28. AE, DC, DISC, MC, V. Mon–Sat noon–3pm and 5:30–10pm.

MODERATE

Bistrot Lepic & Wine Bar 🐀🐀 FRENCH　Bistrot Lepic is the real thing—a charming French restaurant that seems plucked right off a Parisian side street. The atmosphere is bustling and cheery, and you hear a lot of French spoken—not just by the waiters, but also by customers. The Bistrot is a neighborhood place, and you'll often see diners waving hellos across the room to each other, or even leaving their table to visit with those at another. In its 10 years, the restaurant has made some changes to accommodate its popularity, most recently turning the upstairs into a wine bar and lounge; this means that if you arrive early for your reservation, you now have a place to wait (in the past, one had to hover hungry-eyed at the door). Or you can come just to hang out, sip a glass of wine, and munch on delicious little somethings from the wine bar menu, where the most expensive item is the $12 terrine of homemade foie gras. No need to make a reservation at the wine bar unless you plan to order dinner from the regular menu.

This is traditional French cooking, updated. The seasonal menu offers such entrees as grilled rainbow trout with carrot sauce, beef medallions with polenta and shiitake mushroom sauce, and sautéed sea scallops with ginger broccoli mousse. We opted for specials: rare tuna served on fennel with citrus vinaigrette, and grouper with a mildly spicy lobster sauce upon a bed of spinach.

The modest French wine list offers a fairly good range. The house red wine, Le Pic Saint-Loup, is a nice complement to most menu choices and is $23 a bottle.

1736 Wisconsin Ave. NW. ☎ 202/333-0111. www.bistrotlepic.com. Reservations recommended. Lunch main courses $13–$21; dinner main courses $16–$25. AE, DC, DISC, MC, V. Tues–Sun 11:30am–2:30pm; Tues–Thurs 5:30–10pm; Fri–Sat 5:30–10:30pm; Sun 5:30–9:30pm. Wine bar Tues–Thurs and Sun 5:30–11:30pm; Fri–Sat 5:30pm–12:30am ("But if it's not crowded, we close earlier").

Miss Saigon VIETNAMESE　This is a charming restaurant, with tables scattered amid a "forest" of tropical foliage, and twinkly lights strewn upon the fronds of the potted palms and ferns.

The food here is delicious and authentic, though the service can be a trifle slow when the restaurant is busy. To begin, there is the crispy calamari, or the shrimp and pork-stuffed garden rolls. House specialties include steamed flounder, caramel salmon, and "shaking beef" (cubes of tender Vietnamese steak, marinated in wine, garlic, butter, and soy sauce, then sautéed with onions and potatoes and served with rice and salad). There's a full bar. Desserts range from bananas *flambé au rhum* (fried bananas with rum sauce) to ice cream with Godiva liqueur. Not to be missed is drip-pot coffee, brewed table side and served iced over sweetened condensed milk.

3057 M St. NW. ⓒ 202/333-5545. Reservations recommended, especially weekend nights. Lunch main courses $4.50–$8.95; dinner main courses $6.50–$23. AE, DC, MC, V. Mon–Fri 11am–10:30pm (lunch menu served until 3pm); Sat–Sun noon–11pm (dinner menu served all day).

Old Glory Barbecue *Kids* BARBECUE   Raised wooden booths flank one side of the restaurant; an imposing, old-fashioned dark wood bar with saddle-seat stools extends down the other. Recorded swing music during the day, more mainstream music into the night, plays in the background. Old Glory boasts the city's "largest selection of single-barrel and boutique bourbons" and a new rooftop deck with outdoor seating and views of Georgetown.

After 9pm or so, the two-story restaurant becomes packed with the hard-drinkin' young and restless. In early evening, though, Old Glory is prime for anyone—singles, families, or an older crowd—although it's almost always noisy. Come for the messy, tangy, delicious spare ribs; hickory-smoked chicken; tender, smoked beef brisket; or marinated, wood-fired shrimp. Six sauces are on the table, the spiciest being the vinegar-based East Carolina and Lexington. My Southern-raised husband favored the Savannah version, which reminded him of that city's famous Johnny Harris barbecue sauce. The complimentary corn muffins and biscuits; side dishes of collard greens, succotash, and potato salad; and desserts like apple crisp and coconut cherry cobbler all hit the spot.

3139 M St. NW. ⓒ 202/337-3406. www.oldglorybbq.com. Reservations not accepted Fri–Sat. Main courses $7.95–$25; Sun brunch buffet $14, half-price for children 8–11, free for children under 8. AE, DC, DISC, MC, V. Sun 11am–11:30pm (brunch from 11am–3pm); Mon–Thurs 11:30am–11:30pm; Fri–Sat 11:30am–midnight. Bar stays open later nightly.

INEXPENSIVE

Aditi INDIAN   This charming two-level restaurant provides a serene setting in which to enjoy first-rate Indian cooking to the tune of Indian music. A must here is the platter of assorted appetizers, which features *bhajia* (a deep-fried vegetable fritter) and crispy vegetable samosas stuffed with spiced potatoes and peas. Favorite entrees include lamb biryani, which is basmati rice pilaf tossed with savory pieces of lamb, cilantro, raisins, and almonds; and the skewered jumbo tandoori prawns, chicken, lamb, or beef—all fresh and fork tender—barbecued in the tandoor. Sauces are on the mild side, so if you like your food fiery, inform your waiter. A *kachumber* salad, a medley of chopped cucumber, lettuce, green pepper, and tomatoes, topped with yogurt and spices, is a refreshing accompaniment to entrees. For dessert, try *kheer,* a cooling rice pudding garnished with chopped nuts. There's a full bar.

3299 M St. NW. ⓒ 202/625-6825. Reservations recommended. Lunch main courses $8–$16; dinner main courses $8–$30. AE, DC, DISC, MC, V. Sun noon–2:30pm and 5:30–10pm; Mon–Thurs 11:30am–2:30pm and 5:30–10pm; Fri–Sat 11:30am–2:30pm and 5:30–10:30pm.

9 Woodley Park

EXPENSIVE

New Heights ⓕ AMERICAN/INTERNATIONAL   This attractive second-floor dining room has a bank of windows looking out over Rock Creek Park, and walls hung with the colorful artwork by local artists. New Heights attracts a casually upscale clientele, which fills the room every night. An Indian influence will always be found in at least one or two items on the menu, to please the palate of owner Amarjeet (Umbi) Singh, as well as those of his patrons. My husband and I have dined at New Heights a lot over the years, our constancy outlasting a number of fine chefs, who seem to come and go here rather quickly. Recent dinners have treated us to horseradish-crusted halibut with crab-parsnip purée and au poivre rib-eye steak with lobster hash and roasted garlic butter sauce. In the past, I've found New Heights's innovative cuisine to be too adventurous, but these dishes I can handle. Sunday brunch is heavenly, too: brioche French toast, soup of puréed chestnut with foie gras, and the like.

2317 Calvert St. NW (near Connecticut Ave.). ⓒ 202/234-4110. www.newheights restaurant.com. Reservations recommended. Brunch $7–$14; dinner main courses $19–$30. AE, DC, DISC, MC, V. Sun–Thurs 5:30–10pm; Fri–Sat 5:30–11pm; Sun brunch 11am–2:30pm. Metro: Woodley Park–Zoo.

Petits Plats ⓕ FRENCH   Petits Plats is another French bistro, and a very pretty one, ensconced in a town house that's situated directly across from the Woodley Park Metro entrance and the Marriott Wardman Park Hotel. You can sit at the sidewalk cafe, on the porch above, or in the front room, back room, or upstairs rooms of the town house. Watching the passersby on busy Connecticut Avenue is a major amusement. Bistro fare includes shrimp bisque with crabmeat; five different mussels dishes, like the mussels in a mustard, cream, and white wine sauce (each comes with french fries); Provençal-styled shrimp on an artichoke-bottom dish; Belgian endive salad with apples, walnuts, and Roquefort; and roasted rack of lamb with potatoes au gratin. The reasonably priced Petits Plats becomes even more so Monday through Friday at lunch, when a two-course set menu is available for $14; daily at early dinner, 5:30 to 7pm, and after 9pm, when a three-course set menu is available for $25; and at Saturday and Sunday brunch, when $23 gets you a choice of entree (from eggs Benedict to steak *frites*), a house salad, and all the champagne you like. Since it opened in the spring of 2000, Petits Plats has gained a loyal following.

2653 Connecticut Ave. NW. ℂ 202/518-0018. www.petits-plats.com. Reservations recommended. www.petitsplats.com. Lunch main courses $11–$19; dinner main courses $16–$24. AE, MC, V. Mon 11:30am–2:30pm; Tues–Thurs 11:30am–2:30pm and 5:30–10pm; Fri 11:30am–2:30pm and 5:30–11pm; Sat 11:30am–4:30pm and 5:30–11pm; Sun 11:30am–4:30pm and 5:30–10pm. Metro: Woodley Park–Zoo.

MODERATE

Lebanese Taverna MIDDLE EASTERN This family owned restaurant gives you a taste of Lebanese culture—its cuisine, decor, and music. It's very popular on weekends, so expect to stand in line (reservations are accepted for seating before 6:30pm only). Diners, once seated in the courtyardlike dining room, where music plays and prayer rugs hang on the walls, hate to leave. The wood-burning oven in the back bakes the pita breads and several appetizers. Order mezza dishes for the table: hummus, tabbouleh, baba ghanoush, stuffed grape leaves, cheese pastries, couscous, and pastry-wrapped spinach pies *(fatayer bi sabanikh)*, enough for dinner for a couple or as hors d'oeuvres for a table of you. Or consider entrees, such as the roasted half chicken wrapped in bread and served with garlic purée. The wealth of meatless dishes will delight vegetarians, while rotisserie items, especially the chicken and the chargrilled kabobs of chicken and shrimp, will please all others.

There are other Lebanese Tavernas in the area, but this is the only one in the District. It continues to win Restaurant Association of Metropolitan Washington awards for "best casual dining" and "neighborhood gathering place."

2641 Connecticut Ave. NW. ℂ 202/265-8681. www.lebanesetaverna.com. Reservations accepted before 6:30pm. Lunch main courses $7.75–$15; dinner main courses $11–$20. AE, DC, DISC, MC, V. Mon–Thurs 11:30am–2:30pm and 5:30–10:30pm; Fri 11:30am–2:30pm and 5:30–11pm; Sat 11:30am–3pm and 5:30–11pm; Sun 5–10pm. Metro: Woodley Park–Zoo.

5

Exploring Washington, D.C.

To its scores of "must-see" attractions, the nation's capital in 2004 added several more: the National World War II Memorial, the Marian Koshland Science Museum, and the National Museum of the American Indian. It's an exciting time to visit Washington, D.C.; the city is vibrant with the whirl of wonderful new—as well as ongoing—possibilities for learning about our history, the world, and our culture, awaiting you at museums, memorials, and other landmarks all over town.

1 The Three Houses of Government

Three of the most visited sights in Washington have always been the buildings housing the executive, legislative, and judicial branches of the U.S. government. All three—the Capitol, the White House, and the Supreme Court—are stunning and offer fascinating lessons in American history and government. Although these three landmarks are not as freely open to the public as they were before the terrorist attacks of September 11, 2001, all three do allow tours. Here is some information that will help you as you go.

The Capitol 𝒜𝒜𝒜 The Capitol is as majestic up close as it is from afar. For 135 years it sheltered not only both houses of Congress, but also the Supreme Court and, for 97 years, the Library of Congress as well. When you tour the Capitol, you'll learn about America's history as you admire the place in which it unfolded. Classical architecture and embellishments and hundreds of paintings, sculptures, and other artworks are integral elements of the Capitol.

On the massive bronze doors leading to the **Rotunda** are portrayals of events in the life of Columbus. The Rotunda—a huge 96-foot-wide circular hall capped by a 180-foot-high dome—is the hub of the Capitol. The dome was completed, at Lincoln's direction, while the Civil War was being fought. Ten presidents have lain in state here, with former President Ronald Reagan being the most recent; when Kennedy's casket was displayed, the line of mourners stretched 40 blocks. On the circular walls are eight immense oil

Call Ahead

If there were only one piece of advice I could give to a visitor, it would be to call ahead to the places you plan to tour in order to make sure they're open. I don't mean in advance of your trip (although that can't hurt)—I mean before you set out on each day of touring. Many of Washington's government buildings, museums, memorials, and monuments are open to the general public nearly all the time—except when they are not.

Because buildings like the Capitol, the Supreme Court, and the White House are "offices" as well as tourist destinations, the business of the day always poses the potential for closing one of those sites, or at least sections of them, to sightseers. (The White House is probably most vulnerable to this situation.) This caveat is even more important in the wake of the terrorist attack on the Pentagon; touring procedures change and then change again in response to the need for security measures.

In addition to the security issue, there's the matter of maintenance. The steady stream of visitors to Washington's attractions necessitates ongoing caretaking and, sometimes, new construction, which may require closing all or part of a landmark to the public, or new hours of operation or visiting procedures. (Construction of the Capitol's Visitor Center [p. 106] is one such example.)

Finally, Washington's famous museums, grand halls, and public gardens double as settings for press conferences, galas, special exhibits, festivals, and other special events, so you might arrive at, say, the National Air and Space Museum on a Sunday afternoon, as I did not long ago, only to find some of its galleries off limits because caterers were setting up for an event. Want to avoid frustration and disappointment? Call ahead.

paintings of events in American history, such as the presentation of the Declaration of Independence and the surrender of Cornwallis at Yorktown. In the dome is an allegorical fresco masterpiece by Constantino Brumidi, *Apotheosis of Washington,* a symbolic portrayal of George Washington surrounded by Roman gods and goddesses

Washington, D.C. Attractions

Woodley Rd • Devonshire Pl • Klingle Rd. • Cortland Pl. • Hawthorne St • **NATIONAL ZOOLOGICAL PARK** • Lamont St • Kilbourne Pl. • Mt. Pleasant St. • Park Rd • Hiatt Pl. • Lake Rd. • Kenyon St • Irving St • Hobart St. • **Columbia Heights Green Line**

Cathedral Ave • Garfield St • 34th St • 33rd St • 31st St • Garfield Terr. • 28th St • 27th St • Woodley Pl. • **Woodley Park-Zoo/ Adams Morgan Red Line** • Calvert St. • Harvard St. • Ontario Rd • Lanier Pl. • Columbia Rd. • **ADAMS-MORGAN**

Fulton St • Woodland Dr. • Edmunds St • Davis St • 35th Pl. • 36th Pl. • 35th St • Cleveland Ave • McGill Terr. • **ROCK CREEK PARK** • Connecticut Ave. • Euclid St. • Champlain St. • Belmont St • Kalorama Rd. • Ontario Rd • **Belmont St**

Wisconsin Ave • Observatory Circle • **EMBASSY ROW** • **U.S. Naval Observatory** • Massachusetts Ave • Rock Creek • Belmont Rd. • Kalorama Rd. • Wyoming Ave. • Tracy Pl. • California Ave. • Vernon St. • Florida Ave. • U St. • Florida Ave. • W St. • V St.

DUMBARTON OAKS PARK • California Pl. • Bancroft Pl. • Swann St. • T St. • S St. • R St.

T St. • S St. • R St. • Reservoir Rd. • 32nd St. • **MONTROSE PARK** • Decatur Pl. • Riggs Pl. • Q St. • R St. • Q St.

Georgetown University • Dent Pl. • Q St. • Volta Pl. • P St. • O St. • 28th St • 26th St • Dumbarton St • N St. • ③ • **Dupont Circle** M • **Dupont Circle Red Line** • **DUPONT CIRCLE** • Church St. • P St. • Scott Circle • **Logan Circle**

GEORGETOWN • Prospect St • M St • Whitehurst Fwy. • 24th St • 23rd St • 22nd St • Washington Circle • K St. • I St. • Farragut Square • New Hampshire Ave. • 17th St • 16th St • 15th St • **Thomas Circle** • L St. • **Franklin Square**

Francis Scott Key Bridge • **29** • **25th St** • Pennsylvania Ave • **Farragut North Red Line** • **Farragut West Blue & Orange Lines** • **McPherson Square** M • **McPherson Square Blue & Orange Lines**

66 • N. Lynn St • Wilson Blvd • **Theodore Roosevelt Island** • Little River • George Washington Memorial Pkwy. • Rock Creek and Potomac Pkwy. • **Foggy Bottom-GWU Blue & Orange Lines** • **George Washington University** • H St. • G St. • F St. • E St. • ④ • ⑤ • **White House** • ⑥ • ⑦

Rosslyn Blue & Orange Lines • **Kennedy Center** ⑧ • **FOGGY BOTTOM** • C St. • Constitution Ave. • ① 50

VIRGINIA • Theodore Roosevelt Mem. Bridge • ⑭ • Lincoln Memorial ⑬ • ⑫ • **WEST POTOMAC PARK** • ⑮ • ⑯ **Washington Monument** • ⑲

⑨ • **ARLINGTON** • Arlington Mem. Bridge • **Arlington Cemetery Blue Line** • Independence Ave. • W. Basin Dr. • **Tidal Basin** • ⑱ • ⑰

NATIONAL CEMETERY • Jefferson Davis Hwy. • Washington Blvd. • Potomac • FDR Memorial ⑪ • Ohio Dr. • **Cherry Trees** • ⑩ **Jefferson Memorial** • ①

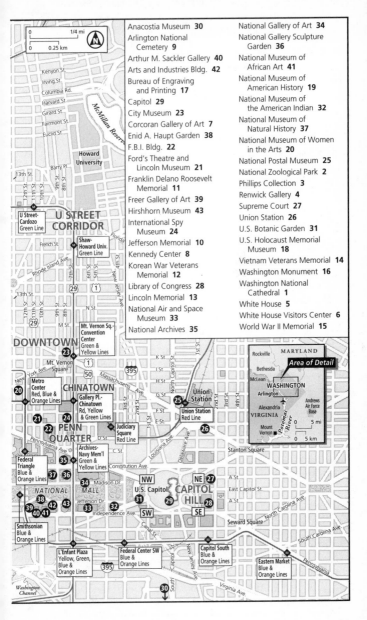

Anacostia Museum **30**
Arlington National Cemetery **9**
Arthur M. Sackler Gallery **40**
Arts and Industries Bldg. **42**
Bureau of Engraving and Printing **17**
Capitol **29**
City Museum **23**
Corcoran Gallery of Art **7**
Enid A. Haupt Garden **38**
F.B.I. Bldg. **22**
Ford's Theatre and Lincoln Museum **21**
Franklin Delano Roosevelt Memorial **11**
Freer Gallery of Art **39**
Hirshhorn Museum **43**
International Spy Museum **24**
Jefferson Memorial **10**
Kennedy Center **8**
Korean War Veterans Memorial **12**
Library of Congress **28**
Lincoln Memorial **13**
National Air and Space Museum **33**
National Archives **35**

National Gallery of Art **34**
National Gallery Sculpture Garden **36**
National Museum of African Art **41**
National Museum of American History **19**
National Museum of the American Indian **32**
National Museum of Natural History **37**
National Museum of Women in the Arts **20**
National Postal Museum **25**
National Zoological Park **2**
Phillips Collection **3**
Renwick Gallery **4**
Supreme Court **27**
Union Station **26**
U.S. Botanic Garden **31**
U.S. Holocaust Memorial Museum **18**
Vietnam Veterans Memorial **14**
Washington Monument **16**
Washington National Cathedral **1**
White House **5**
White House Visitors Center **6**
World War II Memorial **15**

watching over the progress of the nation. Brumidi was known as the "Michelangelo of the Capitol" for the many works he created throughout the building. (Take another look at the dome and find the woman directly below Washington; the triumphant *Armed Freedom* figure is said to be modeled after Lola Germon, a beautiful young actress with whom the 60-year-old Brumidi had a child.) Beneath the dome is a *trompe l'oeil* frieze depicting events in American history, from the arrival of Columbus through the Wright brothers' flight at Kitty Hawk.

The **National Statuary Hall** was originally the chamber of the House of Representatives. In 1864, it became Statuary Hall, and the states were invited to send two statues each of native sons and daughters to the hall. There are 97 statues in all because three states, Nevada, New Mexico, and North Dakota, have sent only one. As the room filled up, statues spilled over into the Hall of Columns, corridors, and any space that might accommodate the bronze and marble artifacts. Many of the statues honor individuals who played important roles in American history, such as Henry Clay, Ethan Allen, and Daniel Webster, and seven women, including Jeannette Rankin, the first woman to serve in Congress.

At this time, self-guided tours and "VIP" tours (tours reserved in advance by individuals through their congressional offices) have been suspended for the foreseeable future. Now the only way to tour the Capitol Building is in groups of 40. A Capitol Guide Service guide conducts each tour, which is free and lasts about 30 minutes.

You have two options: If you are part of an organized bunch, say a school class on a field trip, you may arrange a tour in advance, putting together groups of no more than 40 each, by contacting your congressional office at least 1 month ahead and following the

---

Under Construction

In mid-2002, construction started on a comprehensive, underground **Capitol Visitor Center,** with completion scheduled for 2006. Because the Capitol Visitor Center is being created directly beneath the plaza where people traditionally line up for tours on the east side of the Capitol, touring procedures have changed. The best thing to do is to call ahead (© 202/ 225-6827) to find out the new procedures in place for the time you are visiting, and whether the construction work will temporarily close parts of the building you wish to visit.

Capitol Hill

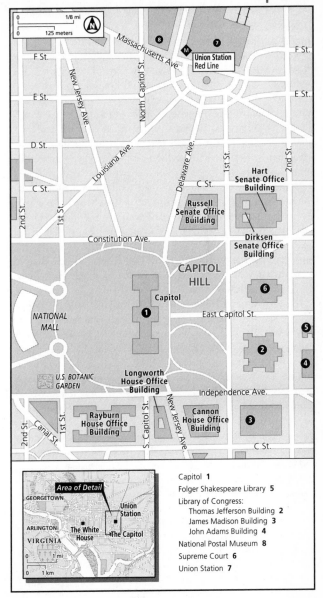

Capitol **1**

Folger Shakespeare Library **5**

Library of Congress:
   Thomas Jefferson Building **2**
   James Madison Building **3**
   John Adams Building **4**

National Postal Museum **8**

Supreme Court **6**

Union Station **7**

procedures that the office outlines for you. If you are on your own, or with family or friends, you will want to get to the Capitol early (by 7:30am) to stand in line for one of a limited number of timed tickets that the Capitol distributes daily starting at 9am. Head to the ticket kiosk at the southwest corner of the Capitol grounds, near the intersection of First Street and Independence Avenue SW, across First Street from the U.S. Botanic Gardens. It's a first-come, first-served system, with only one ticket given to each person, and each person, including children of any age, must have a ticket. The good news is that once you receive your ticket, you are free to go some-where nearby to get a bite to eat, or to sightsee, while you wait for your turn to tour the Capitol. The bad news is that all of you, even 1-year-old baby Louie, have to rise early and get to the Capitol by about 7:30am and then stand in line for another hour or more to be sure of touring the Capitol that day. Still, this is an improvement over the old touring procedure, which required you to stay in the queue until you entered the Capitol. Again, you must call the recorded information line (© **202/225-6827**) on the morning of your planned visit to confirm exactly where you should go and how to obtain your ticket.

Now, if you wish to visit either or both the House and Senate galleries, you follow a different procedure. The Senate Gallery is open to visitors only when it is in session, while the House Gallery is open to visitors whether or not it is in session. I would recommend that you try to visit when both the Senate and House are **in session** ⟨★★★⟩. Either way, in session or not, you must have a pass to visit each gallery. (Families, take note that children under 6 are not allowed in the Senate gallery.) Once obtained, the passes are good through the remainder of the Congress. To obtain visitor passes in advance, contact your representative for a House gallery pass or your senator for a Senate gallery pass; District of Columbia and Puerto Rico residents should contact their delegate to Congress. If you don't receive visitor passes in the mail (not every senator or representative sends them), they're obtainable at your senator's office on the Constitution Avenue, or north side, of the building or at your representative or delegate's office on the Independence Avenue, or south side, of the building. (Visitors who are not citizens can obtain a gallery pass by presenting a passport at the Senate or House appointments desk, located on the first floor of the Capitol.) Call the Capitol switchboard at © **202/224-3121** to contact the office of your senator or congressperson. Your congressional office will issue you a pass and direct you to the House or Senate Gallery line outside the Capitol for entry into the Capitol.

You'll know the House and/or the Senate is in session if you see flags flying over their respective wings of the Capitol (House: south side, Senate: north side), or you can check the weekday "Today in Congress" column in the *Washington Post* for details on times of the House and Senate sessions and committee hearings. This column also tells you which sessions are open to the public. You can also access the Capitol's website at www.aoc.gov ("aoc" stands for "architect of the capitol"). Recently improved, the site provides lots of good information about the history, art, and construction of the Capitol building; an in-depth education on the legislative process; and schedules of bill debates in the House and Senate, committee markups and meetings, and lots of other good stuff. The homepage has links to the individual Senate (www.senate.gov) and House (www.house.gov) pages, or you can go directly to those sites to connect to your senator's or house representative's page.

At the east end of the Mall, entrance on E. Capitol St. and 1st St. NW. ℂ 202/225-6827. www.aoc.gov, www.house.gov, and www.senate.gov. Free admission. Year-round Mon–Sat 9am–4:30pm, with 1st tour starting at 9:30am and last tour starting at 3:30pm. Closed for tours Sun and Jan 1, Thanksgiving, and Dec 25. Parking at Union Station or on neighborhood streets. Metro: Union Station or Capitol South.

The Supreme Court of the United States ☆☆☆   The highest tribunal in the nation, the Supreme Court is charged with deciding whether actions of Congress, the president, the states, and lower courts are in accord with the Constitution, and with applying the Constitution's enduring principles to novel situations and a changing country. The Supreme Court's chief justice and eight associate justices have the power of judicial review—that is, authority to invalidate legislation or executive action that conflicts with the Constitution. Out of the 7,000 or so cases submitted to it each year, the Supreme Court hears only about 100 cases, many of which deal with issues vital to the nation. The Court's rulings are final, reversible only by another Supreme Court decision, or in some cases, an Act of Congress or a constitutional amendment.

Until 1935, the Supreme Court met in the Capitol. Architect Cass Gilbert designed the stately Corinthian marble palace that houses the Court today. The building was considered rather grandiose by early residents: One justice remarked that he and his colleagues ought to enter such pompous precincts on elephants.

If you're in town when the Court is in session, try to **see a case being argued** ☆☆☆ (call ℂ **202/479-3211** for details). The Court meets Monday through Wednesday and hears up to four arguments a day (10am–noon and 1–2 or 3pm) starting the first Monday in October through late April, alternating in approximately 2-week intervals between "sittings" to hear cases and deliver opinions and "recesses" for consideration of Court business and writing opinions. From mid-May to late June, you can attend brief sessions (about 15 min.) at 10am on Monday, when the justices release orders and opinions. Find out what's on the docket by checking the *Washington Post*'s "Supreme Court Calendar." Arrive at least an hour early—even earlier for highly publicized cases—to line up for seats, about 150 of which are allotted to the general public.

Call the Supreme Court information line to find out days and times that arguments will take place. You may view these on a first-come, first-served basis, choosing between the 3-minute line, which ushers visitors in and out of the court every 3 minutes, starting at 10am in the morning and at 1pm in the afternoon; or the "regular" line, which admits visitors who wish to stay for the entire argument, starting at 9:30am and 12:30pm (Arrive about 90 min. early to snag a spot).

When the Court is not in session, you can tour the building and attend a **free lecture** in the courtroom about Court procedure and the building's architecture. Lectures are given every hour on the half-hour from 9:30am to 3:30pm.

1 1st St. NE (between E. Capitol St. and Maryland Ave. NE). 📞 **202/479-3000.** www.supremecourtus.gov. Free admission. Mon–Fri 9am–4:30pm. Closed all federal holidays. Metro: Capitol South or Union Station.

The White House 🌟🌟 This house has served as a residence, office, reception site, and world embassy for every U.S. president since John Adams. The White House is the only private residence of a head of state that is open to the public for tours, free of charge. It was Thomas Jefferson who started this practice, which is stopped only during wartime. Our war on terrorism caused the White House to be closed for public tours for about 2 years. Thankfully, the White House is once again open for public tours, although not walkup tours. See "How to Arrange a White House Tour," below.

Note: Even if you have successfully reserved a White House tour for your group, you should still call 📞 **202/456-7041** before setting out in the morning; in case the White House is closed on short notice because of unforeseen events. If this should happen to you, you should make a point of walking by the White House anyway, since its exterior is still pretty awesome. Stroll past it on Pennsylvania Avenue,

The White House Area

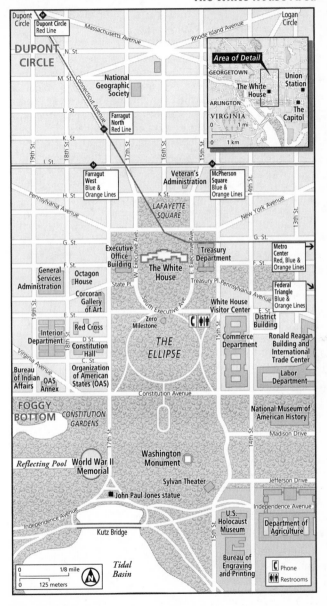

Dupont Circle

Dupont Circle Red Line

Massachusetts Avenue

Logan Circle

Rhode Island Avenue

DUPONT CIRCLE

N. St.

M. St.

National Geographic Society

Connecticut Avenue

L. St.

Farragut North Red Line

K. St.

19th St.

18th St.

17th St.

16th St.

15th St.

I. St.

Farragut West Blue & Orange Lines

Veteran's Administration

McPherson Square Blue & Orange Lines

14th St.

Pennsylvania Avenue

H. St.

K St

New York Avenue

13th St.

LAFAYETTE SQUARE

G. St.

G. St.

Executive Office Building

W. Executive Ave.

Treasury Department

Metro Center Red, Blue & Orange Lines

F. St.

F. St.

General Services Administration

Octagon House

State Pl.

The White House

E. Executive Ave.

Treasury Pl. Pennsylvania Ave.

Federal Triangle Blue & Orange Lines

Corcoran Gallery of Art

South Executive Ave.

White House Visitor Center

District Building

E. St.

Commerce Department

Ronald Reagan Building and International Trade Center

9th St.

Interior Department

Red Cross

18th St.

Zero Milestone

C

THE ELLIPSE

15th St.

D St.

Constitution Hall

C. St.

Virginia Avenue

Bureau of Indian Affairs

OAS Annex

Organization of American States (OAS)

Labor Department

Constitution Avenue

FOGGY BOTTOM

CONSTITUTION GARDENS

National Museum of American History

Madison Drive

14th St.

Reflecting Pool

World War II Memorial

17th St.

Washington Monument

Sylvan Theater

Jefferson Drive

John Paul Jones statue

Independence Avenue

Independence Avenue

U.S. Holocaust Museum

15th St.

Department of Agriculture

Kutz Bridge

Bureau of Engraving and Printing

0 — 1/8 mile
0 — 125 meters

Tidal Basin

C Phone
♦♦ Restrooms

Area of Detail

GEORGETOWN

The White House

Union Station

ARLINGTON

VIRGINIA

The Capitol

0 — 1 mi
0 — 1 km

How to Arrange a White House Tour

The White House allows groups of 10 or more to tour the White House (Tues–Sat 7:30–11:30am). Tours are self-guided and most people take no more than an hour to go through. You must have a reservation to tour the White House. The procedure is simply this: At least 3 or 4 months before your trip, call your senator's or representative's office with the names of the people in your group, and ask for a specific tour date. The tour coordinator passes on this information to White House staff members, who determine whether there is an availability and then notify the tour coordinator. The tour coordinator contacts you and, if your date is available, obtains the names, birth dates, Social Security numbers (for those 14 and up), and other information for the people in your party. The tour coordinator submits this information to the White House, where the Secret Service reviews the information and clears you for the tour, putting the names of the people in your group on a confirmed reservation list. The White House notifies the congressional tour coordinator, who notifies you, usually about 1 month in advance of your trip. On the day of your White House tour, call ✆ **202/456-7041** to make sure that the White House is still open that day to the public. Then off you go, to the south side of East Executive Avenue, near the

down 15th Street past the Treasury Building, and along the backside and South Lawn, on E Street.

1600 Pennsylvania Ave. NW (visitor entrance gate at E St. and E. Executive Ave.). ✆ **202/456-7041** or 202/208-1631. www.whitehouse.gov. Free admission. Tours for groups of 10 or more, who have arranged the tour through their congressional offices. Metro: McPherson Square.

The White House Visitor Center ✵ Even—especially—if you are not able to tour the White House, you should stop here. The Visitor Center opened in 1995 to provide extensive interpretive data about the White House (as well as other Washington tourist attractions) and to serve as a ticket-distribution center (though that function is suspended indefinitely). It is run under the auspices of the National Park Service, and the staff is particularly well informed.

Southeast Gate of the White House, with photo IDs for everyone in your party who is 15 or older.

Do not bring the following prohibited items: backpacks, bookbags, or *handbags or purses;* food and beverages; strollers; cameras, video recorders, or any type of recording device; tobacco products; personal grooming items, from cosmetics to a hairbrush; any pointed objects, whether a pen or a knitting needle; aerosol containers; guns, ammunition, fireworks, or electric stun guns; mace; martial arts weapons/devices; or knives of any description. Cellphones are okay, but not the kind that are also cameras. The White House does not have a coat check facility, so there is no place for you to leave your belongings while you go on the tour. There are no public restrooms or telephones in the White House, and picture-taking and videotaping are prohibited. Best advice: Leave everything but your wallet back at the hotel.

Okay, so what do you do if you're a family of four and you want to tour the White House? My congressional office contact suggests that groups of fewer than 10 people call their congressional office and ask whether it might be possible to join with another family to meet the 10-person minimum. The coordinator also emphasizes that you request a reservation at least 4 months in advance.

1450 Pennsylvania Ave. NW (in the Dept. of Commerce Building, between 14th and 15th sts.). 📞 **202/208-1631** for recorded information. Free admission. Daily 7:30am–4pm. Closed Jan 1, Thanksgiving, and Dec 25. Metro: Federal Triangle.

2 The Major Memorials

Note: Do not be alarmed or put off if you should see construction surrounding the **Washington Monument,** the **Lincoln Memorial,** or the **Jefferson Memorial.** All three sites remain open to the public. The Washington Monument is in the midst of installing a vehicle barrier security system, a process likely to continue into the fall of 2005; the Jefferson Memorial is also planning to install such a system. The Lincoln Memorial is not undergoing any changes; it's the roads encircling the memorial: (Rock Creek Pkwy., Henry

---

(*Tips* **Parking Near the Mall**

First of all: Don't drive. Use Metro. But if you're hell-bent on driving on a weekday, set out early to nab one of the Independence or Constitution avenue spots that become legal at 9:30am, when rush hour ends. Arrive about 9:15am and sit in your car until 9:30am (to avoid getting a ticket), then hop out and stoke the meter. So many people do this that if you arrive after 9:30am, you'll find most of the street parking spots gone.

Bacon Dr., 23rd St., and the approach from the Arlington Memorial Bridge) that are being treated for maintenance purposes.

Washington Monument 𝒜𝒜𝒜 *(Kids*   The idea of a tribute to George Washington first arose at the Continental Congress of 1783, 16 years before his death. But the new nation had more pressing problems, and funds were not readily available. It wasn't until the early 1830s, with the 100th anniversary of Washington's birth approaching, that any action was taken.

Visiting the Washington Monument: The Washington Monument is the world's tallest freestanding work of masonry. It stands at the center of Washington, D.C.'s landmarks, and the 360-degree views from the top are spectacular. Due east are the Capitol and Smithsonian buildings; due north is the White House; due west are the World War II and Lincoln Memorials (with Arlington National Cemetery beyond); and due south is the Jefferson Memorial, overlooking the Tidal Basin and the Potomac River. "On a clear day, you can see west probably 60 miles, as far as the Shenandoah Mountains," says Bill Line, chief information officer for the National Park Service's National Capital Region. It's like being at the center of a compass, and it provides a marvelous orientation to the city.

Climbing the 897 steps is not allowed, but the large elevator whisks visitors to the top in just 70 seconds. As a rule, you are not allowed to walk down the stairs of the monument. If you're absolutely dying to see more of the interior, you must contact the National Park Service at least 1 month ahead of time to arrange for a special walk-down tour. On this tour you'll learn more about the building of the monument and get to see the 193 carved stones inserted into the interior walls. The stones are gifts from foreign countries, all 50 states, organizations, and individuals. The most expensive stone was given by the state of Alaska in 1982—it's pure jade and worth millions. Allow a half-hour here, plus time spent waiting in line.

Ticket Information: "Interest in the Washington Monument is more than sky-high," says National Park Service spokesman Bill Line, which explains why a ticketing system is in place: Admission to the Washington Monument is free, but you'll still have to get a ticket. The ticket booth is located at the bottom of the hill from the monument, on 15th Street NW between Independence and Constitution avenues. It's open daily from 8am to 4:30pm. Tickets are usually gone by 9am, so plan to get there by 7:30 or 8am, especially in peak season, if you really want to ascend to the top of the monument. The tickets grant admission at half-hour intervals between the stated hours on the same day you visit. If you want to save yourself the trouble and get them in advance, call the National Park Reservation Service (☎ **800/967-2283**) or go to http://reservations.nps.gov; the tickets themselves are free, but you'll pay $1.50 per ticket for shipping and handling, plus a 50¢ service charge per transaction. To make sure that you get tickets for your desired date, reserve these tickets at least 2 weeks in advance.

Directly south of the White House (at 15th St. and Constitution Ave. NW). ☎ **202/ 426-6841.** Free admission. Daily 9am–5pm. Last elevators depart 15 min. before closing (arrive earlier). Closed Dec 25, open until noon July 4th. Metro: Smithsonian, then a 10-min. walk.

National World War II Memorial ★★★   When this memorial was dedicated on May 29, 2004, 150,000 people turned out: President Bush; members of Congress; Marine Corps General (retired) P.X. Kelley, who chaired the American Battle Monuments Commission, the group that spearheaded construction of the memorial; celebrities such as actor Tom Hanks and news anchor Tom Brokaw, both of whom had been active in eliciting support for the memorial; and last but most important, thousands of World War II veterans and their families. These legions of veterans, some dressed in uniform, many wearing a cap identifying the name of the veteran's division, turned out to receive the nation's gratitude, 60 years in the making, expressed profoundly in this memorial.

Designed by Friedrich St. Florian and funded mostly by private donations, the memorial fits nicely into the landscape between the Washington Monument and the Lincoln Memorial and its reflecting pool. St. Florian purposely situated the 7.4-acre memorial so as not to obstruct this long view down the Mall: 56 17-foot-high granite pillars representing each state and territory stand to either side of a central plaza and the Rainbow pool. Likewise, 24 bas-relief panels divide down the middle so that 12 line each side of the walkway leading from the entrance at 17th St. The panels to the left illustrate seminal scenes from the war years as they relate to the Pacific theater: Pearl Harbor, amphibious landing, jungle warfare, a field burial, and so on. The panels to the right are sculptured scenes of war moments related to the Atlantic theater: Rosie the Riveter, Normandy Beach landing, the Battle of the Bulge, and the Russians meeting the Americans at the Elbe River. Raymond Kaskey, an architect and sculptor, sculpted the panels based on archival photographs.

Large open pavilions stake out the north and south axes of the memorial, and semicircular fountains create waterfalls on either side. Inscriptions at the base of each pavilion fountain mark key battles. Beyond the center Rainbow Pool is a wall of 4,000 gold stars, one star for every 100 soldiers who died in World War II. People often leave photos and mementos everywhere around the memorial, which the National Park Service gathers up daily (the NPS is currently deciding how best to maintain an archive of these mementos). If you are lucky, you will see World War II veterans when you visit this memorial. My husband and I saw a man of that certain age bend down and touch the word "Okinawa" engraved in the fountain at the base of the Pacific pavilion, and start to cry.

From the 17th St. entrance, walk south around the perimeter of the memorial to reach a ranger station, where there are brochures and registry kiosks, the latter for looking up names of veterans. Better information and faster service is available online at www. wwiimemorial.com.

17th St. and Constitution Ave. NW. ② **800/639-4WW2** or 202/426-6841. www. wwiimemorial.com. Free admission. Rangers on duty daily 8am–11:45pm. Closed Dec 25. Metro: Farragut West, Federal Triangle, or Smithsonian.

Lincoln Memorial ✪✪✪ *(Kids)* This beautiful and moving testament to the nation's greatest president attracts millions of visitors annually. Like its fellow presidential memorials, this one was a long time in the making. Although it was planned as early as 1867—2 years after Lincoln's death—it was not until 1912 that Henry Bacon's design was completed, and the memorial itself was dedicated in 1922.

The neoclassical templelike structure, similar in design to the Parthenon in Greece, has 36 fluted Doric columns representing the states of the Union at the time of Lincoln's death, plus two at the entrance. On the attic parapet are 48 festoons symbolizing the number of states in 1922, when the monument was erected. Hawaii and Alaska are noted in an inscription on the terrace. Due east is the Reflecting Pool, lined with American elms and stretching 2,000 feet toward the Washington Monument and the Capitol beyond.

The memorial chamber has limestone walls inscribed with the Gettysburg Address and Lincoln's Second Inaugural Address. Most powerful, however, is Daniel Chester French's 19-foot-high seated statue of Lincoln, which disappears from your sightline as you get close to the base of the memorial, then emerges slowly into view as you ascend the stairs.

Lincoln's legacy has made his memorial the site of numerous demonstrations by those seeking justice. Most notable was a peaceful demonstration of 200,000 people on August 28, 1963, at which the Rev. Dr. Martin Luther King, Jr., proclaimed, "I have a dream." The words I HAVE A DREAM. MARTIN LUTHER KING, JR., THE MARCH ON WASHINGTON FOR JOBS AND FREEDOM, AUGUST 28, 1963 are inscribed and centered on the granite step, 18 steps down from the chamber, on the precise spot where King stood to deliver his famous speech.

Directly west of the Mall in Potomac Park (at 23rd St. NW, between Constitution and Independence aves.). ℭ **202/426-6842**. Free admission. Daily 8am–11:45pm. Closed Dec 25. Metro: Foggy Bottom, then a 30-min. walk.

Korean War Veterans Memorial ℛ   This privately funded memorial, founded in 1995, honors those who served in Korea, a 3-year conflict (1950–53) that produced almost as many casualties as Vietnam. It consists of a circular "Pool of Remembrance" in a grove of trees and a triangular "Field of Service," highlighted by lifelike statues of 19 infantrymen, who appear to be trudging across fields. In addition, a 164-foot-long black-granite wall depicts the array of combat and support troops that served in Korea (nurses, chaplains, airmen, gunners, mechanics, cooks, and others); a raised granite curb lists the 22 nations that contributed to the U.N.'s effort there; and a commemorative area honors KIAs, MIAs, and POWs. Plan to spend 15 minutes for viewing. Limited parking is available on Ohio Drive.

Just across from the Lincoln Memorial (east of French Dr., between 21st and 23rd sts. NW). ℭ **202/426-6841**. Free admission. Rangers on duty daily 8am–11:45pm. Closed Dec 25. Ranger-led interpretive programs are given throughout the day. Metro: Foggy Bottom.

Vietnam Veterans Memorial ℛℛ   The Vietnam Veterans Memorial is possibly the most poignant sight in Washington: two long, black-granite walls in the shape of a V, each inscribed with

the names of the men and women who gave their lives, or remain missing, in the longest war in American history. Even if no one close to you died in Vietnam, it's wrenching to watch visitors grimly study the directories to find out where their loved ones are listed, or rub pencil on paper held against a name etched into the wall. The walls list close to 60,000 people, many of whom died very young.

Just across from the Lincoln Memorial (east of Henry Bacon Dr. between 21st and 22nd sts. NW). © 202/426-6841. Free admission. Rangers on duty daily 8am–11:45pm. Closed Dec 25. Ranger-led programs are given throughout the day. Metro: Foggy Bottom.

Franklin Delano Roosevelt Memorial ✿✿✿ The FDR
Memorial has proven to be one of the most popular of the presidential memorials since it opened on May 2, 1997. Its popularity has to do as much with its design as the man it honors. This is a 7.5-acre outdoor memorial that lies beneath a wide-open sky. It stretches out, rather than rising up, across the stone-paved floor. Granite walls define the four "galleries," each representing a different term in FDR's presidency from 1933 to 1945. Architect Lawrence Halprin's design includes waterfalls, sculptures (by Leonard Baskin, John Benson, Neil Estern, Robert Graham, Thomas Hardy, and George Segal), and Roosevelt's own words carved into the stone.

In West Potomac Park, about midway between the Lincoln and Jefferson memorials, on the west shore of the Tidal Basin. © 202/426-6841. Free admission. Ranger staff on duty daily 8am–11:45pm. Closed Dec 25. Free parking along W. Basin and Ohio drs. Metro: Smithsonian, with a 30-min. walk; or take the Tourmobile.

Jefferson Memorial ✿✿ The site for the Jefferson Memorial
was of extraordinary importance. The Capitol, the White House, and the Mall were already located in accordance with architect Pierre L'Enfant's master plan for the city, but there was no spot for such a project that would maintain L'Enfant's symmetry. So the memorial was built on land reclaimed from the Potomac River, now known as the Tidal Basin. Franklin Delano Roosevelt, who laid the cornerstone in 1939, had all the trees between the Jefferson Memorial and the White House cut down so that he could see the memorial.

The memorial is a columned rotunda in the style of the Pantheon in Rome, whose classical architecture Jefferson himself introduced to this country (he designed his home, Monticello, and the earliest University of Virginia buildings in Charlottesville). On the Tidal Basin side, the sculptural group above the entrance depicts Jefferson with Benjamin Franklin, John Adams, Roger Sherman, and Robert Livingston, all of whom worked on drafting the Declaration of

Independence. The domed interior of the memorial contains the 19-foot bronze statue of a standing Jefferson.

South of the Washington Monument on Ohio Dr. SW (at the south shore of the Tidal Basin). *Ⓒ* **202/426-6841**. Free admission. Daily 8am–11:45pm. Closed Dec 25. Metro: Smithsonian, with a 20- to 30-min. walk; or take the Tourmobile.

3 The Smithsonian Museums

The Smithsonian's collection of nearly 142 million objects spans the entire world and all of its history, its peoples and animals (past and present), and our attempts to probe into the future. The sprawling institution comprises 14 museums (the opening of the National Museum of the American Indian this year brings that number to 15, with 10 of them on the Mall), as well as the National Zoological Park in Washington, D.C. (there are two additional museums in New York City). Still, the Smithsonian's collection is so vast that its museums display only about 1% or 2% of the collection's holdings at any given time. Its holdings, in every area of human interest, range from a 3.5-billion-year-old fossil to part of a 1902 Horn & Hardart Automat. Thousands of scientific expeditions sponsored by the Smithsonian have pushed into remote frontiers in the deserts, mountains, polar regions, and jungles.

Smithsonian Information Center (the "Castle")   Make this your first stop and enter through the Enid A. Haupt Garden (p. 143) for a pleasurable experience. Built in 1855, this Norman-style red-sandstone building, popularly known as the "Castle," is the oldest building on the Mall, yet it holds the impressively high-tech and comprehensive Smithsonian Information Center.

The main information area here is the Great Hall, where a 24-minute video overview of the institution runs throughout the day in two theaters. There are two large schematic models of the Mall (as well as a third in Braille), and two large electronic maps of Washington allow visitors to locate nearly 100 popular attractions and Metro and Tourmobile stops. Interactive videos, some at children's heights, offer extensive information about the Smithsonian and other capital attractions and transportation.

1000 Jefferson Dr. SW. *Ⓒ* **202/633-1000**. Daily 8:30am–5:30pm, info desk 9am–4pm. Closed Dec 25. Metro: Smithsonian.

Anacostia Museum and Center for African-American History and Culture   This museum is inconveniently located, but that's because it was initially created in 1967 as a neighborhood museum (which makes it unique among the Smithsonian branches). It's devoted to the African-American experience, focusing on Washington, D.C., and the Upper South. The permanent collection includes about 7,000 items, ranging from videotapes of African-American church services to art, sheet music, historic documents, textiles, glassware, and anthropological objects. In addition, the Anacostia produces a number of shows each year and offers a comprehensive schedule of free educational programs and activities in conjunction with exhibit themes. Allow about an hour here.

1901 Fort Place SE (off Martin Luther King Jr. Ave.). ① **202/287-3306.** www.si. edu/anacostia. Free admission. Daily 10am–5pm. Closed Dec 25. Metro: Anacostia, head to the exit marked LOCAL, turn left after exiting, then take a W2 or W3 bus directly to the museum.

Arthur M. Sackler Gallery ⓖ   Asian art is the focus of this museum and the neighboring Freer (together, they form the National Museum of Asian Art in the United States). The Sackler opened in 1987, thanks to a gift from Arthur M. Sackler of 1,000 priceless works. Since then, the museum has received 11th- to 19th-century Persian and Indian paintings, manuscripts, calligraphies, miniatures, and book-bindings from the collection of Henri Vever. In the spring of 2003, art collector Robert O. Muller bequeathed the museum his entire collection of 4,000 Japanese prints and archival materials.

The Sackler's permanent collection displays Khmer ceramics; ancient Chinese jades, bronzes, paintings, and lacquerware; 20th-century Japanese ceramics and works on paper; ancient Near Eastern works in silver, gold, bronze, and clay; and stone and bronze sculptures from South and Southeast Asia. With the addition of Muller's bequest, the Sackler now has a sumptuous graphic arts inventory, covering a century of work by Japanese master printmakers. A visit here is an education in Asian decorative arts and antiquities.

1050 Independence Ave. SW. ① **202/633-4880.** www.asia.si.edu. Free admission. Daily 10am–5:30pm; in summer, museum often stays open Thurs until 8pm, but call to confirm. Closed Dec 25. Metro: Smithsonian.

Arts and Industries Building (Kids)   The building is closed for an extensive, long-term renovation, though its children's theater remains open. Completed in 1881 as the first U.S. National Museum, this red-brick and sandstone structure was the scene of Pres. Garfield's inaugural ball. (It looks quite similar to the Castle, so don't be confused; from the Mall, the Arts and Industries Building is the one on the left.)

900 Jefferson Dr. SW (on the south side of the Mall). www.si.edu/ai. Free admission. Daily 10am–5:30pm. Closed Dec 25. Metro: Smithsonian.

Freer Gallery of Art 🏛   Charles Lang Freer, a collector of Asian and American art from the 19th and early 20th centuries, gave the nation 9,000 of these works for his namesake gallery's opening in 1923. Freer's original interest was American art, but his good friend James McNeill Whistler encouraged him to collect Asian works as well. Eventually the latter became predominant. Freer's gift included funds to construct a museum and an endowment to add to the Asian collection only, which now numbers more than 28,000 objects. It includes Chinese and Japanese sculpture, lacquer, metalwork, and ceramics; early Christian illuminated manuscripts; Iranian manuscripts, metalwork, and miniatures; ancient Near Eastern metalware; and South Asian sculpture and paintings.

The Freer is mostly about Asian art, but it also displays some of the more than 1,200 American works by **Whistler.** Most remarkable and always on view is the famous **Peacock Room.** Originally a dining room designed for the London mansion of F. R. Leyland, the Peacock Room displayed a Whistler painting called *The Princess from the Land of Porcelain.* But after his painting was installed, Whistler was dissatisfied with the room as a setting for his work. When Leyland was away from home, Whistler painted over the very expensive leather interior and embellished it with paintings of golden peacock feathers. Not surprisingly, a rift ensued between Whistler and Leyland. After Leyland's death, Freer purchased the room, painting and all, and had it shipped to his home in Detroit. It is now permanently installed here. Other American painters represented in the collections are Thomas Wilmer Dewing, Dwight William Tryon, Abbott Henderson Thayer, John Singer Sargent, and Childe Hassam. All in all, you could spend a happy 1 to 2 hours here.

On the south side of the Mall (at 1050 Independence Ave. SW). ✆ **202/633-4880.** www.asia.si.edu. Free admission. Daily 10am–5:30pm; in summer, gallery often stays open Thurs until 8pm, but call to confirm. Closed Dec 25. Metro: Smithsonian.

Hirshhorn Museum and Sculpture Garden 🏛   This museum of modern and contemporary art is named after Latvian-born Joseph H. Hirshhorn, who, in 1966, donated his vast art collection—more than 4,000 drawings and paintings and some 2,000 pieces of sculpture—to the United States "as a small repayment for what this nation has done for me and others like me who arrived here as immigrants." At his death in 1981, Hirshhorn bequeathed an additional 5,500 artworks to the museum, and numerous other donors have greatly expanded his legacy.

Constructed 14 feet above ground on sculptured supports, the doughnut-shaped concrete-and-granite building shelters a verdant plaza courtyard where sculpture is displayed. The light and airy interior follows a simple circular route that makes it easy to see every exhibit without getting lost in a honeycomb of galleries. Natural light from floor-to-ceiling windows makes the inner galleries the perfect venue for viewing sculpture—second only, perhaps, to the beautiful tree-shaded sunken **Sculpture Garden** ⊛ across the street (don't miss it). Paintings and drawings are installed in the outer galleries, along with intermittent sculpture groupings.

A rotating show of about 600 pieces is on view at all times. The collection features just about every well-known 20th-century artist, with particular emphasis on our contemporary period. Among the best-known pieces are Rodin's *Monument to the Burghers of Calais* (in the Sculpture Garden), Hopper's *First Row Orchestra,* de Kooning's *Two Women in the Country,* and Warhol's *Marilyn Monroe's Lips.*

On the south side of the Mall (at Independence Ave. and 7th St. SW). ✆ 202/633-4674. http://hirshhorn.si.edu. Free admission. Museum daily 10am–5:30pm; in summer museum often stays open Thurs until 8pm, but call to confirm. Sculpture Garden daily 7:30am–dusk. Closed Dec 25. Metro: L'Enfant Plaza (Smithsonian Museums/Maryland Ave. or Smithsonian exit).

National Air and Space Museum ⊛⊛ *Kids*   With the opening of the Steven F. Udvar-Hazy Center in December 2003, the National Air and Space Museum now bills itself, "One museum, two locations." It's not realistic, however, to think you could visit both museums in one day: The flagship museum on the National Mall consumes 2 or 3 hours—longer, if you attend an IMAX film or planetarium show; the round-trip to the satellite Udvar-Hazy Center, located on the grounds of Washington-Dulles International Airport, takes about 2 hours; and the touring of that museum another 2 or 3 hours. You could do it, but you'd be frantic.

So start with this one, the original Air and Space Museum on the Mall. This museum chronicles the story of the mastery of flight, from Kitty Hawk to outer space. It holds the largest collection of historic aircraft and spacecraft in the world—so many, in fact, that the museum is able to display only about 20% of its artifacts at any one time, hence the opening of the Udvar-Hazy Center.

During the tourist season and on holidays, arrive before 10am to make a beeline for the film ticket line when the doors open. The not-to-be-missed **IMAX films** ⊛ shown here are immensely popular, and tickets to most shows sell out quickly. You can purchase tickets up to 2 weeks in advance, but they are available only at the

Lockheed Martin IMAX Theater box office on the first floor. Two or more films play each day, most with aeronautical or space-exploration themes; *To Fly* and *Space Station 3D* are two that should continue into 2005. Tickets cost $8 for adults, $6.50 for ages 2 to 12 and 55 or older; they're free for children under 2. You can also see IMAX films most evenings after the museum's closing; call for details (© **202/ 357-1686**).

You'll also need tickets to attend a show at the **Albert Einstein Planetarium** ✦, which creates "an astronomical adventure" as projectors display blended space imagery upon a 70-foot diameter dome, making you feel as if you're traveling in 3-D through the cosmos. The planetarium's main feature, called "Infinity Express, A 20-Minute Tour of the Universe," gives you the sensation of zooming through the solar system, as it explores such questions as "how big is the universe?" and "where does it end?" Tickets are $8 for adults, $6.50 for ages 2 to 12 and 55 or older; or buy an IMAX film and planetarium combo ticket for $13 per adult, $11 per child.

Kids love the walk-through **Skylab orbital workshop** on the first floor. Other galleries here highlight the solar system, U.S. manned space flights, sea-air operations, and aviation during both world wars.

Now, to get to the Steven F. Udvar-Hazy Center, you can drive (for directions: © 202/786-2122; www.nasm.si.edu.), or you can take a shuttle bus from the Air and Space Museum on the Mall. The shuttles run six times a day from both locations, at the same times, starting at 9am with the last shuttle departing at 5pm. You must purchase tickets to take the shuttle, which are sold at the IMAX film box office, for $7 round-trip per person. To purchase shuttle bus tickets in advance, call © 202/633-4629. If you drive to the center, you should be aware that parking is a whopping $12 due to the fact that the center lies on airport property.

At the Udvar-Hazy Center, you'll find two hangars (one for a viation artifacts, the other for space artifacts) and an observation tower for watching planes leave and arrive at Dulles Airport.

On the south side of the Mall (at 7th and Independence Ave. SW), with entrances on Jefferson Dr. or Independence Ave. © **202/357-2700** (for both locations), or 202/357-1686 for IMAX ticket information. www.nasm.si.edu. Free admission. Both locations daily 10am–5:30pm. The mall museum often opens at 9am in summer, but call to confirm. Free 1½-hr. highlight tours daily at 10:15am and 1pm. Closed Dec 25. Metro: L'Enfant Plaza (Smithsonian Museums/Maryland Ave. exit) or Smithsonian. The Udvar-Hazy Center is located at 14390 Air and Space Museum Pkwy., Chantilly, VA.

National Museum of African Art ✦   Founded in 1964, and part of the Smithsonian since 1979, the National Museum of

African Art moved to the Mall in 1987 to share a subterranean space with the Sackler Gallery (p. 120) and the Ripley Center. Its above-ground domed pavilions reflect the arch motif of the neighboring Freer Gallery of Art (p. 121).

The museum collects and exhibits ancient and contemporary art from the entire African continent, but its permanent collection of more than 7,000 objects (shown in rotating exhibits) highlights the traditional arts of the vast sub-Saharan region. Most of the collection dates from the 19th and 20th centuries. Also among the museum's holdings are the **"Eliot Elisofon Photographic Archives,"** comprising 300,000 photographic prints and transparencies and 120,000 feet of film on African arts and culture. Permanent exhibits include **"The Ancient West African City of Benin, a.d. 1300–1897"** (cast-metal heads, figures, and architectural plaques that depict kings and attendants); **"The Ancient Nubian City of Kerma, 2500–1500 b.c."** (ceramics, jewelry, and ivory animals); **"The Art of the Personal Object"** (everyday items such as chairs, headrests, snuffboxes, bowls, and baskets); and **"Images of Power and Identity"** (masks, sculptures and other visual arts from Africa, south of the Sahara).

950 Independence Ave. SW. © 202/357-4600. www.nmafa.si.edu. Free admission. Daily 10am–5:30pm. Closed Dec 25. Metro: Smithsonian.

National Museum of American History ★★★ *Kids* This museum deals with "everyday life in the American past" and the external forces that have helped to shape our national character.

Start at the top—that is, the third floor—where **"The American Presidency"** exhibit explores the power and meaning of the presidency by studying those who have held the position. (There's a gift shop just for this exhibit on this floor.) Continue on this floor to an exhibit added to the museum on Veterans Day 2004. Called **"The Price of Freedom: Americans at War,"** the exhibit examines major American military events and explores the idea that America's armed forces reflect American society. Among the items on display here are George Washington's commission from Congress as commander-in-chief of the Continental Army, and the uniform jacket that Andrew Jackson wore during the Battle of New Orleans in the War of 1812.

Head downstairs to the second floor for the intriguing opportunity of viewing the huge **original Star-Spangled Banner** ★★★, whose 30-by-34-foot expanse has just been painstakingly conserved by expert textile conservators. This is the very flag that inspired Francis Scott Key to write the poem that eventually became the U.S.

national anthem in 1931. Conservation work was completed in August 2004 and now the flag remains on view and outstretched, flat, behind glass, in its specially designed conservation lab.

One of the most popular exhibits on the second floor is **"First Ladies: Political Role and Public Image,"** which displays the first ladies' gowns and tells you a bit about each of these women. Infinitely more interesting, I think, is the neighboring exhibit, **"From Parlor to Politics: Women and Reform in America, 1890–1925,"** which chronicles the changing roles of women as they've moved from domestic to political and professional pursuits. Following that, find the exhibit called **"Within These Walls . . .,"** which interprets the rich history of America by tracing the lives of the people who lived in this 200-year-old house, transplanted from Ipswich, MA. If this personal approach to history appeals to you, continue on to **"Field to Factory,"** which tells the story of African-American migration from the South between 1915 and 1940.

Finally, you're ready to hit the first floor, where some exhibits explore the development of farm machinery, power machinery, and timekeeping. A temporary exhibit that opened in August 2002 and ends its popular run in September 2005 is *"Bon Appétit!* **Julia Child's Kitchen at the Smithsonian,"** which is a presentation of the famous chef's actual kitchen from her home in Cambridge, Massachusetts. When she moved to California in late 2001, Child donated her kitchen and all that it contained (1,200 items in all) to the museum. Most of these are on display, vegetable peeler to kitchen sink. Also look here for **"America on the Move,"** which details the story of transportation in America since 1876.

Wind up your visit at the **Palm Court,** where you can stop and have gelato and a sandwich; the Palm Court includes the interior of Georgetown's Stohlman's Confectionery Shop as it appeared around 1900, and part of an actual 1902 Horn & Hardart Automat.

On the north side of the Mall (between 12th and 14th sts. NW), with entrances on Constitution Ave. and Madison Dr. ℃ **202/357-2700.** www.americanhistory.si.edu. Free admission. Daily 10am–5:30pm. Closed Dec 25. Metro: Smithsonian or Federal Triangle.

National Museum of the American Indian ★★★ *Kids*   This staggeringly handsome and supremely fascinating museum opened in September 2004. Consider its exterior: Its burnt sand–colored exterior of kasota limestone wraps around the undulating walls of the museum, making the five-story building a standout among the many white-stone structures on the National Mall. Its interior design incorporates themes of nature and astronomy. For instance, the Potomac (a Piscataway word meaning "where the goods are brought in") is a rotunda that serves as the museum's main gathering place; it is also "the heart of the museum, the sun of its universe" (as noted in the museum's literature). Measuring 120 feet in diameter, with an atrium rising 120 feet to the top of the dome overhead, the Potomac is the central entryway into the museum; a venue for performances; and a hall filled with celestial references, from the equinoxes and solstices mapped on the floor beneath your feet to the sights of sky visible through the oculus in the dome above your head.

The National Museum of the American Indian is very much a "living" museum, with performances, events, and exhibits that aim at giving Native peoples the chance to tell their own stories. Exhibits explore Native life and history, and showcase works of individual artists. Most importantly, the museum is a giant display case for a collection of objects representing 1,000 Native communities. A wealthy New Yorker named George Gustav Heyer (1874–1957) assembled the collection of these 800,000 pieces, including wood- and stone carvings, masks, pottery, feather bonnets, and so on; the museum displays about 8,000 of these at any given time.

Anticipating that many people will want to visit this museum, the Smithsonian Institution established a same-day/timed-pass admission procedure. You should arrive no later than 10am to stand in line to obtain a pass, which will be printed with the time you will be able to enter the museum. You pass is free, but if you want to order yours in advance you can call ✆ 866/400-6624 or go online to www.tickets.com to order tickets (the ticket agency, not the museum, charges you a nominal fee for the service).

Fourth St. and Independence Ave. SW. ✆ **202/633-1000.** www.nmai.si.edu. Free admission. Daily 10am–5:30pm. Closed Dec 25. Metro: Federal Center Southwest or L'Enfant Plaza.

National Museum of Natural History ★★ (Kids)   Children refer to this Smithsonian showcase as "the dinosaur museum" because there's a dinosaur hall, or sometimes "the elephant museum" because a huge, stuffed African bush elephant is the first amazing thing you see if you enter the museum from the Mall. Whatever you call it, the National Museum of Natural History is the largest of its kind in the world, and one of the most visited museums in Washington, D.C. It contains more than 124 million artifacts and specimens, everything from Ice Age mammoths to the legendary Hope Diamond. The same warning applies here as at the National

Museum of American History: You're going to suffer artifact over-load, so take a reasoned approach to sightseeing.

If you have children in your crew, you might want to make your first stop the first-floor **Discovery Room,** which is filled with creative hands-on exhibits "for children of all ages." Call ahead or inquire at the information desk about hours. Also popular among little kids is the second floor's **O. Orkin Insect Zoo** 👫, where they enjoy looking at tarantulas, centipedes, and the like, and crawling through a model of an African termite mound. The Natural History museum, like its sister Smithsonian museums, is struggling to overhaul and modernize its exhibits, some of which are quite dated in appearance, if not in the facts presented. So a renovation of the gems and minerals hall has made the **Janet Annenberg Hooker Hall of Geology, Gems, and Minerals** 👫👫 worth a stop. You can learn all you want about earth science, from volcanology to the importance of mining in our daily lives. Interactive computers, animated graphics, and a multimedia presentation of the "big picture" story of the earth are some of the things that have moved the exhibit and the museum a bit further into the 21st century.

The **Kenneth E. Behring Hall of Mammals** is an example of an updated section of the museum. Here, visitors can operate interactive dioramas that explain how mammals evolved and adapted to changes in habitat and climate over the course of millions of years.

Other rotunda-level displays include the **fossil collection,** which traces evolution back billions of years and includes a 3.5-billion-year-old stromatolite (blue-green algae clump) fossil—one of the earliest signs of life on Earth—and a 70-million-year-old dinosaur egg. **"Life in the Ancient Seas"** features a 100-foot-long mural depicting primitive whales, a life-size walk-around diorama of a 230-million-year-old coral reef, and more than 2,000 fossils that chronicle the evolution of marine life. The **Dinosaur Hall** displays giant skeletons of creatures that dominated the earth for 140 million years before their extinction about 65 million years ago.

Don't miss the **Discovery Center,** funded by the Discovery Channel, featuring the Johnson **IMAX theater** with a six-story-high screen for 2-D and 3-D movies (*T-Rex: Back to the Cretaceous* was among recent offerings). Purchase tickets as early as possible, or at least 30 minutes before the screening. The first-floor box office is open daily from 9:45am through the last show. Ticket prices are $8 for adults and $6.50 for children (2–12) and seniors 55 or older. On Friday from 6 to 10pm, the theater stages live jazz nights, starring excellent local musicians ($5 cover).

On the north side of the Mall (at 10th St. and Constitution Ave. NW), with entrances on Madison Dr. and Constitution Ave. ℭ **202/357-2700**, or 202/633-4629 for information about IMAX films. www.mnh.si.edu. Free admission. Daily 10am–5:30pm. In summer the museum often stays open until 8pm, but call to confirm. Closed Dec 25. Free highlight tours Mon–Thurs 10:30am and 1:30pm, Fri 10:30am. Metro: Smithsonian or Federal Triangle.

National Postal Museum ✪　This museum is, somewhat surprisingly, a hit for the whole family. Bring your address book and you can send postcards to the folks back home through an interactive exhibit that issues a postcard and stamps it. That's just one feature that makes this museum visitor-friendly. Many of its exhibits involve easy-to-understand activities, like postal-themed video games.

The museum documents America's postal history from 1673 (about 170 years before the advent of stamps, envelopes, and mailboxes) to the present. In the central gallery, titled **"Moving the Mail,"** three planes that carried mail in the early decades of the 20th century are suspended from a 90-foot atrium ceiling. Here, too, are a railway mail car, an 1851 mail/passenger coach, a Ford Model-A mail truck, and a replica of an airmail beacon tower. In **"Binding the Nation,"** historic correspondence illustrates how mail kept families together in the developing nation. Several exhibits deal with the famed Pony Express, a service that lasted less than 2 years but was romanticized by Buffalo Bill and others. In the Civil War section, you'll learn about Henry "Box" Brown, a slave who had himself "mailed" from Richmond to a Pennsylvania abolitionist in 1856.

2 Massachusetts Ave. NE (at 1st St.). ℭ **202/357-2991.** www.si.edu/postal. Free admission. Daily 10am–5:30pm. Closed Dec 25. Metro: Union Station.

National Zoological Park ✪✪ *Kids*　Established in 1889, the National Zoo is home to some 500 species, many of them rare and/or endangered. A leader in the care, breeding, and exhibition of animals, it occupies 163 beautifully landscaped and wooded acres and is one of the country's most delightful zoos. You'll see cheetahs; zebras; camels; elephants; tapirs; antelopes; brown pelicans; kangaroos; hippos; rhinos; giraffes; apes; and, of course, lions, tigers, and bears (oh my).

Pointers: Enter the zoo at the Connecticut Avenue entrance; you'll be right by the Education Building, where you can pick up a map and find out about feeding times and any special activities. Note that from this main entrance, you're headed downhill; the return uphill walk can prove trying if you have young children and/or it's a hot day. But the zoo rents strollers, and snack bars and ice-cream kiosks are scattered throughout the park.

The zoo animals live in large, open enclosures—simulations of their natural habitats—along two easy-to-follow numbered paths: **Olmsted Walk** and the **Valley Trail.** You can't get lost, and it's hard to miss a thing. Be sure to catch **"Amazonia,"** where you can hang out for an hour peering up into the trees and still not spy the sloth (do yourself a favor and ask the attendant where it is).

New at the zoo is the Kids' Farm, which offers children 3 to 8 a chance to observe farm animals up close. Ducks, chickens, goats, cows, and miniature donkeys are among the animals milling around. Children might also enjoy the vegetable garden and pizza sculpture.

Adjacent to Rock Creek Park, main entrance on the 3000 block of Connecticut Ave. NW. ⓒ 202/673-4800 (recording), or 202/673-4717. www.si.edu/natzoo. Free admission. Daily Apr–Oct (weather permitting): grounds 6am–8pm, animal buildings 10am–6pm. Daily Oct–Apr: grounds 6am–6pm, animal buildings 10am–4:30pm. Closed Dec 25. Metro: Woodley Park–Zoo or Cleveland Park.

Renwick Gallery of the Smithsonian American Art Museum ⓡ (Finds

A department of the Smithsonian American Art Museum, the Renwick Gallery is a showcase for American creativity in crafts, housed in a historic mid-1800s landmark building of the French Second Empire style. The original home of the Corcoran Gallery, it was saved from demolition by First Lady Jacqueline Kennedy in 1963, when she recommended that it be renovated as part of the Lafayette Square restoration. In 1965, it became part of the Smithsonian and was renamed for its architect, James W. Renwick, who also designed the Smithsonian Castle.

Although the setting—especially the magnificent Victorian Grand Salon with its wainscoted walls and 38-foot skylight ceiling—evokes another era, the museum's contents are mostly contemporary. On the first floor are temporary exhibits of American crafts and decorative arts. On the second floor, the museum's rich and diverse displays boast changing crafts exhibits and contemporary works from the museum's permanent collection, such as Larry Fuente's *Game Fish,* or Wendell Castle's *Ghost Clock.* The **Grand Salon** on the second floor, styled in 19th-century opulence, is newly refurbished and currently displays 170 paintings and sculptures from the American Art Museum, which is closed for renovation. The great thing about this room, besides its fine art and grand design, is its cushiony, velvety banquettes, perfect resting stops for the weary sightseer.

750 9th St. NW (at Pennsylvania Ave. and 17th St. NW). ⓒ 202/357-2700. http://americanart.si.edu. Free admission. Daily 10am–5:30pm. Closed Dec 25. Metro: Farragut West or Farragut North.

4 Elsewhere on the Mall

National Archives   The Rotunda of the National Archives displays our country's most important original documents: the Declaration of Independence, the Constitution of the United States, and the Bill of Rights (collectively known as the Charters of Freedom). Until recently, however, it wasn't possible to get a very good look at these documents, and when you did, you had to view the Constitution one page at a time. A superb renovation, known as "The National Archives Experience," has transformed the Rotunda and installed new display cases that allow all visitors, but especially children and those in wheelchairs, much better viewing of the Charters. And, for the first time, you are able to see all four pages of the Constitution in one visit. The renovation adds 14 new document cases that trace the story of the creation of the Charters and the ongoing influence of these fundamental documents on the nation and the world. Further, a restoration of Barry Faulkner's two larger-than-life murals brings the scenes to vivid life. One mural entitled *The Declaration of Independence,* shows Thomas Jefferson presenting a draft of the Declaration to John Hancock, the presiding officer of the Continental Congress; the other, entitled *The Constitution,* shows James Madison submitting the Constitution to George Washington and the Constitutional Convention.

Phase II of the renovation, completed in late 2004, debuts new exhibition space in the National Archives' public vaults. Exhibits here feature interactive technology and displays of documents and artifacts to explain our country's development in the use of records, from Indian treaties to presidential websites.

As a federal institution, the National Archives is charged with sifting through the accumulated papers of a nation's official life—billions of pieces a year—and determining what to save and what to destroy. The Archives' vast accumulation of census figures, military records, naturalization papers, immigrant passenger lists, federal documents, passport applications, ship manifests, maps, charts, photographs, and motion picture film (and that's not the half of it) spans 2 centuries. Anyone is welcome to use the National Archives center for genealogical research—this is where Alex Haley began his work on *Roots*—and it's all available for the perusal of anyone 16 or over (call for details). If you're interested, visit the building, entering on Pennsylvania Avenue, and head to the fourth floor, where a staff member can advise you about the time and effort that will be involved, and, if you decide to pursue it, exactly how to proceed.

The National Archives building itself is worth an admiring glance. The neoclassical structure, designed by John Russell Pope (also the architect of the National Gallery of Art and the Jefferson Memorial) in the 1930s, is an impressive example of the Beaux Arts style. Seventy-two columns create a Corinthian colonnade on each of the four facades. Great bronze doors mark the Constitution Avenue entrance, and four large sculptures representing the Future, the Past, Heritage, and Guardianship sit on pedestals near the entrances. Huge pediments crown both the Pennsylvania Avenue and Connecticut Avenue entrances to the building.

700 Pennsylvania Ave. NW (between 7th and 9th sts. NW; enter on Pennsylvania Ave.). ℭ 866/272-6272 or 202/501-5000 for general information, or 202/501-5400 for research information. www.nara.gov. Free admission. Daily 10am–7pm. Call for research hours. Closed Dec 25. Metro: Archives–Navy Memorial.

National Gallery of Art 𝕬𝕬𝕬   Most people don't realize it, but the National Gallery of Art is not part of the Smithsonian complex. Housing one of the world's foremost collections of Western painting, sculpture, and graphic arts, spanning from the Middle Ages through the 20th century, the National Gallery has a dual personality. The original West Building, designed by John Russell Pope (architect of the Jefferson Memorial and the National Archives), is a neoclassical marble masterpiece with a domed rotunda over a colonnaded fountain and high-ceilinged corridors leading to delightful garden courts. It was a gift to the nation from Andrew W. Mellon, who also contributed the nucleus of the collection, including 21 masterpieces from the Hermitage, two Raphaels among them. The ultramodern East Building, designed by I. M. Pei and opened in 1978, is composed of two adjoining triangles with glass walls and lofty tetrahedron skylights. The pink Tennessee marble from which both buildings were constructed was taken from the same quarry; it forms an architectural link between the two structures.

The West Building: On the main floor of the West Building, about 1,000 paintings are on display at any one time. To the right and left of the rotunda are sculpture galleries. On view are more than 800 works from the museum's permanent collection, mostly European sculptures from the Middle Ages to the early 20th century.

The **National Gallery Sculpture Garden** 𝕬, just across 7th Street from the West Wing, takes up 2 city blocks and features open lawns; a central pool with a fountain (the pool turns into an ice rink in winter); an exquisite glassed-in pavilion housing a cafe; 17 sculptures by renowned artists like Roy Lichtenstein and Ellsworth Kelly (and Scott Burton, whose *Six-Part Seating* you're welcome to sit upon); a Paris Metro sign; and informally landscaped shrubs, trees, and plants. Friday evenings in summer, the gallery stages live jazz performances here.

The East Building: Inside this wing is a showcase for the museum's collection of 20th-century art, including works by Picasso, Miró, Matisse, Pollock, and Rothko; this is also the home of the art history research center. Always on display is an exhibit called **"Small French Paintings."**

The National Gallery is in the midst of finishing up a renovation, so some galleries and favorite works of art may not be on view. For instance, the famous, massive aluminum Alexander Calder mobile that usually dangles in the seven-story skylit atrium of the East Building was being cleaned at the time of this writing (to be re-hung in the summer of 2005). Call ✆ **202/842-6179** for information.

4th St. and Constitution Ave. NW, on the north side of the Mall (between 3rd and 7th sts. NW). ✆ **202/737-4215**. www.nga.gov. Free admission. Mon–Sat 10am–5pm; Sun 11am–6pm. Closed Jan 1 and Dec 25. Metro: Archives, Judiciary Square, or Smithsonian.

United States Holocaust Memorial Museum ✮✮ This museum remains a top draw, as it has been since it opened in 1993. If you arrive without a reserved ticket specifying an admission time, you'll have to join the line of folks seeking to get one of the 1,575 day-of-sale tickets the museum makes available each day. The museum opens its doors at 10am and the tickets are usually gone by 10:30am. Get in line early in the morning (around 8am).

When you enter, you will be issued an identity card of an actual victim of the Holocaust; at several points in the tour, you can find out the location and status of person on your card—by 1945, 66% of those whose lives are documented on these cards were dead.

The tour begins on the fourth floor, where exhibits portray the events of 1933 to 1939, the years of the Nazi rise to power. On the third floor (documenting 1940–44), exhibits illustrate the narrowing choices of people caught up in the Nazi machine. You board a Polish freight car of the type used to transport Jews from the Warsaw ghetto to Treblinka and hear recordings of survivors telling what life in the camps was like. This part of the museum documents the details of the Nazis' "Final Solution" for the Jews.

The second floor recounts a more heartening story: It depicts how non-Jews throughout Europe, by exercising individual action and responsibility, saved Jews at great personal risk. Denmark—led by a king who swore that if any of his subjects wore a yellow star, so would he—managed to hide and save 90% of its Jews. Exhibits follow on the liberation of the camps, life in Displaced Persons camps, emigration to Israel and America, and the Nuremberg trials. A highlight at the end of the permanent exhibition is a 30-minute film called *Testimony*, in which Holocaust survivors tell their personal stories. The tour concludes in the hexagonal Hall of Remembrance, where you can meditate on what you've experienced and light a candle for the victims. The museum notes that most people take 2 to 3 hours on their first visit; many people take longer.

The museum recommends not bringing children under 11; for older children, it's advisable to prepare them for what they'll see. You can see some parts of the museum without tickets. These include two special areas on the first floor and concourse: **"Daniel's Story: Remember the Children"** and the **"Wall of Remembrance"** (Children's Tile Wall), which commemorate the 1.5 million children killed in the Holocaust, and the **Wexner Learning Center.**

100 Raoul Wallenberg Place SW (formerly 15th St. SW; near Independence Ave., just off the Mall). © **202/488-0400.** www.ushmm.org. Free admission. Daily 10am–5:30pm, until 8pm Tues and Thurs mid-Apr to mid-June. Closed Yom Kippur and Dec 25. Metro: Smithsonian.

5 Other Government Agencies

Bureau of Engraving & Printing *Kids*   This is where they will literally show you the money. A staff of 2,600 works around the clock churning it out at the rate of about $700 million a day. Everyone's eyes pop as they walk past rooms overflowing with new greenbacks. But the money's not the whole story. The bureau prints many other products, including 25 billion postage stamps a year, presidential portraits, and White House invitations.

Tickets for general public tours are required every day, and every person taking the tour must have a ticket. To obtain a ticket, go to the ticket booth on the 15th Street side of the building and show a valid photo ID. You will receive a ticket specifying a tour time for that same day, and be directed to the 14th Street entrance of the bureau; you are allowed as many as eight tickets per person. Booth hours are from 8am to 2pm, staying open until 7pm in summer.

The 40-minute guided tour begins with a short introductory film. Then you'll see the processes that go into the making of paper money: the inking, stacking of bills, cutting, and examination for defects. Most printing here is done from engraved steel plates in a

---

The F.B.I. Gets a Makeover

The **Federal Bureau of Investigation** has been closed to public tours during its renovation, but it is slated to re-open sometime in 2005. Call ✆ **202/324-3447** for the latest information.

---

process known as *intaglio,* the hardest to counterfeit, because any alteration will cause a noticeable change in the portrait in use.

14th and C sts. SW. ✆ **800/874-3188** or 202/874-2330. www.moneyfactory.com. Free admission. Mon–Fri 10am–2pm (last tour begins at 1:40pm); in summer, extended hours 5–6:40pm. Closed Dec 25–Jan 1 and federal holidays. Metro: Smithsonian (Independence Ave. exit).

Library of Congress ✪   The question most frequently asked by visitors to the Library of Congress is: Where are the books? They're on the 532 miles of shelves located throughout the library's three buildings: the **Thomas Jefferson, James Madison Memorial,** and **John Adams** buildings. Established in 1800, "for the purchase of such books as may be necessary for the use of Congress," the library today serves the nation, with holdings for the visually impaired, research scholars, college students—and tourists. Its first collection of books was destroyed in 1814 when the British burned the Capitol (where the library was then housed) during the War of 1812. Thomas Jefferson then sold the institution his personal library of 6,487 books as a replacement, and this became the foundation of what would grow to become the world's largest library.

Today, the collection contains a mind-boggling 128 million items, including more than 29 million cataloged books, 57 million manuscripts, 12 million prints and photographs, 2.7 million audio holdings (discs, tapes, talking books, and so on), about a million movies and videotapes, musical instruments from the 1700s, and the letters and papers of everyone from George Washington to Groucho Marx. The library offers a year-round program of free concerts, lectures, and poetry readings, and houses the Copyright Office.

Just as impressive as the scope of the library's holdings is its architecture. Most magnificent is the ornate Italian Renaissance–style **Thomas Jefferson Building,** which was erected between 1888 and 1897 to hold the burgeoning collection and establish America as a cultured nation with magnificent institutions equal to anything in Europe. Fifty-two painters and sculptors worked for 8 years on its interior. There are floor mosaics of Italian marble, allegorical paintings on the overhead vaults, more than 100 murals, and numerous ornamental cornucopias, ribbons, vines, and garlands within. The building's exterior has 42 granite sculptures and yards of bas-reliefs. Especially impressive are the exquisite marble **Great Hall** and the **Main Reading Room,** the latter under a 160-foot dome. Originally intended to hold the fruits of at least 150 years of collecting, the Jefferson Building was, in fact, filled up in a mere 13 years. It is now supplemented by the James Madison Memorial Building and the John Adams Building.

On permanent display in the Great Hall are several exhibits: The **"American Treasures of the Library of Congress"** rotates a selection of more than 300 of the rarest items from the library's collection—such as Thomas Jefferson's rough draft of the Declaration of Independence with notations by Benjamin Franklin and John Adams in the margins, and the contents of Lincoln's pockets when he was assassinated. Be sure to obtain a free audio wand before you view the American Treasures exhibit, so that you can listen to audio treasures: a Duke Ellington recording, an excerpt from Martin Luther King's delivery of his "I have a dream" speech, and so on.

1st St. SE (between Independence Ave. and E. Capitol St.). ✆ **202/707-8000.** www.loc.gov. Free admission. Madison Building Mon–Fri 8:30am–9:30pm; Sat 8:30am–6pm. Jefferson Building Mon–Sat 10am–5:30pm. Adams Building Mon and Wed–Thurs 8:30am–9:30pm; Tues and Fri–Sat 8:30am–5:30pm. Closed federal holidays. Stop at the information desk inside the Jefferson Building's west entrance on 1st St. to obtain same-day free tickets to tour the Library. Tours of the Great Hall: Mon–Fri 10:30 and 11:30am, and 1:30, 2:30, and 3:30pm; Sat 10:30 and 11:30am, and 1:30 and 2:30pm. Contact your congressional representatives to obtain tickets for a congressional, or "VIP" tour, a more personal tour given weekdays at 8:30am and 2pm. Metro: Capitol South.

6 More Museums

City Museum ✿   Long overdue, this museum, which opened in May 2003, presents the story of "the people, events, and communities" of Washington, D.C. A main feature is the 25-minute multimedia show, in which historical figures and contemporary characters come to life, going backwards and forwards in time, as they reveal the main events and personalities that formed this city.

An exhibit on the first floor entitled "Washington Perspectives" covers the history of the city through displays of old ticket stubs, photographs, advertisements, and other artifacts, with printed explanations and sometimes recorded voices. The room is divided into four chronological sections, and as you move through each time period, you pick up details—whether it's about the bustle of market life in the 18th century or segregation in the 1950s. Also on this floor are two galleries that introduce you to two longtime Washington communities: "Chinatown, Place or People?" and "Mount Vernon Square Communities: Generations of Change."

Upstairs are two more exhibits. "Sandlots to Stadiums" basically traces the history of sports and recreation in the city. To me, the much more interesting exhibit is "Taking a Closer Look," which displays old maps, receipts, and drawings; headphones on stands in front of many of the artifacts provide audio recordings of historians giving context to and information about what you are seeing.

801 K St. NW (at Mount Vernon Sq., between 7th and 9th sts.). © 202/383-1800. www.citymuseumdc.org. Admission to exhibits $3 adults, $2 students and seniors; to multimedia show $6 adults, $5 students and seniors; combination ticket $8 adults, $6 students and seniors. Tues–Sun 10am–5pm; 3rd Thurs every month until 9pm. Closed Mon and major holidays. Metro: Mount Vernon Square/Convention Center or Gallery Place/Chinatown.

The Corcoran Gallery of Art ★★

The first art museum in Washington, the Corcoran Gallery was housed from 1869 to 1896 in the red-brick and brownstone building that is now the Renwick. The collection outgrew its quarters and was transferred in 1897 to its present Beaux Arts building, designed by Ernest Flagg.

The collection focuses chiefly on American art. A prominent Washington banker, William Wilson Corcoran was among the first wealthy American collectors to realize the importance of encouraging and supporting this country's artists. Enhanced by further gifts and bequests, the collection spans American art from 18th-century portraiture to 20th-century moderns like Nevelson, Warhol, and Rothko. Nineteenth-century works include Bierstadt's and Remington's imagery of the American West; Hudson River School artists; expatriates like Whistler, Sargent, and Mary Cassatt; and two giants of the late 19th century, Homer and Eakins.

The Corcoran is not exclusively an American art museum. On the first floor is the collection from the estate of Sen. William Andrews Clark, an eclectic grouping of Dutch and Flemish masters, European painters, French Impressionists, Barbizon landscapes, Delft porcelains, a Louis XVI *salon dore* transported in toto from Paris, and more. Don't miss the small walnut-paneled room known as "Clark Landing," which showcases 19th-century French Impressionist and American art; a room of exquisite Corot landscapes; another of medieval Renaissance tapestries; and numerous Daumier lithographs donated by Dr. Armand Hammer. Allow an hour for touring the collection.

500 17th St. NW (between E St. and New York Ave.). © 202/639-1700. www. corcoran.org. $6.75 adults, $4.75 seniors, $3 students 13–18, $8 families, free for

children under 12; free admission all day Mon, and Thurs after 5pm. Wed–Mon 10am–5pm, with extended hours Thurs until 9pm. Free walk-in tours daily (except Tues) at noon, as well as at 7:30pm Thurs and 2:30pm Sat–Sun. Closed Jan 1 and Dec 25. Metro: Farragut West or Farragut North.

Ford's Theatre & Lincoln Museum (Kids)   On April 14, 1865, Pres. Abraham Lincoln was in the audience at Ford's Theatre, one of the most popular playhouses in Washington. Everyone was laughing at a funny line from Tom Taylor's celebrated comedy, *Our American Cousin,* when John Wilkes Booth crept into the president's box, shot the president, and leapt to the stage, shouting *"Sic semper tyrannis!"* ("Thus ever to tyrants!") With his left leg broken from the vault, Booth mounted his horse in the alley and galloped off. Doctors carried Lincoln across the street to the house of William Petersen, where the president died the next morning.

The theater was closed after Lincoln's assassination and used as an office by the War Department. It remained in disuse until the 1960s, when it was remodeled and restored to its appearance on the night of the tragedy. Except when rehearsals or matinees are in progress (call before you go), visitors can see the theater and retrace Booth's movements on that fateful night. Free 15-minute talks on the history of the theater and the story of the assassination are given throughout the day. Be sure to visit the Lincoln Museum in the basement, where exhibits—including the Derringer pistol used by Booth and a diary in which he outlines his rationalization for the deed—focus on events surrounding Lincoln's assassination and the trial of the conspirators. Thirty minutes is plenty of time here.

517 10th St. NW (between E and F sts.). (C) 202/426-6925. www.nps.gov/foth. Free admission. Daily 9am–5pm. Closed Dec 25. Metro: Metro Center.

International Spy Museum (🔭🔭)   After several visits to the Spy Museum, my 12-year-old and I like to test each other's powers of observation. We'll be standing in a store or other public place and look around for signs of "hostile surveillance, security systems, and unexpected risk or unlucky breaks." We're putting into practice some tips we picked up at the museum, in a section called "Tricks of the Trade," where interactive monitors teach you what to look for when it comes to suspicious activity. This tradecraft area is the first you come to in the museum. In addition to the surveillance games, the section displays trick equipment (such as a shoe transmitter used by Soviets as a listening device and a single-shot pistol disguised as a lipstick tube) and runs film in which spies talk about bugging devices and locks and picks. You can watch a video that shows individuals being made up for disguise, from start to finish, and you can crawl on your belly through ductwork in the ceiling overhead.

Try to pace yourself, though, because there's so much more to see, and you can easily reach your personal limit before you get through the 68,000-square-foot museum. The next section covers the history of spying ("the second oldest profession") and tells about famous spymasters over time—from Moses; to Sun Tzu, the Chinese general who wrote *The Art of War* in 400 B.C.; to George Washington, whose Revolutionary War letter of 1777 setting up a network of spies in New York is on view. You learn about the use of codes and code-breaking in spying.

Much more follows: artifacts from all over; a re-created tunnel beneath the divided city of Berlin during the Cold War; the intelligence-gathering stories of those behind enemy lines and of those involved in planning D-Day in World War II; an exhibit on escape and evasion techniques in wartime; the tales of spies of recent times, told by the CIA and FBI agents involved in identifying them; and a mockup of a 21st-century intelligence operations center.

The International Spy Museum has been immensely popular since its 2002 opening, which often means long lines for admission. Consider ordering advance tickets for next-day or future-date tours through Ticketmaster (© **202/432-SEAT**), which you can pick up at the Will Call desk inside the museum. You can also purchase advance tickets, including those for later in the day, at the box office.

800 F St. NW (at 8th St. NW). © **866/779-6873** or 202/393-7798. www.spymuseum.org. Admission $13 adults (ages 12–65), $12 for seniors and college students, $10 for children 5–11. Mar 20–Oct 31 daily 10am–8pm; Nov 1–Mar 19 daily 10am–6pm; museum closes 1 hr. after last admission. Closed Thanksgiving, Dec 25, and Jan 1. Metro: Gallery Place/Chinatown or National Archive/Navy Memorial.

Marian Koshland Science Museum 🅡   The National Academy of Sciences operates this museum, which was conceived of by molecular biologist Daniel Koshland in memory of his wife, the immunologist and molecular biologist, Marian Koshland, who died in 1997. The museum opened in April 2004 in the heart of downtown D.C. Recommended for children over 13, and especially for those with a scientific bent, the museum presents state-of-the-art exhibits that explore the complexities of science. Three exhibits currently on show are "Wonders of Science," which includes animations of groundbreaking research and an introductory film about the nature of science; "Global Warming Facts and Our Future"; and "Putting DNA to Work," which covers the details of current approaches to DNA sequencing, from tracking the origins of SARS to criminal forensics.

6th and E sts. NW. ℂ 202/334-1201. www.koshlandsciencemuseum.org. Admission $5 adults, $3 children 5–18 and seniors (65 and up). Wed–Mon 10am–6pm. Closed Tues and Thanksgiving, Dec 25, and Jan 1. Metro: Gallery Place/Chinatown or Judiciary Square.

National Museum of Women in the Arts   Eighteen years after it opened, this stunning collection remains the foremost museum in the world dedicated to celebrating "the contribution of women to the history of art."

Since its opening, the collection has grown to more than 3,000 works by more than 800 artists, including Rosa Bonheur, Frida Kahlo, Helen Frankenthaler, Barbara Hepworth, Georgia O'Keeffe, Camille Claudel, Mary Cassatt, Elaine de Kooning, Käthe Kollwitz, and many other lesser known artists from earlier centuries.

1250 New York Ave. NW (at 13th St.). ℂ 800/222-7270 or 202/783-5000. www. nmwa.org. $8 adults, $6 students over 18 with ID and seniors over 60; free for 18 and under. Mon–Sat 10am–5pm; Sun noon–5pm. Closed Thanksgiving, Dec 25, and Jan 1. Metro: Metro Center (13th St. exit).

Phillips Collection ⟡⟡   Conceived as "a museum of modern art and its sources," this intimate establishment, occupying an elegant 1890s Georgian Revival mansion and a more youthful wing, houses the exquisite collection of Duncan and Marjorie Phillips, avid collectors and proselytizers of modernism. Carpeted rooms with leaded- and stained-glass windows, oak paneling, plush chairs and sofas, and fireplaces establish a comfortable, homelike setting. Today the collection includes more than 2,500 works, including superb Daumier, Dove, and Bonnard paintings; some splendid small Vuillards; five van Goghs; Renoir's *Luncheon of the Boating Party;* seven Cézannes; and six works by Georgia O'Keeffe. Ingres, Delacroix, Manet, El Greco, Goya, Corot, Constable, Courbet, Giorgione, and Chardin are among the forerunners of modernism represented. Modern notables include Rothko, Hopper, Kandinsky, Matisse, Klee, Degas, Rouault, Picasso, and many others.

1600 21st St. NW (at Q St.). ℂ 202/387-2151. www.phillipscollection.org. Admission Sat–Sun $8 adults, $6 students and seniors, free for children 18 and under; contribution accepted Tues–Fri. Special exhibits may require an additional fee. Tues–Sat 10am–5pm (Thurs until 8:30pm); Sun noon–5pm. Free tours Wed and Sat at 2pm. Closed Jan 1, July 4th, Thanksgiving, and Dec 25. Metro: Dupont Circle (Q St. exit).

7 Other Attractions

Arlington National Cemetery ⟡⟡   Upon arrival, head over to the **Visitor Center,** where you can view exhibits, pick up a detailed map, use the restrooms (there are no others until you get to Arlington

House), and purchase a **Tourmobile ticket** ($6 per adult, $3 for children 3–11), which allows you to stop at all major sites in the cemetery and then reboard whenever you like. Service is continuous and the narrated commentary is informative; this is the only guided tour of the cemetery offered. If you've got plenty of stamina, consider doing part or all of the tour on foot. Remember as you go that this is a memorial frequented not just by tourists but also by those attending burial services or visiting the graves of beloved relatives and friends who are buried here.

This shrine occupies approximately 612 acres on the high hills overlooking the capital from the west side of the Memorial Bridge. It honors many national heroes and more than 260,000 war dead, veterans, and dependents. Cemetery highlights include **The Tomb of the Unknowns,** containing the unidentified remains of service members from both world wars, the Korean War, and, until 1997, the Vietnam War; **Arlington House** (© **703/235-1530;** www.nps.gov/arho), whose structure was begun in 1802, by Martha and George Washington's grandson, George Washington Parke Custis (actually, Custis was George Washington's adopted grandson); **Pierre Charles L'Enfant's grave;** and the **Gravesite of John Fitzgerald Kennedy.**

In 1997, the **Women in Military Service for America Memorial** (© **800/222-2294** or 703/533-1155; www.womensmemorial.org) was added to Arlington Cemetery to honor the more than 1.8 million women who have served in the armed forces from the American Revolution to the present. The impressive new memorial lies just beyond the gated entrance to the cemetery, a 3-minute walk from the Visitor Center.

Just across the Memorial Bridge from the base of the Lincoln Memorial. © **703/607-8000.** www.arlingtoncemetery.org. Free admission. Apr–Sept daily 8am–7pm; Oct–Mar daily 8am–5pm. Metro: Arlington National Cemetery. Parking is $1.25 an hour for the 1st 3 hr., $2 an hour thereafter. The cemetery is also accessible via Tourmobile.

John F. Kennedy Center for the Performing Arts ✇

Opened in 1971, the Kennedy Center is both the national performing arts center and a memorial to John F. Kennedy. Set on 17 acres overlooking the Potomac, the striking facility, designed by noted architect Edward Durell Stone, encompasses an opera house, a concert hall, two stage theaters, a theater lab, and a film theater. The best way to see the Kennedy Center is to take a free 50-minute guided tour (which takes you through some restricted areas).

2700 F St. NW (at New Hampshire Ave. NW and Rock Creek Pkwy.). © **800/444-1324,** or 202/467-4600 for information or tickets. www.kennedy-center.org. Free

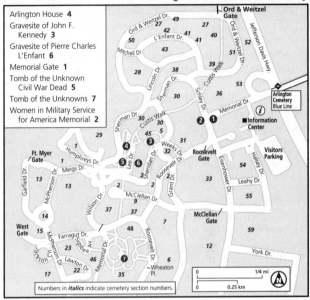

Arlington House **4**

Gravesite of John F.
Kennedy **3**

Gravesite of Pierre Charles
L'Enfant **6**

Memorial Gate **1**

Tomb of the Unknown
Civil War Dead **5**

Tomb of the Unknowns **7**

Women in Military Service
for America Memorial **2**

Numbers in *italics* indicate cemetery section numbers.

admission. Daily 10am–midnight. Free guided tours Mon–Fri 10am–5pm; Sat–Sun 10am–1pm. Metro: Foggy Bottom (there's a free shuttle service between the station and the center, running every 15 min. Mon–Fri 9:45am–midnight, Sat 10am–midnight, and Sun noon–midnight). Bus: 80 from Metro Center.

Union Station   In Washington, D.C., even the very train station where you arrive is an attraction. When it opened in 1907, Union Station was the largest train station in the world. The Ionic colonnades outside were fashioned from white granite. The facade contains 100 eagles. In the front of the building, a replica of the Liberty Bell and a monumental statue of Columbus hold sway. Six carved fixtures over the entranceway represent Fire, Electricity, Freedom, Imagination, Agriculture, and Mechanics. You enter the station through graceful 50-foot Constantine arches and walk across an expanse of white-marble flooring. The **Main Hall** is a massive rectangular room with a 96-foot barrel-vaulted ceiling and a balcony adorned with 36 Augustus Saint-Gaudens sculptures of Roman legionnaires. Off the Main Hall is the **East Hall,** shimmering with scagliola marble walls and columns, and stunning murals of classical scenes inspired by ancient Pompeiian art.

Today, Union Station is once again a vibrant entity patronized by locals and visitors alike, all 25 million of them yearly. About 120 retail and food shops on three levels offer a wide array of merchandise. The sky lit **Main Concourse,** which extends the entire length of the station, is the primary shopping area as well as a ticketing and baggage facility. A nine-screen **cinema complex** lies on the lower level, across from the Food Court. You could spend half a day here shopping, or about 20 minutes touring.

50 Massachusetts Ave. NE. *C* **202/371-9441.** www.unionstationdc.com. Free admission. Daily 24 hr. Shops Mon–Sat 10am–9pm; Sun noon–6pm. Parking: $1 for 2 hr. with store or restaurant's stamped validation; for 2–3 hr., you pay $6 with validated ticket. Without validation, parking rates start at $5 for the 1st hr., and go up from there. Metro: Union Station.

Washington National Cathedral *C*   Pierre L'Enfant's 1791 plan for the capital city included "a great church for national purposes," but possibly because of early America's fear of mingling church and state, more than a century elapsed before the foundation for Washington National Cathedral was laid. Its actual name is the Cathedral Church of St. Peter and St. Paul. The church is Episcopal, but it has no local congregation and seeks to serve the entire nation as a house of prayer for all people.

A church of this magnitude—it's the sixth largest cathedral in the world, and the second largest in the U.S.—took a long time to build. The foundation stone was laid in 1907 using the mallet with which George Washington set the Capitol cornerstone. Construction was interrupted by both world wars and by periods of financial difficulty. The cathedral was completed with the placement of the final stone on September 29, 1990, 83 years (to the day) after it was begun.

English Gothic in style (with several distinctly 20th-c. innovations, such as a stained-glass window commemorating the flight of *Apollo 11* and containing a piece of moon rock), the cathedral is built in the shape of a cross, complete with flying buttresses and 110 gargoyles. It is, along with the Capitol and the Washington Monument, among the dominant structures on the Washington skyline.

The best way to explore the cathedral is to take a 30- to 45-minute **guided tour;** they leave continually from the west end of the nave. You can also walk through on your own, using a self-guiding brochure available in several languages.

Massachusetts and Wisconsin aves. NW (entrance on Wisconsin Ave.). *C* **202/ 537-6200.** www.cathedral.org/cathedral. Donation $3 adults, $2 seniors, $1 children. Cathedral Mon–Fri 10am–5:30pm; Sat 10am–4:30pm; Sun 8am–6:30pm; May 1 to Labor Day, the nave level stays open Mon–Fri until 8pm. Gardens daily until dusk. Regular tours Mon–Sat 10–11:30am and 12:45–3:15pm; Sun 12:45–2:30pm. No tours on Palm Sunday, Easter, Thanksgiving, Dec 25, or during services. Metro: Tenleytown, with a 20-min. walk. Bus: Any N bus up Massachusetts Ave. from Dupont Circle or any 30-series bus along Wisconsin Ave. This is a stop on the Old Town Trolley Tour.

8 Gardens & Parks

GARDENS

Enid A. Haupt Garden   Named for its donor, a noted supporter of horticultural projects, this stunning garden presents elaborate flower beds and borders, plant-filled turn-of-the-20th-century urns, 1870s cast-iron furnishings, and lush baskets hung from reproduction 19th-century lampposts. Although on ground level, the garden is actually a 4.2-acre rooftop garden above the subterranean Ripley Center and the Sackler and African Art museums. An **"Island Garden"** near the Sackler Gallery, entered via a 9-foot moon gate, has benches backed by English boxwoods set under the canopy of weeping cherry trees.

10th St. and Independence Ave. SW. ✆ 202/357-2700. Free admission. Late May to Aug daily 7am–9:15pm; Sept to mid-May daily 7am–5:45pm. Closed Dec 25. Metro: Smithsonian.

United States Botanic Garden The Botanic Garden reopened in late 2001 after a major, 5-year renovation. In its new incarnation, the grand conservatory devotes half of its space to exhibits that focus on the importance of plants to people, and half to exhibits that focus on ecology and the evolutionary biology of plants. The conservatory holds 4,000 living species; 26,000 plants; a high-walled enclosure, called "The Jungle," of palms, ferns, and vines; an Orchid Room; and, outside the conservatory, a First Ladies Water Garden, formal rose garden, and a lawn terrace. You'll also find a Meditation Garden and gardens created especially for children.

245 1st St. ✆ 202/225-8333. www.usbg.gov. Free admission. Daily 10am–5pm. Metro: Federal Center SW.

PARKS
POTOMAC PARK

West and East Potomac parks, their 720 riverside acres divided by the Tidal Basin, are most famous for their spring display of **cherry blossoms.** So much attention is lavished on Washington's cherry blossoms that the National Park Service devotes a Web page to the subject at **www.nps.gov/nacc/cherry**. You can access this site to find out forecasts for the blooms and assorted other details. You can also call the National Park Service (✆ **202/485-9880**) for information.

To get to the Tidal Basin by car (*not* recommended in cherry-blossom season), get on Independence Avenue and follow the signs near the Lincoln Memorial that show you where to turn for parking and the FDR Memorial. If you're walking, cross Independence Avenue where it intersects with West Basin Drive, and follow the path to the Tidal Basin. There is no convenient Metro stop near here.

West Potomac Park encompasses Constitution Gardens; the Vietnam Veterans, Korean War Veterans, Lincoln, Jefferson, and FDR memorials; a small island where ducks live; and the Reflecting Pool (see "The Major Memorials" [p. 113] for full descriptions of the memorials). It has 1,628 cherry trees bordering the Tidal Basin. The blossoming of the cherry trees is the focal point of a 2-week-long celebration. The trees bloom for a little less than 2 weeks beginning sometime between March 20 and April 17; April 4 is the average date. Planning your trip around the blooming of the cherry blossoms is an iffy proposition—one good rain and those blossoms are gone.

East Potomac Park has 1,681 cherry trees in 11 varieties. The park also has picnic grounds, tennis courts, three golf courses, a large swimming pool, and biking and hiking paths by the water.

ROCK CREEK PARK

Created in 1890, **Rock Creek Park** ✵ (**www.nps.gov/rocr**) is a 1,750-acre valley within the District of Columbia. Extending 12 miles from the Potomac River to the Maryland border, it's one of the biggest and finest city parks in the nation. Parts of it are still wild; it's not unusual to see a deer scurrying through the woods in more remote sections.

9 Organized Tours

ON FOOT

TourDC, Walking Tours of Georgetown, Dupont Circle & Embassy Row (℅ **301/588-8999;** www.tourdc.com) conducts 90-minute ($12) walking tours of Georgetown, telling about the neighborhood's history up to the present and taking you past the homes of notable residents.

Guided Walking Tours of Washington ✵ (℅ **301/294-9514;** www.dcsightseeing.com) offers 2-hour walks through the streets of Georgetown, Adams-Morgan, and other locations, guided by author/historian Anthony S. Pitch. Inquire about private tours. Rates are $15 per person.

BY BUS

TOURMOBILE   Best-known and least expensive, **Tourmobile Sightseeing** (© **888/868-7707** or 202/554-5100; www.tour mobile.com) is a good choice if you're looking for an easy-on/ easy-off tour of major sites. The comfortable sightseeing trams travel to as many as 24 attractions (the company changes its schedule and number of stops, depending on whether sites are open for public tours), including Arlington National Cemetery. Tourmobile is the only narrated sightseeing shuttle tour authorized by the National Park Service.

BY BOAT

Spirit of Washington Cruises, Pier 4 at Sixth and Water streets SW (© **866/211-3811** or 202/554-8000; www.spiritcruises.com; Metro: Waterfront), offers evening dinner, lunch, brunch, and moonlight dance cruises, as well as a half-day excursion to Mount Vernon and back. Lunch and dinner cruises include a 40-minute high-energy musical revue. Prices start at $40 for a lunch excursion and $70 for a dinner cruise. Call to make reservations.

The **Capitol River Cruise**'s *Nightingale I* and *Nightingale II* (© **800/405-5511** or 301/460-7447; www.capitolrivercruises.com) are historic 65-foot steel riverboats that can accommodate up to 90 people. The *Nightingale*'s narrated jaunts depart Georgetown's Washington Harbour every hour on the hour, from noon to 9pm, April through October (the 9pm outing is offered in summer months only). The 50-minute tour travels past the monuments and memorials as you head to National Airport and back. A snack bar sells light refreshments, beer, wine, and sodas; or you can bring your own picnic. The price is $10 per adult, $5 per child 3 to 12. To get here, take Metro to Foggy Bottom and then take the Georgetown Metro Connection Shuttle or walk into Georgetown, following Pennsylvania Avenue, which becomes M Street. Turn left on 31st Street NW, which dead-ends at the Washington Harbour complex.

6

Shopping

Washington-area stores are usually open daily from 10am to 5 or 6pm Monday through Saturday, with one late night (usually Thurs) when hours extend to 9pm. Sunday hours are usually from noon to 5 or 6pm. Exceptions are the malls, which are open late nightly, and antiques stores and art galleries, which tend to keep their own hours. Play it safe and call ahead if there's a store you really want to get to.

Sales tax on merchandise is 5.75% in the District, 5% in Maryland, and 4.5% in Virginia.

Most gift, arts, and crafts stores, including those at the Smithsonian museums, will handle shipping for you; clothes stores generally do not.

If you're a true bargain hunter, scope out the *Washington Post* website (**www.washingtonpost.com**) in advance of your trip to see which stores are having sales. Once you get to the *Post*'s home page, hit "Arts and Living" at the top of your screen, click on "Fashion and Beauty," and then click on "Sales and Bargains," a column that's updated weekly.

ANTIQUES

Brass Knob Architectural Antiques   When old homes and office buildings are demolished in the name of progress, these savvy salvage merchants spirit away saleable treasures, from chandeliers to wrought-iron fencing. 2311 18th St. NW. © 202/332-3370. www.thebrass knob.com. Metro: Woodley Park or Dupont Circle. There's a 2nd location across the street called **Brass Knob's Back Doors Warehouse**, 2329 Champlain St. NW (© 202/265-0587).

cherry   This is an antiques store, all right, but as its name suggests, it's a little offbeat. Expect affordable eclectic furnishings and decorative arts, and lots of mirrors and sconces. 1526 Wisconsin Ave. NW. © 202/342-3600. Metro: Foggy Bottom, then walk or take the Georgetown Metro Connection shuttle.

Gore-Dean   Though its offerings include some American pieces, the store specializes in 18th- and 19th-century European furnishings, decorative accessories, paintings, prints, and porcelains. Recently added are a lampshade shop, garden shop, and framing studio. 1525 Wisconsin Ave. NW. ℂ 202/625-9199. www.gore-dean.com. Metro: Foggy Bottom, then take the Georgetown Metro Connection.

ART GALLERIES

Art galleries abound in Washington, but especially in the Dupont Circle and Georgetown neighborhoods, and along 7th Street downtown.

For a complete listing of local galleries, get your hands on a copy of **"Galleries,"** a monthly guide to major galleries and their shows; the guide is available free at many hotel concierge desks and at many galleries.

DUPONT CIRCLE

For all galleries listed below, the closest Metro stop is Dupont Circle.

Elizabeth Roberts Gallery   A 20-something American University grad opened this gallery in March 2003 to showcase the works of local artists working in different media, from pottery to prints. The gallery has quickly caught the eye of critics. 2108 R St. NW. ℂ 202/328-0828. www.elizabethroberts.net.

Kathleen Ewing Gallery   This gallery features vintage and contemporary photography. 1609 Connecticut Ave. NW. ℂ 202/328-0955. www.kathleenewinggallery.com.

GEORGETOWN

For all the galleries listed below, the closest stop is Foggy Bottom, with a transfer to the Georgetown Metro Connection bus to get you the rest of the way.

Addison/Ripley Fine Art   This gallery represents both nationally and regionally recognized artists, from the 19th century to the present; works include paintings, sculpture, photography, and fine arts. 1670 Wisconsin Ave. NW. ℂ 202/338-5180. www.addisonripleyfineart.com.

Govinda Gallery   This place, a block from the campus of Georgetown University, generates a lot of media coverage, since it often shows artwork created by famous names and features photographs of celebrities. My husband and I wandered in last winter, and we had the gallery to ourselves as we enjoyed the photographs of a young Bob Dylan, taken by the renowned Barry Feinstein. 1227 34th St. NW. ℂ 202/333-1180. www.govindagallery.com.

SEVENTH STREET ARTS CORRIDOR

To get here, take Metro to either the Archives/Navy Memorial (Blue–Orange Line) or Gallery Place/Chinatown/MCI Center (Red–Yellow Line) stations.

406 Art Galleries Several first-rate art galleries, some of them interlopers from Dupont Circle, occupy this historic building, with its 16-foot-high ceilings and spacious rooms. Look for the **David Adamson Gallery** (*(C)* 202/628-0257; www.adamsoneditions. com), which showcases digital printmaking and photography and the works of contemporary artists, like local Kevin MacDonald, as well as national and international artists Jim Dine, Chuck Close, and William Wegman. The **Touchstone Gallery** (*(C)* 202/347-2787; www.touchstonegallery.com), on the second floor, is a self-run co-op of 35 to 40 artists, each of whom has at least one work on display at all times; and the third floor **Eklektikos Gallery of Art** (*(C)* 202/783-8444; www.eklektikos.com) represents regional, national, and international artists. 406 7th St. NW, between D and E sts.

Zenith Gallery Across the street from the 406 Group, the 27-year-old Zenith shows diverse works by contemporary artists—most American, about half of whom are local. You can get a good deal here, paying anywhere from $50 to $50,000 for a piece. Among the things you'll find are annual humor shows, neon exhibits, realism, abstract expressionism, and landscapes. 413 7th St. NW. *(C)* 202/783-2963. www.zenithgallery.com.

BOOKS

Barnes & Noble This wonderful three-story shop in Georgetown has sizable software, travel book, and children's title sections. A cafe on the second level sometimes hosts concerts. 3040 M St. NW. *(C)* 202/965-9880. www.barnesandnoble.com. Metro: Foggy Bottom, then take the Georgetown Metro Connection shuttle. Other area locations include 555 12th St. NW (*(C)* 202/347-0176) and 4801 Bethesda Ave., in Bethesda, Maryland (*(C)* 301/986-1761).

Borders With its overwhelming array of books, records, videos, and magazines, this outpost of the expanding chain has taken over the town. Many hardcover bestsellers are 30% off. The store often hosts performances by local musicians. 1800 L St. NW. *(C)* 202/466-4999. www.borders.com. Metro: Farragut North. Other Borders stores in the District include 5333 Wisconsin Ave. NW (*(C)* 202/686-8270), in upper northwest D.C.; and 600 14th St. NW (*(C)* 202/737-1385).

Chapters, A Literary Bookstore Chapters is strong in new and backlisted fiction (no discounts, though), and is always hosting author readings. Tea is always available, and on Friday afternoons they break out the sherry and cookies. 445 11th St. NW (inside building at 1001 Pennsylvania Ave.). *(C)* 202/737-5553. www.chaptersliterary.com. Metro: Archives-Navy Memorial or Federal Triangle.

Kramerbooks & Afterwords Café *(Finds)*   The first bookstore/cafe in Washington, maybe in the country, this place has launched countless romances. It's jammed and often noisy, stages live music Wednesday through Saturday evenings, and is open all night on weekends. Paperback fiction takes up most of its inventory, but the store carries a little of everything. No discounts. 1517 Connecticut Ave. NW. ℂ 202/387-1400. www.kramers.com. Metro: Dupont Circle.

Olsson's Books and Records   This 33-year-old independent, quality bookstore chain has about 60,000 to 70,000 books on its shelves. Members of its helpful staff know what they're talking about and will order books they don't have in stock. Some discounts are given on books, tapes, and CDs, and their regular prices are pretty good, too.

Besides this 7th St. NW store, there is one other Olsson's bookstore in the District at 1307 19th St. NW (ℂ 202/785-1133). 418 7th St. NW. ℂ 202/638-7610. www.olssons.com. Metro: Gallery Place or Archive-Navy Memorial.

Trover Shop   This family-owned and -operated shop is close to 50 years old, and is the only general-interest bookstore on Capitol Hill; specializations include political selections and magazines. The store discounts 30% on the *Washington Post* hardcover fiction and nonfiction bestsellers. 221 Pennsylvania Ave. SE. ℂ 202/547-BOOK. www.trover.com. Metro: Capitol South.

CAMERAS & FILM DEVELOPING

Ritz Camera Centers   Ritz sells camera equipment for the average photographer and offers 1-hour film processing. Call for other locations; there are many throughout the area. 1740 Pennsylvania Ave. NW. ℂ 202/466-3470. www.ritzpix.com. Metro: Farragut West.

CRAFTS

A mano   Owner Adam Mahr frequently forages in Europe and returns with the unique handmade, imported French and Italian ceramics, linens, and other decorative accessories that you'll covet here. 1677 Wisconsin Ave. NW. ℂ 202/298-7200. www.amanoinc.com. Metro: Foggy Bottom, then take the Georgetown Metro Connection shuttle.

American Studio Plus   This store features exquisite contemporary handcrafted American ceramics and jewelry, plus international objets d'art. 2906 M St. NW. ℂ 202/965-3273. Metro: Foggy Bottom, then take the Georgetown Metro Connection shuttle.

Emergency Shopping

You've just arrived in town, but your luggage hasn't—the airline lost it. Or you're about to depart for home or another destination and you notice that the zipper to your suitcase is broken. Or you've arrived at your hotel all in one piece, only to discover you've forgotten something essential: underwear, allergy medicine, an umbrella. What's a lonesome traveler to do? If you find yourself in a similar situation, one of the following might be able to come to your rescue.

CVS: This is Washington's main pharmacy and essentials chain. Among the items sold at CVS stores are pantyhose, over-the-counter and prescription medicines, toys, greeting cards, wrapping paper and ribbon, magazines, film and 1-hour photo developing, batteries, candy, some refrigerated food such as milk and orange juice, and office supplies. The stores are ubiquitous, so chances are you'll find one near you. Two centrally located branches are a 24-hour store at 801 7th St. NW (© **202/842-3567** or 202/842-3627 for the pharmacy; www.cvs.com; Metro: Gallery Place/MCI Center) and a store open until 10pm at 435 8th St. NW (© **202/ 783-4292** or 202/783-4293 for the pharmacy; Metro: Gallery Place/MCI Center or Archives/Navy Memorial).

Indian Craft Shop *(Finds* The Indian Craft Shop has represented authentic Native American artisans since 1938, selling their handwoven rugs and handcrafted baskets, jewelry, figurines, paintings, pottery, and other items. You need a photo ID to enter the building. Use the C Street entrance, which is the only one open to the public. Department of the Interior, 1849 C St. NW, Room 1043. © 202/208-4056. Weekdays and the third Sat of each month. www.indiancraftshop.com. Metro: Farragut West or Foggy Bottom.

FARMER'S & FLEA MARKETS

Dupont Circle FreshFarm Market *(Kids* Fresh flowers, produce, eggs, and cheeses are for sale here. The market also features kids' activities and guest appearances by chefs and owners of some of Washington's best restaurants: Bis, Vidalia, Restaurant Nora, Tosca, and 1789. Held Sunday from 9am to 1pm, rain or shine, year-round. The FreshFarm Market organization stages other farmers

Doudaklian Leather: Ever since a little shop in Baltimore sewed up my suitcase a few short hours before my husband and I were about to fly to London on our honeymoon (20 years ago), I've had a soft spot for shops like this one, which not only sells major brands of luggage, but repairs them as well—and quickly—if staff members are able. Doudaklian, at 921 19th St. NW (© 202/293-0443; Metro: Farragut West), is open Monday through Saturday.

Hecht's: This old reliable is the only department store located downtown. And though it's been around a while, the store continually updates its merchandise to keep up with the times. Run here if you need cosmetics, clothes (for men, women, and children), shoes (but not for children), electronics, appliances, lingerie, luggage, raincoats, and countless other need-immediately goods. Located at 1201 G St. NW (© 202/628-6661; www.hechts.com; Metro: Metro Center), it's open daily.

Metro stations: If it starts raining and you're scrambling to find an umbrella, look no further than your closest Metro station, where vendors are at the ready selling umbrellas and other handy things.

markets on other days around town; go to www.freshfarmmarkets.org for locations, dates and times. On 20th St. NW, between Q St. and Massachusetts Ave., and in the adjacent Riggs Bank parking lot. © 202/362-8889. Metro: Dupont Circle, Q St. exit.

Eastern Market *Value*   This is the one everyone knows about, even if they've never been here. In continuous operation since 1873, this Capitol Hill institution holds an inside bazaar Tuesday through Sunday, where greengrocers, butchers, bakers, farmers, artists, craftspeople, florists, and other merchants sell their wares. Saturday morning is the best time to go. On Sunday, outside stalls become a flea market. Operates Tuesday through Saturday from 7am to 6pm, Sunday from 10am to 5pm. 225 7th St. SE, between North Carolina Ave. and C St. SE. © 202/544-0083. www.easternmarket.net. Metro: Eastern Market.

Georgetown Flea Market *Finds*   Grab a coffee at Starbucks across the lane and get ready to barter. The Georgetown Flea Market is frequented by all types of Washingtonians looking for a good deal—they often get it—on antiques, painted furniture, vintage clothing, and decorative garden urns. Nearly 100 vendors sell their wares here. Open year-round on Sunday from 9am to 5pm. In the Hardy Middle School parking lot bordering Wisconsin Ave., between S and T sts. NW. ✆ 202/775-FLEA. www.georgetownfleamarket.com. Metro: Foggy Bottom, then take the Georgetown Metro Connection shuttle.

MEN'S CLOTHING

Brooks Brothers   Brooks sells traditional menswear, as well as the fine line of Peal's English shoes. This store made the news as the place where Monica Lewinsky bought a tie for President Clinton. It also sells an extensive line of women's clothing. 1201 Connecticut Ave. NW. ✆ 202/659-4650. www.brooksbrothers.com. Metro: Dupont Circle or Farragut North. Other locations are at Potomac Mills (✆ 703/491-2950), at National Airport (✆ 703/417-1071), and at 5504 Wisconsin Ave., in Chevy Chase, MD (✆ 301/654-8202).

Thomas Pink   For those who like beautifully made, bright-colored shirts, this branch of the London-based high-end establishment should please. The store also sells ties, boxer shorts, women's shirts, cufflinks, and other accessories. 1127 Connecticut Ave. NW (inside the Mayflower Hotel). ✆ 202/223-5390. www.thomaspink.com. Metro: Farragut North.

Urban Outfitters   For the latest in casual attire, from fatigue pants to tube tops. The shop has a floor of women's clothes, a floor of men's clothes, as well as housewares, inflatable chairs, books, cards, and candles. 3111 M St. NW. ✆ 202/342-1012. www.urbn.com. Metro: Foggy Bottom, then take the Georgetown Metro Connection shuttle.

MUSIC

Tower Records   When you need a record at 10 minutes to midnight on Christmas Eve, you go to Tower. This large, funky store, across the street from George Washington University, has a wide choice of records, cassettes, and CDs in every category—but the prices are high. 2000 Pennsylvania Ave. NW. ✆ 202/223-3900. www.tower.com. Metro: Foggy Bottom.

WINE & SPIRITS

Barmy Wine and Liquor   Located near the White House, this store sells it all, with a special emphasis on fine wines and rare cordials. 1912 L St. NW. ✆ 202/833-8730. Metro: Farragut North.

WOMEN'S CLOTHING

Betsey Johnson   New York's flamboyant flower-child designer personally decorated the bubble-gum pink walls in her Georgetown shop. Her sexy, offbeat play-dress-up styles are great party and club clothes for the young and the still skinny young at heart. This is the only Betsey Johnson store in D.C. 1319 Wisconsin Ave. NW. © 202/338-4090. www.betseyjohnson.com. Metro: Foggy Bottom, then take the Georgetown Metro Connection shuttle.

Betsy Fisher   A walk past the store is all it takes to know that this shop is a tad different. Its windows and racks show off whimsically feminine fashions by new American designers. 1223 Connecticut Ave. NW. © 202/785-1975. www.betsyfisher.com. Metro: Dupont Circle.

Zara   This cheery store is an outpost of a popular chain started in Spain, but with many locations in Europe. Clothes are both dress-up and casual, but all trendy. A sprinkling of coats is also found here, when the season calls for it. My 17-year-old loves Zara. 1234-44 Wisconsin Ave. NW. © 202/944-9797. www.zara.com. Metro: Foggy Bottom, then take the Georgetown Metro Connection Shuttle.

7

Washington, D.C., After Dark

Washingtonians can't get enough drama, it seems: All of our major theaters are expanding, big time. The Kennedy Center for the Performing Arts, the Shakespeare Theatre, and Arena Stage—all are undergoing changes so extensive that they won't be complete for years—in the case of the Kennedy Center, a decade. These theaters remain open throughout the various phases of construction, continuing to draw you to enjoy high entertainment.

Washington's bars, nightclubs, concert halls, dance clubs, and amphitheaters proliferate, so read over the listings that follow to see which forms of amusement most appeal. For schedules of events—from live music and theater to children's programs and flower shows—check the Friday "Weekend" section of the *Washington Post,* or browse the *Post*'s nightlife information at **www.washington post.com**. The *City Paper,* available free at restaurants, bookstores, and other places around town, and at www.washingtoncitypaper.com, is another good source.

TICKETS

TICKETplace, Washington's only discount day-of-show ticket outlet has one location: 407 7th St. NW (*(C)* **202/TICKETS** [842-5387]; www.ticketplace.org; Metro: Gallery Place/MCI Center or Archives/ Navy Memorial). On the day of performance (except Sun–Mon; see below), you can buy half-price tickets (American Express, Discover, MasterCard, and Visa debit and credit cards are accepted; cash and traveler's checks are not accepted) to performances with tickets still available at most major Washington-area theaters and concert halls, as well as for performances of opera, ballet, and other events. TICKET-place is open Tuesday through Friday from 11am to 6pm and Saturday from 10am to 5pm; half-price tickets for Sunday and Monday shows are sold on Saturday. Although tickets are half-price, there's a service charge of 12% of the full face value of each ticket.

Tickets are available online Tuesday through Friday, between noon and 4pm. Again, the tickets sold are for same-day performances, at half-price plus the per-ticket service charge (which for online sales is 17% of the full face value of the ticket). You must pay by credit card (MasterCard or Visa only), then pick up the tickets at the "Will Call" booth of the theater you're attending; bring your credit card and a photo ID. TICKETplace is a service of the Cultural Alliance of Washington, in partnership with the Kennedy Center, the *Washington Post,* and Ticketmaster.

You can buy full-price tickets for most performances in town through **Ticketmaster** (© 202/432-7328; www.ticketmaster.com) if you're willing to pay a hefty service charge. Purchase tickets to Washington theatrical, musical, and other events before you leave home by going online or by calling © **800/551-SEAT.**

1 The Performing Arts

THE TOP THEATERS

Arena Stage   This outpost on the unattractive Washington waterfront is worth seeking out, despite its poor location. (Dine at a downtown restaurant, then drive or take a taxi here; or you can take Metro, but be careful walking the block or so to the theater.)

Founded by the brilliant Zelda Fichandler in 1950, the Arena Stage is home to one of the oldest acting ensembles in the nation. Several works nurtured here have moved to Broadway, and many graduates have gone on to commercial stardom, including Ned Beatty, James Earl Jones, and Jane Alexander. The excellence of Arena productions has brought the theater much success, to the extent that a major expansion is planned; construction is set to start mid- to late 2005, and may result in productions being staged at alternate locations.

Arena presents eight productions annually on two stages: the **Fichandler** (a theater-in-the-round) and the smaller, fan-shaped **Kreeger.** In addition, the Arena houses the **Old Vat,** a space used for new play readings and special productions. 1101 6th St. SW (at Maine Ave.). © 202/488-3300. www.arenastage.org. Tickets $40–$66; discounts available for students, seniors, people with disabilities, and groups. Metro: Waterfront.

John F. Kennedy Center for the Performing Arts   This 34-year-old theater complex strives to be not just the hub of Washington's cultural and entertainment scene, but also a performing arts theater for the nation. It is constantly evolving, and right now that evolution involves an immense expansion, which will add two buildings to the 8-acre plaza in front of the center, and better connect the center to the rest of the city. The center lies between the Potomac River and a crisscross of major roadways, which makes it

Washington, D.C., After Dark

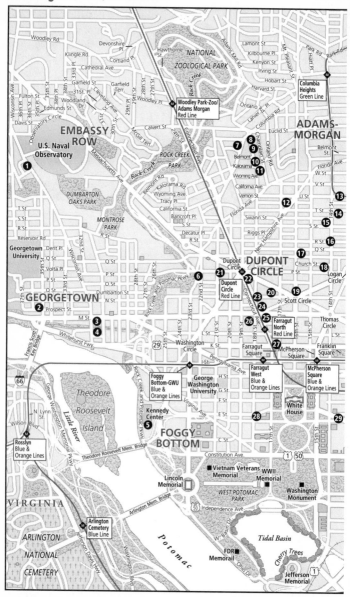

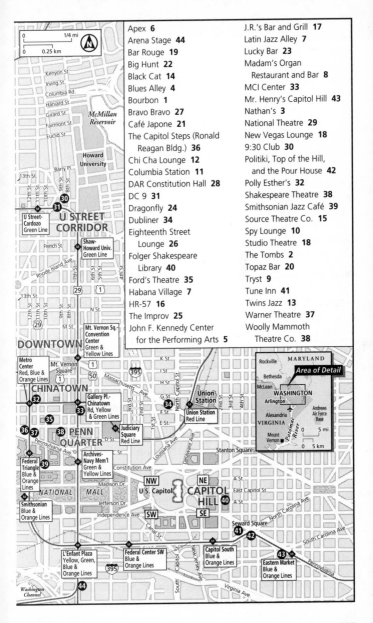

sound like it's easily accessible when, in fact, it is not, for its location actually isolates it from the rest of town. The center's performances, meanwhile, continue uninterrupted.

These are top-rated performances by the best ballet, opera, jazz, modern dance, musical, and theater companies in the world. The best costs the most, and you are likely to pay more for a ticket here than at any other theater in D.C.—from $14 for a children's play to more than $285 for a box seat on a Saturday night at the opera, although most ticket prices run in the $50 to $75 range. 2700 F St. NW (at New Hampshire Ave. NW and Rock Creek Pkwy.). *C* 800/444-1324 or 202/467-4600 for tickets and information. www.kennedy-center.org. 50% discounts are offered (for select performances) to students, seniors 65 and over, people with permanent disabilities, enlisted military personnel, and persons with fixed low incomes (call *C* 202/416-8340 for details). Garage parking $15. Metro: Foggy Bottom (though it's a fairly short walk, there's a free shuttle between the station and the Kennedy Center, departing every 15 min. Mon–Sat 9:45am–midnight, Sun noon–midnight). Bus: 80 from Metro Center.

National Theatre   The splendid Federal-style National Theatre is the oldest continuously operating theater in Washington (since 1835) and the third oldest in the nation. It's exciting just to see the stage on which Sarah Bernhardt, John Barrymore, Helen Hayes, and so many other notables have performed. The 1,672-seat National is the closest thing Washington has to a Broadway-style playhouse.

One thing that has never flagged at The National is its commitment to offering free programs: Saturday morning children's theater (puppets, clowns, magicians, dancers, and so on) and Monday night showcases of local performers September through May, plus free summer films. Call *C* **202/783-3372** for details. 1321 Pennsylvania Ave. NW. *C* 800/447-7400 or 202/628-6161 to charge tickets. www.national theatre.org. Tickets $30–$75; discounts available for students, seniors, military personnel, and people with disabilities. Metro: Metro Center.

Shakespeare Theatre   This is top-level theater, with superb acting. Try to snag tickets to a play here, for the productions are reliably outstanding. Season subscriptions claim many of the seats and the plays almost always sell out, so if you're interested in attending a play here, you'd better buy your tickets now. This internationally renowned classical ensemble company offers five plays, usually three Shakespearean and two modern classics each September-to-June season. 450 7th St. NW (between D and E sts.). *C* 202/547-1122. www. shakespearetheatre.org. Tickets $20–$66, $10 for standing-room tickets sold 1 hr.

before sold-out performances; discounts available for students, seniors, and groups. Metro: Archives–Navy Memorial or MCI Center/Gallery Place.

SMALLER THEATERS

The **Source Theatre Company,** 1835 14th St. NW, between S and T streets (© **202/462-1073;** www.sourcetheatre.com), is Washington's major producer of new plays. The **Studio Theatre,** 1333 P St. NW, at 14th Street (© **202/332-3300;** www.studiotheatre.org), showcases contemporary plays and nurtures Washington acting talent; the 2004–05 lineup marks the theater's 28th season, in expanded quarters. The **Woolly Mammoth Theatre Company** (© **202/393-3939;** www.woollymammoth.net), offers as many as six productions each year, specializing in new, offbeat plays. In the fall of 2004, the Woolly took up residence in its new 265-seat state-of-the-art facility, at 7th and D sts. NW, in downtown Washington, just down the street from the Shakespeare Theatre.

In addition, I highly recommend productions staged at the **Folger Shakespeare Library,** 201 E. Capitol St. SE (© **202/544-7077;** www.folger.edu). Plays take place in the library's Elizabethan Theatre, which is styled after the inn-yard theater of Shakespeare's time. The theater is intimate and charming, the theater company is remarkably good, and an evening spent here guarantees an absolutely marvelous experience. The Elizabethan Theatre is also the setting for musical performances, lectures, readings, and other events.

Finally, there's **Ford's Theatre,** 511 10th St. NW, between E and F streets (© **202/347-4833;** www.fordstheatre.org), the actual theater where, on the evening of April 14, 1865, actor John Wilkes Booth shot President Lincoln. Though popular among Washingtonians for its annual holiday performance of Dickens's *A Christmas Carol,* Ford's stages generally mediocre presentations, usually intertwined with American history themes.

INDOOR ARENAS & OUTDOOR PAVILIONS

When Madonna, U2, Britney Spears, or the Dixie Chicks come to town, they usually play at one of the huge indoor or outdoor arenas. The 20,600-seat **MCI Center,** 601 F St. NW, where it meets 7th Street (© **202/628-3200;** www.mcicenter.com), in the center of downtown, hosts plenty of concerts and also is Washington's premier indoor sports arena (home to the NBA Wizards, the WNBA Mystics, the NHL Capitals, and Georgetown NCAA basketball).

My favorite summer setting for music is also the closest to D.C. and the easiest to get to: **Wolf Trap Farm Park for the Performing**

Arts, 1551 Trap Rd., Vienna, Virginia (© **703/255-1860;** www.wolftrap.org). The country's only national park devoted to the performing arts, Wolf Trap, 30 minutes by car from downtown D.C., offers performances by the National Symphony Orchestra (it's their summer home) and has hosted Lucinda Williams, Lyle Lovett, The Temptations, Ani DiFranco, and many others. Performances take place in the 7,000-seat Filene Center, about half of which is under the open sky. You can also buy cheaper lawn seats on the hill, which is sometimes the nicest way to go. Arrive early (the lawn opens 90 min. before the performance) and bring a blanket and a picnic dinner—it's a tradition. Wolf Trap also hosts a number of popular **festivals,** including an Irish music festival in May; the Louisiana Swamp Romp Cajun Festival and a jazz and blues weekend in June; and the International Children's Festival each September.

The **Carter Barron Amphitheater,** 16th Street and Colorado Avenue NW (© **202/426-0486**), is in Rock Creek Park, close to the Maryland border. This is the area's smallest outdoor venue, with 4,250 seats. Summer performances include a range of gospel, blues, and classical entertainment. The shows are usually free, but tickets are required. You can always count on Shakespeare: The **Shakespeare Theatre Free For All** takes place at the Carter Barron usually for 2 weeks in June, Tuesday through Sunday evenings; the free tickets are available the day of performance only, on a first-come, first-served basis (call © **202/334-4790** for details).

SMALLER AUDITORIUMS

DAR Constitution Hall, on 18th Street NW, between C and D streets (© **202/628-4780;** www.dar.org), is housed within a beautiful turn-of-the-20th-century Beaux Arts–style building and seats 3,746. Its excellent acoustics have supported an eclectic (and I mean eclectic) group of performers: Sting, the Buena Vista Social Club, John Hiatt, the Count Basie Orchestra, the Los Angeles Philharmonic, Lil Bow Wow, Ray Charles, Trisha Yearwood, The Strokes, and the *O Brother Where Art Thou?* tour.

The **Warner Theatre,** 1299 Pennsylvania Ave. NW, with the entrance on 13th Street, between E and F streets (© **202/783-4000;** www.warnertheatre.com), opened in 1924 as the Earle Theatre (a movie/vaudeville palace) and was restored to its neoclassical-style appearance in 1992 at a cost of $10 million. It's worth coming by just to see its ornately detailed interior. The 2,000-seat auditorium offers year-round entertainment, alternating dance performances (from Baryshnikov to the Washington Ballet's Christmas performance of *The Nutcracker*) and Broadway/off-Broadway shows *(Grease)* with headliner entertainment (Hanson, Bob Dylan).

2 The Club & Music Scene

COMEDY

The Capitol Steps *(Moments* This political satire troupe is made up of former Congressional staffers, equal-opportunity spoofers all, who poke endless fun through song and skits at politicians on both sides of the aisle, and at government goings-on in general. Shows take place in the Amphitheater, on the concourse level of the Ronald Reagan Building and International Trade Center, Friday and Saturday at 7:30pm. 1300 Pennsylvania Ave. NW (in the Ronald Reagan Building). © 202/312-1555. www.capsteps.com. Tickets $34. Metro: Federal Triangle.

The Improv The Improv features top performers on the national comedy club circuit as well as comic plays and one-person shows. *Saturday Night Live* performers David Spade, Chris Rock, and Adam Sandler have all played here, as have comedy bigs Ellen DeGeneres, Jerry Seinfeld, and Robin Williams. Shows are about 1½ hours long and include three comics (an emcee, a feature act, and a headliner). Show times are Sunday at 8pm, Tuesday through Thursday at 8:30pm, and Friday and Saturday at 8 and 10:30pm. 1140 Connecticut Ave. NW (between L and M sts.). © 202/296-7008. www.dcimprov.com. Cover $15–$35 Sun–Thurs, $15 Fri–Sat, plus a 2-item minimum. Metro: Farragut North.

POP/ROCK/RAVE/ALTERNATIVE

Black Cat This comfortable, low-key club draws a black-clad crowd to its concert hall, which features national, international, and local indie and alternative groups. The place is made for dancing, accommodating more than 600 people. Adjoining the hall is the Red Room Bar, a large, funky lounge with booths, tables, a red-leather sofa, pinball machines, a pool table, and a jukebox stocked with an eclectic collection. A college crowd collects on weekends, but you can count on seeing a 20- to 30-something bunch here most nights. Black Cat also hosts film screenings, poetry readings, and other quiet forms of entertainment in its ground floor room called "Backstage," and serves vegetarian food in its smoke-free cafe. The Red Room Bar is open until 2am Sunday through Thursday, and until 3am Friday and Saturday. Concerts take place 4 or 5 nights a week, beginning at about 8:30pm (call for details). 1811 14th St. NW (between S and T sts.). © 202/667-7960. www.blackcatdc.com. Cover $5–$20 for concerts; no cover in the Red Room Bar. Metro: U St.–Cardozo.

Tips **Metro Takes You There**

Recognizing that Washingtonians are keeping later hours these days, Metro not only keeps its trains running until 3am on weekends, but has also inaugurated special shuttle service to Adams-Morgan (home to lots of nightclubs, but no Metro stations).

Here's what you do: Take Metro to the Red Line's Woodley Park/Zoo–Adams-Morgan Station or to the Green Line's U St.–Cardozo Station, and hop on the no. 98 Adams-Morgan/ U St. Link Shuttle, which travels through Adams-Morgan between these two stations after 6pm daily, except on Saturday, when service starts at 10am. The U Link Shuttle operates every 15 minutes and costs only 25¢.

DC 9   This medium-size venue—which holds 250—debuted in the spring of 2004 with a commitment to offering both live music and DJ shows. Open nightly, DC9 features indie rock bands Thursday through Saturday from 8 to 11pm, and DJs for dancing until 2am or 3am those nights and from 9:30pm to midnight other nights. (That schedule may change, however.) The two-story club includes a bar downstairs with couches, booths, bar stools, and a digital jukebox of 130,000 tunes; the hall upstairs is reserved for music. 1940 9th St. NW. ℂ 202/483-5000. www.dcnine.com. No cover downstairs; $5–$10 cover upstairs, depending on show. Metro: U St.–Cardozo.

Eighteenth Street Lounge   This place maintains its "hot" status. First you have to find it, and then you have to convince the bouncer to let you in. So here's what you need to know: Look for the mattress shop south of Dupont Circle, then look up. "ESL" (as those in the know call it) sits above the shop, and hangs only a tiny plaque at street level to advertise its existence. Wear something exotic and sexy. If you pass inspection, you'll find yourself in a restored mansion (Teddy Roosevelt once lived here) with fireplaces, high ceilings, and a deck out back. Get right out there on the hardwood floors to dance to acid jazz, hip-hop, reggae, or Latin jazz tunes spun by a DJ. 1212 18th St. NW. ℂ 202/466-3922. Cover $5–$20 Tues–Sat. Metro: Dupont Circle or Farragut North.

9:30 Club   Housed in yet another converted warehouse, this major live-music venue hosts frequent record-company parties and features a wide range of top performers. You might catch Sheryl

Crow, Simple Minds, The Clarks, Luna, The Tragically Hip, or even Tony Bennett. It's only open when there's a show on, which is almost every night, and the crowd (as many as 1,200) varies with the performer. It's best to buy tickets ($10–$50) in advance, whether at the box office or online. The sound system is state of the art and the sight lines are excellent. There are four bars: two on the main dance-floor level, one in the upstairs VIP room (anyone is welcome here unless the room is being used for a private party), and another in the distressed-looking cellar. The 9:30 Club is a standup place, literally—there are few seats. 815 V St. NW (at Vermont Ave.). © 202/393-0930. www.930.com. Metro: U St.–Cardozo, 10th St. exit.

Polly Esther's This is a three-dance-clubs-in-one emporium with '70s disco music (think ABBA and the BeeGees) blaring from the sound system on the Polly Esther's dance floor, '80s tunes by artists like Madonna and Prince playing in the Culture Club, and current radio hits blasting throughout Club Expo. Decor for each floor matches the music of that era, so, for instance, you'll see such artifacts as a John Travolta memorial and Brady Bunch memorabilia in the Polly Esther's club. Open Thursday through Saturday. 605 12th St. NW. © 202/737-1970. www.pollyesthers.com. Cover $7 Thurs, $8 Fri, $10 Sat. Metro: Metro Center.

JAZZ & BLUES

Blues Alley Blues Alley, in Georgetown, has been Washington's top jazz club since 1965, featuring such artists as Nancy Wilson, McCoy Tyner, Sonny Rollins, Wynton Marsalis, Rachelle Ferrell, and May-nard Ferguson. There are usually two shows nightly, at 8 and 10pm; some performers also do midnight shows on weekends. Reservations are essential (call after noon); because seating is on a first-come, first-served basis, it's best to arrive no later than 7pm and have dinner. Entrees on the steak and Creole seafood menu are in the $17 to $23 range, snacks and sandwiches are $5.25 to $10, and drinks are $5.35 to $9. The decor is classic jazz club: exposed brick walls; beamed ceiling; and small, candlelit tables. Sometimes well-known visiting musicians get up and jam with performers. 1073 Wisconsin Ave. NW (in an alley below M St.). © 202/337-4141. www.bluesalley.com. Cover $16–$40, plus $9 food or drink minimum, plus $2.25 surcharge. Metro: Foggy Bottom, then take the Georgetown Metro Connection Shuttle.

Columbia Station (Value) This intimate club in Adams-Morgan showcases live blues and jazz nightly. The performers are pretty good, which is amazing considering there's no cover. Columbia

Station is also a bar/restaurant, with the kitchen usually open until midnight, serving pastas, seafood, and Cajun cuisine. 2325 18th St. NW. ℂ 202/462-6040. Metro: U St.–Cardozo or Woodley Park–Zoo–Adams-Morgan and catch the U Link Shuttle.

HR-57   This cool club is named for the House Resolution passed in 1987 that designated jazz "a rare and valuable national American treasure." More than a club, HR-57 is also the Center for the Preservation of Jazz and Blues. Step inside Wednesday through Saturday evenings for a jazz jam session or star performance. 1610 14th St. NW. ℂ 202/667-3700. www.hr57.org. Cover $6–$10. Metro: U St.–Cardozo or Woodley Park–Zoo–Adams-Morgan and catch the U Link Shuttle.

Madam's Organ Restaurant and Bar *Finds*   This beloved Adams-Morgan hangout fulfills owner Bill Duggan's definition of a good bar: great sounds and sweaty people. The great sounds feature jazz, blues, bluegrass, and salsa during the week, and regional blues groups on weekends. The bar is decorated eclectically with a gilded mirror, stuffed fish and animal heads, and paintings of nudes. The second-floor bar is called Big Daddy's Love Lounge & Pick-Up Joint, which tells you everything you need to know. For what it's worth, *Playboy's* May 2000 issue named Madam's Organ one of the 25 best bars in America. Food is served, but I'd eat elsewhere. 2461 18th St. NW. ℂ 202/667-5370. www.madamsorgan.com. Cover $3–$7. Metro: U St.–Cardozo or Woodley Park–Zoo–Adams-Morgan and catch the Adams-Morgan/U St. Link Shuttle.

Mr. Henry's Capitol Hill   Almost every Friday night at 8pm, Mr. Henry's features a jazz group—maybe the Kevin Cordt Quartet—that plays on the second floor of this cozy restaurant. There's no cover, but it's expected that you'll order something off the menu (perhaps a burger or gumbo). Mr. Henry's has been around for at least 30 years and has always attracted a gay and lesbian clientele, although it's a comfortable place for everyone. 601 Pennsylvania Ave. SE. ℂ 202/546-8412. No cover, but a minimum food/drink charge of $8. Metro: Eastern Market.

New Vegas Lounge   This small club closed for a time to clean up its act, re-opening in November 2003, much improved in appearance: exposed brick walls, slate fireplace, hardwood dance floor, L-shaped bar. The music, thank God, is the same: blues and more blues, mostly played by the Out of Town Blues Band, who favor soulful hits by the likes of Otis Redding. The word is, though, that service is bad. 1415 P St. NW. ℂ 202/483-3971. www.newvegaslounge.com. $15 cover most nights. Metro: Dupont Circle.

Smithsonian Jazz Café *(Value* What a treat! The museum that's a must during the day is also a must Friday evenings, when the Atrium Café features performances of local jazz pros. Food and drink are also available. In the National Museum of Natural History, 10th St. NW and Constitution Ave. NW. ✆ 202/357-2700. www.si.edu/imax. $5 cover. Metro: Federal Triangle or Smithsonian.

Twins Jazz This intimate jazz club offers live music nearly every night—it's closed on Monday. On weeknights, you'll hear local artists; weekends are reserved for out-of-town acts, such as Bobby Watson, Gil Scott Heron, and James William. Musicians play two shows on Friday and Saturday nights at 9pm and 11pm. Sunday night is a weekly jam session attended by musicians from all over town. The menu features American, Ethiopian, and Caribbean dishes. 1344 U St. NW. ✆ 202/234-0072. www.twinsjazz.com. Cover $10–$30, with a $10–$20 table minimum, plus a 2-drink-per-person minimum. Metro: U St.–Cardozo.

Late-Night Bites

If your stomach is grumbling after the show is over, the dancing has ended, or the bar has closed, you can always get a meal at one of a growing number of late-night or all-night eateries.

In Georgetown, the **Bistro Francais**, 3128 M St. NW (✆ 202/338-3830), has been feeding night owls for years; it even draws some of the area's top chefs after their own establishments close. Open until 4am Friday and Saturday, until 3am every other night, the Bistro is thoroughly French, serving steak *frites*, omelets, and pâtés.

On U Street, **Ben's Chili Bowl** (p. 85) serves up chili dogs, turkey subs, and cheese fries until 4am on Friday and Saturday nights.

In Adams-Morgan one all-night dining option is the **Diner**, 2453 18th St. NW (✆ 202/232-8800), which serves some typical (eggs and coffee, grilled cheese) and not-so-typical (a grilled fresh salmon club sandwich) diner grub.

Finally, in Dupont Circle, stop in at **Kramerbooks & Afterwords Café**, 1517 Connecticut Ave. NW (✆ 202/387-1400), for big servings of everything, from quesadillas to french fries to French toast. The bookstore stays open all night on weekends, and so does its kitchen.

INTERNATIONAL SOUNDS

Bravo Bravo *(Finds)*   Wildly popular among Latin music fans, this club has been open for more than a decade. In fact, the crowd itself is mostly Latino and Spanish-speaking, including the DJs. The club holds 500 people, all of whom stay to dance until 4am on Friday and Saturday nights. The club offers salsa lessons on Wednesday nights, when the action is a little tamer. 1001 Connecticut Ave. NW. ℂ 202/223-5330. www.bravobravo.com. Cover $15 (minimum). Metro: Farragut West or Farragut North.

Chi Cha Lounge *(Finds)*   You can sit around on couches, eat Ecuadorian tapas, and listen to live Latin music, which is featured Sunday through Thursday. Or you can sit around on couches and smoke Arabic tobacco through a 3-foot-high arguileh pipe. Or you can just sit around. This is a popular neighborhood place. 1624 U St. NW. ℂ 202/234-8400 (call after 4:30pm). No cover, but sometimes a $15 minimum. Metro: U St.–Cardozo.

Habana Village   This nightclub has a bar/restaurant on the first floor, a bar/dance floor with DJ on the second level, and a live music space on the third floor. Salsa and merengue lessons are given Wednesday through Friday evenings, $10 per lesson. Otherwise, a DJ or live band plays danceable Latin jazz tunes. 1834 Columbia Rd. NW. ℂ 202/462-6310. Cover $5 Fri–Sat after 9:30pm (no cover for women). Metro: U St.–Cardozo or Woodley Park–Zoo–Adams-Morgan, and catch the Adams-Morgan/ U St. Link Shuttle.

Latin Jazz Alley   This Adams-Morgan hot spot is another place to get in on Washington's Latin scene. At the Alley, you can learn to salsa and merengue Wednesday and Thursday nights; each lesson costs $5 to $10. The club features live Brazilian music Thursday from 10pm to 1am. Friday and Saturday from about 10pm to 2am, a DJ plays Latin jazz. Dinner is served until midnight. 1721 Columbia Rd. NW, on the 2nd floor of the El Migueleno Cafe. ℂ 202/328-6190. $5–$10 for dance lessons; 2-drink minimum. Metro: U St.–Cardozo or Woodley Park–Zoo–Adams-Morgan and catch the Adams-Morgan/U St. Link Shuttle.

GAY CLUBS

Apex   Apex (used to be called "Badlands") is an institution and still going strong as a favorite dance club for gay men. In addition to the parquet dance floor in the main room, the club has at least six bars throughout the first level. Upstairs is the Annex bar/lounge/pool hall, and a show room where karaoke performers commandeer the mike Friday night. 1415 22nd St. NW, near P St. ℂ 202/ 296-0505. www.apex-dc.com. Sometimes a cover of $3–$12, depending on the event. Metro: Dupont Circle.

J.R.'s Bar and Grill This casual and intimate all-male Dupont Circle club draws a crowd that is friendly, upscale, and attractive. The interior—not that you'll be able to see much of it, because J.R.'s is always sardine-packed—has a 20-foot-high pressed-tin ceiling and exposed brick walls hung with neon beer signs. The big screen over the bar area airs music videos, showbiz singalongs, and favorite TV shows. Thursday from 5 to 8pm is all-you-can-drink for $8; at midnight, you get free shots. The balcony, with pool tables, is a little more laid-back. Food is served daily until 5pm Sunday and until 7pm all other days. 1519 17th St. NW (between P and Q sts.). ℂ 202/328-0090. www.jrsdc.com. Metro: Dupont Circle.

3 The Bar Scene

Bar Rouge Hopping, popping Bar Rouge lies just inside the Hotel Rouge (p. 47) but also has its own entrance from the street— you must pass under the watchful eyes of the stone Venuses arrayed in front to reach it. As acid jazz or international music pulses throughout the narrow room, a large flat-screen monitor on the back wall of the bar presents visions of flowers blooming, snow falling, and other photographically engineered scenes. The place is full of attitude-swaggering patrons tossing back drinks with names like the Brigitte Bardot Martini. A lucky few have snagged seats on the white leather-cushioned barstools at the deep red mahogany bar. Others lounge on the 20-foot-long tufted banquette and munch on little dishes of scallop ceviche sopapillas, roasted pumpkin ravioli, and other Latin-inspired tastings served by waitresses in patent leather go-go boots and seductive black attire. Bar Rouge aims to be a scene and succeeds. 1315 16th St. NW (at Massachusetts Ave. and Scott Circle). ℂ 202/232-8000. Metro: Dupont Circle.

Big Hunt This casual Dupont Circle hangout for the 20- to 30-something crowd bills itself as a "happy hunting ground for humans" (read: meat market). It has a kind of *Raiders of the Lost Ark*/jungle theme. A downstairs room (where music is the loudest) is adorned with exotic travel posters and animal skins; another area has leopard skin–patterned booths under canvas tenting. Amusing murals grace the balcony level, which adjoins a room with pool tables. The candlelit basement is the spot for quiet conversation.

The menu offers typical bar food, and the bar offers close to 30 beers on tap, most of them microbrews. An outdoor patio lies off the back poolroom. 1345 Connecticut Ave. NW (between N St. and Dupont Circle). © 202/785-2333. Metro: Dupont Circle.

Bourbon *(Finds)* North of Georgetown, in the area known as "Glover Park" is this neighborhood bar that has a comfortable feel to it, even though it's only about a year old. The owners have invited their regulars to bring in black-and-white family photos, so that's what on the walls. Downstairs is a narrow room and long bar, upstairs is a dining room with leather booths. Fifty bourbons are on offer, along with 12 wines on draft, 10 beers on tap, as well as the usual bar beverages. Another plus is the rooftop deck. 2348 Wisconsin Ave. NW. © 202/625-7770. Take a taxi.

Café Japone This place is a hoot. The upstairs is a karaoke bar, where locals and tourists seem to be competing for most humorous performance. The downstairs is a respectable restaurant, serving sushi and Japanese fusion dishes. Beyond the restaurant is a club, featuring loud DJ music. Take your pick. 2032 P St. NW. © 202/223-1573. Metro: Dupont Circle or Foggy Bottom.

Dragonfly Expect to wait in line to get in here and the other hip clubs along this stretch of Connecticut Avenue. Dragonfly is a club, with music playing, white walls glowing, white-leather chairs beckoning, and people in black vogueing. And Dragonfly is a restaurant, with serious aspirations to please sushi-lovers. 1215 Connecticut Ave. NW. © 202/331-1775. Metro: Dupont Circle or Farragut North.

The Dubliner This is your typical old Irish pub. It's got the dark-wood paneling and tables, the etched- and stained-glass windows, an Irish-accented staff, and, most importantly, the Auld Dubliner Amber Ale. You'll probably want to stick to drinks here, but you can grab pub fare; the kitchen is open until 1am. Irish music groups play nightly. In the Phoenix Park Hotel, 520 N. Capitol St. NW, with its own entrance on F St. NW. © 202/737-3773. www.dublinerdc.com. Metro: Union Station.

Lucky Bar Lucky Bar is a good place to kick back and relax. But, in keeping with the times, it also features free salsa lessons on Monday night. Sometimes the music is live, but mostly it's courtesy of a DJ. Other times the jukebox plays, but never so loud that you can't carry on a conversation. The bar has a front room overlooking Connecticut Avenue and a back room decorated with good-luck signs, couches, hanging TVs, booths, and a pool table. Lucky Bar is known in the area as a "soccer bar," with its TVs tuned to soccer matches going on around the world. 1221 Connecticut Ave. NW. ⓒ 202/ 331-3733. Metro: Dupont Circle or Farragut North.

Nathans   Nathans is in the heart of Georgetown. If you pop in here in the midafternoon, it's a quiet place to grab a beer or glass of wine and watch the action on the street. Visit at night, though, and it's a more typical bar scene, at least in the front room. The back room is a civilized, candlelit restaurant serving classic American fare. After 11:30pm on Friday and Saturday, this room turns into a dance hall, playing DJ music and attracting the 20-somethings Friday night, an older crowd Saturday night. 3150 M St. NW (at the corner of Wisconsin Ave.). ⓒ 202/338-2600. Metro: Foggy Bottom, then take the Georgetown Metro Connection shuttle.

Politiki, Top of the Hill, and the Pour House   This is three separate bars in one, hardly the traditional approach favored by other pubs along this stretch of Capitol Hill. The Pour House, on the first floor, plays on a Pittsburgh theme (honoring the owner's roots), displaying Steeler and Penguin paraphernalia, and drawing Iron City drafts from its tap and pierogis from the kitchen. Downstairs is Politiki, a tiki bar: Think piña coladas, pupu platters, and hula dancer figurines. The basement has pool tables, a bar, and a lounge area; the street level has booths and a bar. On the top floor is "Top of the Hill," promoted as "hip and upscale," but it's not really, although you will find leather chairs, art, and chandeliers here. 319 Pennsylvania Ave. SE. ⓒ 202/546-1001. Metro: Capitol South.

Spy Lounge   You enter this cool bar through the Felix Restaurant and Lounge, and that's because Alan Popowsky owns them both. The Spy attempts a modern European feel, with metal stools and white walls, and builds upon a spy theme, showing scenes from James Bond movies continually on its TVs. Popowsky keeps the place from getting too crowded or riffraffy by allowing only a certain number of people in at a time (and only those who are dressed attractively). 2406 18th St. NW. ⓒ 202/483-3549. Metro: U St.–Cardozo or Woodley Park–Zoo–Adams-Morgan, and catch the Adams-Morgan/U St. Link Shuttle.

The Tombs   Housed in a converted 19th-century Federal-style home, The Tombs, which opened in 1962, is a favorite hangout for students and faculty of nearby Georgetown University. (Bill Clinton came here during his college years.) They tend to congregate at the central bar and surrounding tables, while local residents head for "the Sweeps," the room that lies down a few steps and has red-leather banquettes.

Arlington Row

As unlikely as it seems, one of the hottest spots for Washington nightlife is a stretch of suburban street in Arlington, Virginia. I'm talking about a section of Wilson Boulevard in the Clarendon neighborhood, roughly between Highland and Danville streets. People used to refer to this area as "Little Vietnam," for the many Vietnamese cafes and grocery stores that have flourished here. But more recently, this specific patch of Arlington has gained renown as a musical mecca, because of the profusion of live music venues that have sprung up.

Let's get one thing straight: Arlington is not Adams-Morgan. Adams-Morgan is urban, ethnic, and edgy, full of the requisite black clothes, body piercings, colorful hair, tattoos, and bad attitudes. Arlington Row is a lot tamer, attracting (so far anyway) a crowd of all ages, usually dressed for comfort. You don't feel like your presence has to make a statement. Certainly, the clubs are more accessible: Metro stops are nearby, parking is easier, streets are safer, and clubs front the streets with picture windows and aren't as exclusive.

I wouldn't recommend that you visit Arlington Row if it weren't for one key element: the music. It's live, it's good (most of the time), and it's here almost nightly. So take Metro to the Clarendon stop and walk down Wilson, or drive up Wilson from Key Bridge, turn left on Edgewood Road or another side street, and park on the street. Then walk to these spots, all of which serve food:

If you're a teetotaler, or just in the mood for the mellowest of experiences, head to **Common Grounds Coffeehouse,** 3211 Wilson Blvd, which is 1 block west of the Clarendon Metro station (© 703/312-0427; www.cgespresso.com). The coffeehouse serves up yummy comfort food and live music Thursday to Saturday. The atmosphere is folksy, and the music is usually country, acoustic guitar, or indie. Cover ranges from $6 to $9.

The smallest of the bunch, **Galaxy Hut,** 2711 Wilson Blvd. (© 703/525-8646; www.galaxyhut.com), is a comfortable

Directly below the upscale 1789 restaurant (p. 96), The Tombs benefits from 1789 chef Riz Lacoste's supervision. The menu offers burgers, sandwiches, and salads, as well as more serious bar with far-out art on the walls and a patio in the alley. Look for live alternative rock most nights.

At **IOTA**, 2832 Wilson Blvd. (© **703/522-8340;** iotaclubandcafe.com), up-and-coming local bands take the stage nightly in a setting with minimal decor (cement floor, exposed brick walls, and a wood-beamed ceiling); there's a patio in back. There's live music nightly. If there's a cover, it's usually $8 to $18.

Whitlow's on Wilson, 2854 Wilson Blvd. (© **703/276-9693;** www.whitlows.com), is the biggest spot on the block, spreading throughout four rooms, the first showcasing the music (usually blues, with anything from surfer music to rock thrown in). The place has the appearance of a diner, from booths with Formica tables to a soda fountain, and serves retro diner food. (Mon half-price burger nights are a good deal.) The other rooms hold coin-operated pool tables, dartboards, and air hockey. Cover is usually $3 to $5 Thursday through Saturday after 9pm.

Clarendon Grill, 1101 N. Highland St. (© **703/524-7455;** www.cgrill.com), wins a best decor award for its construction theme: murals of construction workers, building materials displayed under the glass-covered bar, and so forth. Music is a mix of modern rock, jazz, and reggae. Cover is $3 to $5 Wednesday through Saturday.

Now, get in your car, hop Metro, or get out your rambling shoes to visit one other place, about a mile south of this stretch of Wilson:

Rhodeside Grill, 1836 Wilson Blvd. (© **703/243-0145;** www.rhodesidegrill.com), 3 blocks from the Courthouse Metro stop, is a well-liked American restaurant on the first floor. The rec room–like bar downstairs features excellent live bands playing roots rock, jazz funk, Latin percussion, country rock, reggae—you name it. Cover averages $5 or more Thursday through Saturday starting at 9:30pm.

fare. 1226 36th St. NW. © **202/337-6668.** Metro: Foggy Bottom, then take the Georgetown Metro Connection shuttle into Georgetown, with a walk from Wisconsin Ave.

Topaz Bar   This is Bar Rouge's sister (they are owned and managed by the same companies) and also lies within a hotel, the Topaz. The decor here emphasizes cool sensuality, hence the Philippe Starck bar stools, blue velvet settees, zebra-patterned ottomans, and leopard-print rugs. A lighting scheme fades into and out of colors: blue to pink to black, and so on. Everyone here is drinking the Blue Nirvana, a combo of champagne, vodka, and a touch of blue curacao liqueur—a concoction that tends to turn your tongue blue, by the way. The Topaz Bar serves small plates of delicious Asian-inspired tastes. 1733 N St. NW. ⓒ 202/393-3000. Metro: Dupont Circle or Farragut North.

Tryst   This is the most relaxed of Washington's lounge bars. The room is surprisingly large for Adams-Morgan, and it's jam-packed with worn armchairs and couches, which are usually occupied, no matter what time of day. People come here to have coffee or a drink, get a bite to eat, read a book, or meet a friend. The place feels almost like a student lounge on a college campus except that alcohol is served. A bonus: Tryst offers free wireless Internet service. 2459 18th St. NW. ⓒ 202/232-5500. www.trystdc.com. Metro: U St.–Cardozo or Woodley Park–Zoo–Adams-Morgan and catch the Adams-Morgan/U St. Link Shuttle.

Tune Inn *(Finds)*   Capitol Hill has a number of bars that qualify as institutions, but the Tune Inn is probably the most popular. Capitol Hill staffers and their bosses, apparently at ease in dive surroundings, have been coming here for cheap beer and greasy burgers since it opened in 1955. (All the longtime Capitol Hillers know that Fri is crab cake day at the Tune Inn, and they all show up.) 33½ Pennsylvania Ave. SE. ⓒ 202/543-2725. Metro: Capitol South.

Index

See also Accommodations and Restaurant indexes, below.

FROMMER'S® COMPLETE TRAVEL GUIDES

FROMMER'S® DOLLAR-A-DAY GUIDES

FROMMER'S® PORTABLE GUIDES

FROMMER'S® NATIONAL PARK GUIDES

Algonquin Provincial Park
Banff & Jasper
Family Vacations in the National
    Parks

Grand Canyon
National Parks of the American
    West
Rocky Mountain

Yellowstone & Grand Teton
Yosemite & Sequoia/Kings
    Canyon
Zion & Bryce Canyon

FROMMER'S® MEMORABLE WALKS

Chicago
London

New York
Paris

San Francisco

FROMMER'S® WITH KIDS GUIDES

Chicago
Las Vegas
New York City

Ottawa
San Francisco
Toronto

Vancouver
Walt Disney World® & Orlando
Washington, D.C.

SUZY GERSHMAN'S BORN TO SHOP GUIDES

Born to Shop: France
Born to Shop: Hong Kong,
    Shanghai & Beijing

Born to Shop: Italy
Born to Shop: London

Born to Shop: New York
Born to Shop: Paris

FROMMER'S® IRREVERENT GUIDES

Amsterdam
Boston
Chicago
Las Vegas
London

Los Angeles
Manhattan
New Orleans
Paris
Rome

San Francisco
Seattle & Portland
Vancouver
Walt Disney World®
Washington, D.C.

FROMMER'S® BEST-LOVED DRIVING TOURS

Austria
Britain
California
France

Germany
Ireland
Italy
New England

Northern Italy
Scotland
Spain
Tuscany & Umbria

THE UNOFFICIAL GUIDES®

Beyond Disney
California with Kids
Central Italy
Chicago
Cruises
Disneyland®
England
Florida
Florida with Kids
Inside Disney

Hawaii
Las Vegas
London
Maui
Mexico's Best Beach Resorts
Mini Las Vegas
Mini Mickey
New Orleans
New York City
Paris

San Francisco
Skiing & Snowboarding in the
    West
South Florida including Miami &
    the Keys
Walt Disney World®
Walt Disney World® for
    Grown-ups
Walt Disney World® with Kids
Washington, D.C.

SPECIAL-INTEREST TITLES

Athens Past & Present
Cities Ranked & Rated
Frommer's Best Day Trips from London
Frommer's Best RV & Tent Campgrounds
    in the U.S.A.
Frommer's Caribbean Hideaways
Frommer's China: The 50 Most Memorable Trips
Frommer's Exploring America by RV
Frommer's Gay & Lesbian Europe
Frommer's NYC Free & Dirt Cheap

Frommer's Road Atlas Europe
Frommer's Road Atlas France
Frommer's Road Atlas Ireland
Frommer's Wonderful Weekends from
    New York City
The New York Times' Guide to Unforgettable
    Weekends
Retirement Places Rated
Rome Past & Present

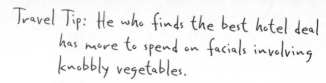

Travel Tip: He who finds the best hotel deal has more to spend on facials involving knobbly vegetables.

Hello, the Roaming Gnome here. I've been nabbed from the garden and taken round the world. The people who took me are so terribly clever. They find the best offerings on Travelocity. For very little cha-ching. And that means I get to be pampered and exfoliated till I'm pink as a bunny's doodah.

travelocity®

1-888-TRAVELOCITY / travelocity.com / America Online Keyword: Travel

Travel Tip: Make sure there's customer service
for any change of plans — involving
friendly natives, for example.

One can plan and plan, but if you don't book with the
right people you can't seize le moment and canoodle
with the poodle named Pansy. I, for one, am all for
fraternizing with the locals. Better yet, if I need to
extend my stay and my gnome nappers are willing, it
can all be arranged through the 800 number at, oh look,
how convenient, the lovely company coat of arms.